Mediaspeak

Also by Donna Woolfolk Cross:

Word Abuse: How the Words We Use Use Us

with William Woolfolk

Daddy's Little Girl

with James Mackillop

Speaking of Words: A Language Reader

Mediaspeak

How Television Makes Up Your Mind

Donna Woolfolk Cross

Coward-McCann, Inc.

NEW YORK

The author gratefully acknowledges permission from *The
New Yorker* to reprint material from "The Bobby Bison
Buy" by George Trow, © 1976, The New Yorker
Magazine, Inc.

Library of Congress Cataloging in Publication Data

Cross, Donna Woolfolk.
  Mediaspeak: how television makes up your mind.

  1. Television broadcasting—Language. 2. Television advertising—United States. 3. English
language—Usage. I. Title.
PN1992.8.L35C7 1983   302.2′345   82-12587
ISBN 0-698-11131-1

PRINTED IN THE UNITED STATES OF AMERICA

Acknowledgments

Special thanks go to my father, William Woolfolk, whose contributions to this book have been so many and so varied that I cannot possibly list them all . . . my editor at Coward-McCann, Tom Miller, whose careful reading of the manuscript and many thoughtful suggestions were indispensable . . . my agent, Mitch Douglas, who provided unflagging encouragement and support . . . Onondaga Community College librarians Lil Kinney, Liz Liddy, and Frank Doble, who gave more of their time to researching this book than anyone could reasonably expect . . . Tracy Ferguson, who went to no small amount of trouble to help me set up several important interviews . . . Tom Friedmann, who was a veritable fount of information about some of television's sillier moments . . . Reema Khan and Sandra Rwambuya, whose skilled and loving child care gave me the time I needed to work . . . Finally, to my husband Richard and my daughter Emily, whose tolerance and love make all things possible.

For my mother, Dorothy Woolfolk,
whose remarkable talents for life, for love, for laughter
have ever been my inspiration and support

Contents

Introduction

The Establishment is a general term for those people in finance, business, and the professions . . . who hold the principal measure of power and influence in this country. . . . The Establishment has very nearly unchallenged power in deciding what is and what is not respectable in this country.

Richard Rovere
The American Establishment

In American society . . . those who wish to control opinions and beliefs turn less to physical force than to mass persuasion in the form of news and views and entertainment. They use the advertising campaign and the public-relations program instead of the threat of firing squad or concentration camp. . . . Never before has public opinion been so completely at the mercy of whoever may control the instrument.

Theodore B. Peterson

If a lie comes from all sides to me, if the number of persons on my side who doubt it becomes smaller each day with no one left at the end, then I will be overpowered by it at some time too.

Victor Klemperer

Television is the quintessential form of media. Paddy Chayevsky called it "the most awesome godless force" in the modern world. Television has become so important a part of our daily routine that for most of us life without it is not imaginable. The New York State legislature recently passed a bill that declared the television set to be a "utensil necessary for a family" to survive in this society and so, along with other

11

necessities such as clothes, furniture, dishes, and kitchen equipment, it is now immune from appropriation should that family go bankrupt.

Our work, our play, our sleep, our lovemaking—all are regulated by television. So are our bathroom habits. Municipal water departments report that water pressure dips dramatically during commercials and at the end of television programs as people leave their sets to go to the bathroom. During the first TV broadcast of the movie *Airport*, the Lafayette, Louisiana, water department reported that for an entire half hour, from the moment a bomb exploded on board a plane to the moment the pilot landed safely at the end, almost nobody left the television set. Then, at the conclusion of the broadcast, twenty thousand people flushed eighty thousand gallons of water at the same time, causing a twenty-five-pound drop in water pressure! Oddly enough, this alternative to the Nielson rating has been overlooked by advertisers who want to judge how successful a television program is.

Surveys reveal that the average American now watches television for an average of six and one half hours a day. It would be surprising if the effects of what we see and hear for more than one-third of our waking hours did *not* shape our opinions. Yet we seem oddly unaware that much of what we believe to be true derives from television. TV messages have become so familiar to us that they appear to be The Simple Truth. This confirms what propagandists have always known: people accept as true those ideas which are repeated to them most often.

In fact, we do not see the world as it is. We see it as television presents it to us.

It's as if We the People all lived in a single house in the middle of a busy street. Outside, life goes on as usual: people meet and make deals, quarrel, make up, break agreements, and form new alliances. There's friendship and honor on the street, but also injustice, misery, and corrupt dealing by the acknowledged rulers of the walk. Some of the things going on, if we were to witness them, might attract or outrage us enough to drive us out onto the street to try to influence events. But the windows in our house are few and small, and the views that we get are limited. We never see anything that goes on outside the walls that have no windows.

The language of television, which I call Mediaspeak, is the house we all live in. Mediaspeak is not merely a way of communicating; it is a way of *perceiving* reality. It provides us with our windows on the world. As Walter Lippmann says, "We do not first see, and then define, we define first and then see. In the great booming, buzzing confusion of the outer world, we pick out what our culture has already defined for us, and we tend to perceive that which we have picked out in the form stereotyped for us by our culture."[1]

This phenomenon gives enormous, unprecedented power to media managers: the power to show and tell the rest of us how to live, what to be afraid of, what to be proud of, how to be successful, how to be loved. More than media managers, they are mind managers.

Of course, human society has always had mind managers of one sort or another, from witch doctors to kings. The difference today is in the mass media. Never before in human history have so few imposed so much of their thinking on so many. Theodore White has said, "You can take a compass with a one-mile radius and put it down at the corner of Fifth Avenue and 51st Street, and you have . . . 95 percent of the entire opinion and influence in the U.S.A."[2]

In America, and throughout the modern world, communication is big business. Like any business, its needs and interests are directed toward increasing profit, not toward promoting the welfare of society as a whole. No less than Adam Smith, the patron saint of modern capitalism, argued that a merchant's necessary self-interest was bound to blind him to "the public interest." Therefore, Smith believed, merchants should never be given monopolistic or governmental power: "The government of an exclusive company of merchants," he said, "is perhaps the worst of all governments."[3]

That is, however, a reasonably accurate description of the state of the American mass media today. Network television has been described by *Advertising Age,* the trade journal of advertising and public relations firms, as being "largely the creation of the one hundred largest companies in the country." As Jerry Mander points out, this means, "What we get to see on television is what suits the mentality and purposes of one hundred corporations."[4]

Consider the "public service announcements" regularly offered on network television as one small but representative example of that corporate mentality. These announcements—called PSAs in the trade—are under the supervision and control of the Advertising Council, a group of businessmen and advertising agency executives who volunteer their time to design and approve messages they judge to be "in the public interest"—urging people to donate blood to the Red Cross, for example, or to help prevent forest fires, or to drive carefully. All very praiseworthy causes. And indeed, the work of the Advertising Council has been highly praised by government and business alike. Charles E. Wilson, former president of General Electric, says, "Through the Advertising Council, American business supports more causes, solves more problems, and serves more people than is possible through any other single organization."[5]

A closer look at PSAs might lead us to question whose problems are really being solved and whose interests are really being served. Recently I watched an anti-pollution PSA that featured an American Indian mournfully regarding a badly littered highway. "People start pollution; people can stop it," the caption read. "Next time you see someone polluting, point it out." As the caption rolled, a single tear trickled down from the corner of the Indian's eye.

It was a very effective ad. I, for one, vowed never again to throw another candy wrapper on the ground.

Only later did I realize how perfectly that ad served the

purposes of the business interest that had created it. My attention had been directed entirely toward small individual acts of pollution and away from other more important sources. The vast amounts of industrial waste dumped in the nation's rivers, the massive disposal problems created by the billions of non-returnable bottles and cans produced each year—these were not mentioned. The business interest who designed this PSA may not have deliberately sought to influence public opinion to their own advantage; nonetheless the focus of the ad was hardly surprising, considering that those responsible for producing and passing approval on the PSA spots included executives from the American Can Company, the National Soft Drink Association, the United States Brewers Association, Pepsi-Cola, and Coca-Cola.

Similarly, PSAs on the subject of crime invariably stress personal precautionary measures such as not leaving keys in the car or carrying a whistle to blow in case of mugging. Fundamental anti-crime measures that might raise taxes on profits are ignored. After one series of anti-delinquency spots, a United Auto Workers spokesman commented: "This is wonderful, and good-hearted people are inclined to applaud this public-spirited action, but when you look at the directors of the Advertising Council, you find that they . . . stand four-square against federal aid to education, against a federal housing program, and against city improvements that would tend to cut the breeding ground out from under juvenile delinquency."[6]

Business crime is not addressed either. Recently, oil companies operating on "the honor system" underreported by $650 million the royalties due the government for oil taken from public lands. That shortfall in federal revenues has to be made up by taking someone else's $650 million—and that someone else is you and me. There have never been public service announcements alerting us to *this* form of theft.

The situation is much the same in other media. Magazines, dependent on advertising revenues, are easily influenced by business interests. When, for example, a bill designed to end deceptive pricing and weighing practices in food packaging was under consideration in the Senate, the president of the Grocery Manufacturers of America met with the publishers of sixteen national magazines. As he tells it, "We suggested to the publishers that the day was here when their editorial department and business department might better understand their interdependency relationships . . . how their operations may affect the advertiser . . . their bread and butter." Later, he pointed out with pleasure how well most of the publishers had "responded" to this not so subtle threat.[7] At the same time, Senator Philip Hart, who sponsored the bill, had a scheduled television appearance canceled because sponsors objected.

Newspapers, also dependent on advertising revenues, rely increasingly on public relations releases as sources of news stories. An American business magazine has noted that "PR plays a unique and quite startling role in the whole flow of communications. . . . This role is often glossed over, but the simple fact is that much of the current news coverage of business by the American press . . . is subsidized by company PR efforts."[8] One study group has concluded that "the portion of the contents of our newspapers that is originated from public relations offices . . . is probably quite remarkable."[9]

Business domination of the media exerts a clear and unmistakable influence on the nature of the communication we receive. "The mass media everywhere are organs of the Establishment," says Pulitzer Prize-winning journalist Harry Ashmore. "In a Communist country, it is their function to defend and propagate the official faith; in a capitalist society they enjoy guarantees against state control and are expected to perform a critical role, but their economic dependence upon the prevailing system fixes limits to the range of dissent."[10]

Business has a natural and understandable inclination to support the status quo. Most business executives are members of a high-income social group and the status quo is perfectly fine with them. They are properly appreciative of the system that has put them where they are, and their view of the world supports, justifies, even glamorizes that system.

This is, you might say, only to be expected. Why should any group act against its own interests? But the question is, do other social groups get an equivalent opportunity to support, justify, and glamorize *their* ideas about society?

Media critic James Monaco comments, "Whole classes of people are effectively prevented from using the media to record and disseminate their own versions of myth and history, and even those few dissenting views that do get through are subtly, but significantly, attenuated."[11] Alternative ways of looking at things cease to be considered, because the mass media teach us, through their omission, that such views are not worth considering.

Surrounded by an abundance of media, we believe we have an abundance of choice. We can choose to subscribe to *Playboy* or *Penthouse; Good Housekeeping, Redbook,* or *Ladies Home Journal; Reader's Digest* or *Life; Newsweek* or *Time.* We can tune in to ABC, NBC, CBS, PBS, or any of a host of cable and "pay-TV" stations. We can listen to over 6700 different commercial radio stations. We can see a different movie each day of the week. Merely reciting these statistics tends to reassure us that we are indeed subjected to a wide and representative spectrum of opinion. It is all too easy to confuse the sheer quantity of media with a diversity of viewpoint. We do not notice that essentially the same messages are being repeated. As Herbert Schiller says, "The fact of the matter is that . . . most Americans are basically, though unconsciously, trapped in what amounts to a no-choice informational bind. Variety of opinion . . . scarcely exists in the media." He adds, "It is not so much that the medium is the message but that *all* the media transmit the same message."[12]

A thorough examination of all the media is beyond the

scope of this book. Instead, I hope by focusing on a single medium to explore the character of its messages in some detail.

Television is the obvious choice. It is the most seductive, the most pervasive, the most influential form of mass communication today. We don't seem to *like* it very much—most of us would probably agree with Fred Allen's comment that "Television is called a medium because anything good on it is rare"—but we watch it. More significantly, we trust it. Recent Roper reports show that we believe television's picture of the world more than any other. Years of conditioning to the kinds of ideas TV sanctions have fortified us against contrary ideas. "The average American," says Schiller, "will accept information which affirms the consumer society and reject material which views it critically. When an American has been properly 'prepared,' he or she is relatively invulnerable to dissonant messages, however accurate they may be."[13] Herbert Marcuse takes this line of reasoning one step further: there is no need for Moscow-style government repression in this country, he says, because the mass media have shaped our consciousness so successfully that we no longer conceive of ideas or values that contradict the established political order.

We can hardly be expected to defend ourselves against propaganda if we aren't even aware that it is being used. Our society surrounds us, a fundamental part of our lives. We function within it and cannot conceive of functioning anywhere else. As philosophers are fond of pointing out, we cannot be sure who first explored the various properties of water, but we do know that it wasn't a fish.

In order to improve our society, we must first understand the nature of the mass media that play so large a part in defending and maintaining it as it is. In that belief, and with the profound hope that such change is still possible, I have written this book.

I

The Pitchmen

1

Profits Without Honor

Advertising: what is it? Education. Modern education, nothing more or less. The airs schoolmasters and college dons give themselves are extraordinary. They think they're the only people who teach. We teach ten times as much. . . .

> Dickon Clissold, fictional
> adman in H.G. Wells's *The
> World of William Clissold*

What a beautiful place, if only one could not read!

> Frenchman seeing Times
> Square for the first time

P.T. Barnum first perfected the carnival barker's art of luring buyers while deliberately withholding information. Once, to advertise his new American Museum in New York City, Barnum hired a man and instructed him to place four bricks in specified locations in front of the museum. With a fifth brick in hand, the man was then told to march purposefully from one brick to another, each time exchanging the brick on the street for the one in his hand, and to keep it up without stopping for an hour, by which time a large crowd had gathered to watch the man's movements. Once an hour, he would enter the museum. Each time a dozen or more spectators would follow him hoping to find out the purpose of his activity. To add excitement to the mystery, Barnum hired a man dressed as a policeman to make a scene by threatening to arrest the "brick man" for obstructing traffic. Barnum later boasted, "This trivial incident excited considerable talk and amusement; it advertised me; and it materially advanced my purpose of making a lively corner near the museum."[1]

Television has turned this kind of huckstering into a veritable art form. Far more time and talent are invested in most television commercials than in the programs they surround. A single thirty-second commercial can cost as much as $250,000 to produce (and that doesn't even include the cost of buying time to broadcast it). If television programs were produced at those rates, a ninety-minute show would cost $45 million—more than the entire budget for such large-scale movies as *Star Wars, Apocalypse Now,* and *Annie.*

There is no apparent limit to the lengths an advertising agency is willing to go in order to create a "catchy" spot. There have been commercials showing sports cars parachuting eight hundred feet into the desert and then driving away in good condition, cameras exploding and then magically reassembling their shattered fragments into a newer, better model, Fiats driving over waterfalls, sports heroes "flying" through airport lobbies to an awaiting car. Occasionally, however, a gimmick backfires. Brian Olesky of the Bozell and Jacobs Agency in New York City tells of one such occurrence:

> Somebody was shooting an airline commercial and they were going to use a condor to simulate flight. Everyone was ready— they were below a plateau where they were going to let the bird go, and the director gave the signal, and they yelled, "Release the condor!" Well, they threw the bird up and somehow they had gotten a bird that didn't fly. Film crews from New York don't know much about birds. These guys couldn't have told a condor from a Mercury Montego. So this bird went up in the air and plummeted about two hundred feet straight down. The

crew was filming and the actors were acting and the bird went straight down and splattered. From then on, "Release the condor!" has been a standing joke in the business.[2]

Still another ad agency once decided to feature their detergent by creating a five-story-high replica of their soap box and placing it on an open plain to be worshiped as an idol by adoring throngs. It took weeks to put the thing together. As soon as the replica was completed, it began to rain. It rained for three days, at the end of which the entire cardboard colossus wilted and collapsed.

Disasters like this are less amusing when you pause to reflect that 20 to 40 percent of the price you pay for the products you buy goes into the production costs for commercials such as these. As everyone in the business will tell you, "It is the consumer who pays in the end." This amounts to double shafting: first manufacturers convince you to purchase products you might not ordinarily want or need, then they charge you for the cost of their advertising efforts.

The fact is that advertising is institutionalized lying. The lies are tolerated—even encouraged—because they serve the needs of the corporate establishment. Even the government indulges in it for its own profit and benefit. Recently an enlisted soldier, upset at the discrepancy between the promises of army advertisements and the reality of his military life, sued the government for "false advertising." The government's defense was that the man had been ridiculously "naive" to take the ads seriously; he should have realized that the promises made were "puffery" and "simply braggings on the part of the government." That made sense to the federal judge; the man lost his case.

By now the falsity—either direct or inferential—of most television commercials is a matter of well-documented fact. Most people accept that ads are not true and yet, because they do not understand the methods by which they are influenced, are still taken in. Can *you* detect the deception behind the following statements?

- *"Ford's LTD is over 700% quieter."*

The clear implication is that the LTD is quieter than cars of comparable size and price. What is really meant is that the *inside* of the car is 700% quieter than the *outside*—a great advantage for those who prefer not to ride on the hood.[3]

- *"All aspirin is not alike. In tests for quality, Bayer proved superior."*

Most people assume this means that Bayer aspirin has been shown to relieve pain better than other aspirin. In fact the "tests for quality," which were conducted by Bayer and not an independent testing agency, showed that Bayer was superior, in its own manufacturer's opinion, because the tablets were whiter and less breakable than the other aspirins tested.[4] Nevertheless, this claim is so effective that a recent FTC survey revealed that forty percent of consumers believe Bayer is the most effective aspirin.

- *"Sominex makes you drowsy so you can sleep."*

Time and again the advertising agencies peddling over-the-counter remedies for insomnia have been rebuked for stating or implying that these products insure a good night's sleep. Undaunted, the nimble admen simply found a new way of making the same claim: The remedies still do not insure a good night's sleep, but they purport to make us drowsy so we *can* sleep. Reading a dull book or watching an uninteresting TV show would probably have the same effect. It is even possible that ads for insomnia cures can put you to sleep sooner than their product will.

- *"Lots of things have changed, but Hershey's goodness hasn't."*

The logical conclusion to draw from this would be that

through the years Hershey's hasn't changed its recipe for making chocolate. But it has; it's the "goodness" that has remained the same. And "goodness" is so subjective a word as to be almost meaningless. As G.K. Chesterton said, "A man who shoots his grandmother at 500 yards may be a good shot but not necessarily a good man."

- *"Count Chocula cereal is part of your child's nutritious breakfast."*

True enough. But then your child's napkin and spoon could also be said to be "part" of her nutritious breakfast. The ad doesn't say that the cereal *itself* is particularly nutritious. Indeed, many of the sugared cereals pitched at the kids' market are almost worthless nutritionally, except for the added vitamins and minerals (which you can get just as effectively from a vitamin pill). One study conducted by the University of Georgia in the late 60s showed that if kids ripped up their cardboard cereal boxes and ate them they'd be getting as much nutrition as they did from the cereal itself!

Many advertising claims are so vague and illusive that it's impossible to tell what is really meant:

- *"Harley-Davidson motorcycles: more than a machine."*

(Maybe there's a little person inside who cooks you chicken soup when you're on the road?)

- *"I can practically set my clock by Senokot [a laxative]."*

    Scene: Family gathered in cozy living room. Suddenly:
    Mom: Oh-oh! (dashes out)
    Son: Must be 8:30, Dad—Mom's going to the bathroom again!

- *"Gallo: because the wine remembers."*

If true, this should put a crimp in dinnertime conversations: "Hush dear, not in front of the Hearty Burgundy."

The late August Sebastiani, who scorned selling techniques such as this, would not allow his wines to be advertised on TV, saying, "If you spend enough on advertising, you can get people to drink sauerkraut juice, juice you couldn't get a thirsty hog to drink."

The rich and beguiling charm of some advertisements appears to reside in their total lack of sense:

- *"Purina Mainstay Dogfood has flavor you can actually see!"*

- *"Milk Mate: Real Instant Chocolate Syrup with Artificial Flavor!"*

- *"Irish Spring Soap: 5 bars for $1. Assorted flavors."*

- *"Amer-glas furnace filters: Save up to 100% on fuel bills!"*

- *Our vacuum cleaner has full power . . . cleans upstairs and downstairs!"*

- *"Clairol Herbal Essence Shampoo. Your hair will get very, very excited!"*

The job of the television commercial is to promote "special" qualities a product doesn't have, and to cloak its defects in a smokescreen. In advertising, as in war, truth is the first casualty. As Helen Woodward, a leading copywriter of the 1920s, once advised fellow ad writers, "If you are advertising any product, never see the factory in which it was made . . . don't watch the people at work . . . because, you see, when you know the truth about anything—the real inner truth—it is very hard to write the surface fluff which sells it."[5]

If there is absolutely no need for a particular product, the adman must invent one. He must convince you that your health and happiness will be in jeopardy if you don't buy his product.

Believe it or not, In the Beginning there was no mouthwash. Proper oral hygiene consisted of a thorough brushing with a good toothpaste. Then one day an enterprising stranger rode into town peddling a new product, a liquid made of water, alcohol, and assorted additives that would "freshen your breath." People weren't interested. "What can this stuff do for me that toothpaste can't?" they asked. Not to be deterred, the stranger hired himself an advertising agency.

Soon the television disease-control center was informing people about a new and terrible disease. No one was immune from it: Housewives and clerics, teenagers, cab drivers, lawyers, new mothers, were being struck down with a devastating malady. Far from eliciting sympathy, a person who contracted this disease was sure to lose his promotion, friends, loved ones, and paper boy. The sufferer himself was always the last to learn, usually from a hastily departing relative, that his affliction was . . . *halitosis.*

Bad breath was smiting the land, the righteous along with the sinners. A great panic might have ensued but for the miraculously timed appearance, at that very moment, of a cure: *mouthwash.* Soon Americans were buying bottles of it by the millions, and many could discourse knowledgeably about the virtues of various brands: "mediciney" vs. "sweet," etc. Skeptical about claims for the product, the American Dental Association and the National Academy of Sciences, after several intensive studies, issued a report stating that mouthwash has no lasting effect on bad breath, and that rinsing one's mouth with salt water is just as beneficial as using mouthwash. But medical science delivered its verdict too late. People had been taught to *believe* in mouthwash. The stranger rode out of town a very rich man.

Corporate America is continually inventing new ailments

in order to create a demand for their manufactured ministrations. The rate at which our human frailty is advancing is truly alarming. We are afflicted by "underarm wetness," "dandruff shoulders," and "feminine itching"—not to mention "that occasional discomfort."

Russell Baker, always an acute observer of the American scene, filed this report on the sickening of America:

> You can always tell what ails America at any given time by measuring the volume of cures being advertised. A few years ago, for instance, the nation was clearly swept by an epidemic of acid distress. This apparently now has subsided, thanks no doubt to the tons of stomach powder recommended during interludes between automobile chases. The ingestion of so much alkaline material was followed by an alarming outbreak of loose dentures, or "wobbly choppers," as the affliction is described in Gray's *Anatomy*. For a long time you couldn't sit through the network evening news without hearing of another poor wretch whose dentures had slipped off his gums and caused intense embarrassment during beefsteak or taffy consumption.
>
> It is my contention, not yet verified by research at the National Institutes of Health, that millions of American dentures were having their glue loosened by the alkaline powder traveling through the mouth en route to the stomach to quell the acid-indigestion epidemic . . .[6]

The art of inventing new consumer needs is not limited to imagined ailments and unnecessary cures. Look, for example, at the way Gleem is marketing its toothpaste these days:

> *Gleem. Adult-strength toothpaste. Eat like an adult. Drink like an adult. But protect your mouth like an adult. With Gleem. The tooth cleaning system.*

Potent stuff, that Gleem. Can you OD on it? Should it be Xrated? Is there *really* any difference between grownup fluoride and kiddie fluoride? Most important, if this selling hook proves to be effective will we soon be seeing ads for other products like "Adult Orange Juice," "Adult Cola," or "Adult Ovaltine?" Will the urge for more "adult" products spread to other areas? Adult Polyester? Adult Deodorants? Adult Gin and Scotch? Or even Adult Diapers? (for the older baby, of course).

In order to keep corporate profits rolling in, consumers must keep buying. And it's not enough for you to buy a product only once: Advertising must make you feel dissatisfied so you will discard what you have bought and buy a newer version. Recently, for example, the Huffy Corporation, the nation's number one bike manufacturer, brought out a new 12-speed bike, even though market research has revealed that most people don't need even 10 speeds. Why did they do it? Corporation President Harry A. Shaw explains: "People don't really need the two extra speeds . . . The bike may not do much for you but it should help to obsolete the 10-speeder."[7] One "product" that advertising really knows how to promote is obsolescence.

If there's one kind of consumer a TV adman hates, it's the person who buys only what he really needs or wants, and not what the adman tells him he needs. Admen call this renegade the "inner-directed consumer," and Edward N. Ney, the chairman of Young and Rubicam, explained the difficulty with him:

> This highly educated person, who now accounts for 14 percent of the population . . . buys only to satisfy his own needs or pleasures and cares little for middle-class status symbols. He is also the least affected by advertising . . . Creative approaches, whether graphics, copy, or sound track, or even the concept itself, would have to be crafted under a jeweler's loupe so that these recalcitrants can be made susceptible to reasonable advertising.[8]

See, Want, Buy is the holy trinity of the advertising faith. You can't sell anything to a person if he isn't even at the market. You can't talk him into believing he needs something if he isn't listening. Therefore, most television commercials begin with an attention-getting "lure" that often has nothing to do with the product. The 1982 Lincoln Continental was introduced with a commercial described in the following Young and Rubicam scenario:

> A man's hand unclasps a sparkling necklace from a woman's neck. The woman's hand cradles the necklace, which suddenly and magically floats out of her hand as though it were a feather caught by a sudden breeze.
>
> We cut to see a beautiful road of chrome leading to a vanishing point. There it forms a jewel-like arch. We rush toward the arch. We now reveal that the "jewels" are actually huge, gleaming chrome letters. They spell "Continental."[9]

The ad gives no information about the car. We learn nothing about its relative quality, price, size, or performance in comparison to other models. Yet the ad has served its purpose. As the senior vice president in charge of the account says, "A commercial has got to stop you, and it's got to stop you real fast, or it's a horrible waste of the client's money."[10]

The best way to "stop" a viewer is with a sexual come-on—a practice dating all the way back to the old Clairol "Does she or doesn't she?" ads. Today, the sexual lure is far more direct. There is the ad that begins with a sultry-looking brunette announcing, "I don't wear panties anymore," in tones that carry the clear suggestion that this fact will allow her to spring into instant action. But now that she has your interest, she goes on to explain, "Under all my dresses, under all my slightly tight pants, I wear Underalls." A concupiscent male barely recovering from the shock of this disappointment may run right into the shaving cream commercial that begins with a blonde saying, "Men, take it off. Take it all off," in throaty cadences. Imagine his distress when he learns that all he is being asked to remove is his beard! Another commercial shows a teenage girl inviting her boyfriend to "come on over to my pad"—which turns out to mean her medicated acne-prevention pad. The young man's descent from passion to pustule is positively dizzying.

How about the Grossinger's bread commercial that reads, "You had it at Grossinger's, now have it at home." In Canada another version of this was used to market a ketchup once sold only to restaurants but now being sold in supermarkets: "He gets it downtown, now give it to him at home!" That unintentional double-entendre was taken off the air when outraged homemakers protested. Other examples of double-entendres that never made it off the storyboard: a BBD&O campaign for a brand of to-the-knee stockings beginning with the line "14 inches of sheer delight." In England, a Young and Rubicam ad for round malt candies ran: "Reach for the best balls in Britain." To understand the reason another British ad was stillborn, you must realize that in England people speak of a "rise" in salary, not a "raise." The ad read, "How to help your husband get a rise. Give him Grape Nuts every morning."[11]

Sexuality is not the only bait a television commercial uses to lure a consumer's attention. There is also ghoulishness. A thirty-second spot for a men's clothing store in Philadelphia pictures the president of the company rising vampire-like from a coffin to announce, "If you gotta go, go in a Krass Brothers suit." In the same spirit, a metropolitan cemetery is advertised as being "conveniently located six feet under Cleveland." And in Los Angeles, the Forest Lawn Cemetery beckons consumers to "come meet our new arrivals"—which turns out to mean their new shrubs and greenery.

Even the staid legal profession is not immune from resorting to a little black humor in its advertising. A Madison, Wisconsin, lawyer named Ken Hur starred in a commercial that showed him driving around in a hearse and cheerily offering "no-frill wills." In another ad, to the accompaniment of the music of *Swan Lake,* Hur rises slowly out of the water,

his 250 pounds stuffed into full diving gear, only to announce, "If you're in over your head, call the Legal Clinic."

After enduring the dull drumbeat of ordinary commercials, we may welcome these touches of macabre humor.
But—if the basic function of advertising, as the admen tell
us, is to inform—just how much have we learned about the
price, quality, and effectiveness of these services or products
that we didn't know *before* viewing the commercials?

Even after our attention has been caught, we're likely to
have a certain amount of built-in skepticism toward the product being advertised. Television commercials overcome this
skepticism by constructing little "dramas" featuring "real"
people like you and me who start out doubting the superiority
of the advertised product, but who are invariably won over
with "persuasive" testimony or demonstrations. The form is
by now so familiar that we know, from the very first words,
what will follow. I call these waiting-for-the-other-shoe-to-
drop lines:

- "C'mon, they're all the same!"

- "Oh, he's a meat and potatoes man. He'll want the potatoes,
  not the stuffing."

- "Don't tell *me*, I've been doing laundry for fifty years!"

Of course, what you never get to see are all the people who do
not oblige the manufacturers by coming to the "correct" conclusion. Those who think the product is *not* good never get on
the air to tell you so—though it would make for more honest,
not to say entertaining, advertising if they did so.

Challenged about the unfairness of broadcasting only favorable testimonials, an adman defends himself by pointing
to a "truth in advertising" agreement among the networks
which requires 80 percent of people used for hidden-
camera testimonials to like the product in order for the com-

mercial to be aired. But this regulation does not apply to *all* the people interviewed, just to those who have been pre-screened. If an ad agency asks one hundred people whether they like their product and seventy-five of them hate it, there's no problem: All they have to do is use the twenty-five people who liked the product, throw in five of those who didn't for the sake of credibility—and among *those* thirty people, there's an 80 percent favorable rating!

This may seem outrageous, but it goes on in consumer testimonial ads all the time. Once, for example, Batten Barton Durstine & Osborn surveyed all the people who had bought Black and Decker power tools in one year. Out of two hundred and fifty people contacted, only thirty liked the product well enough to do a commercial for it (even though they presumably knew they could make money by doing so). The commercial was produced, using the satisfied minority. Of this kind of distortion, Allen Funt, who originated hidden-camera interviews with his "Candid Camera" show, says, "The intrinsic material may be honest, but the lie is in the omission or the selection. In 'Candid Camera,' the omission ratio is the same, but we're not trying to prove anything. The way 'Candid Camera' is done is to hope you'll get the unexpected. The way real-people commercials are done is to ensure you'll get the expected."[12]

Semanticists call this creating a false "map" for the "territory." Conclusions favorable to the needs of corporate sponsors are substituted for what actually happens to be true. "Real people" subjects are happy to help media card sharks turn up whatever card is called for; they know they will be well paid for their efforts. One woman who did a hidden-camera testimonial for Cold Power detergent says, "Last year we made $15,000 (from residuals for the commercial) . . . Cold Power—I'd eat it at the price!"[13]

I was once guilty of the same deception. When I was a struggling graduate student, I participated in a "hidden-camera" commercial. I was alerted in advance that while the "interview" would appear to be a routine consumer survey of a number of products, it was in truth a hidden-camera commercial for Scope. If I was "good," my friendly informant told me, I could earn a lot of money. I had never used Scope, but I was not about to let that stand between me and a down payment on next semester's tuition.

When I arrived for the interview, I was led into a small room in which one wall was covered by an enormous mirror. "Sit over there," said my interviewer, motioning to a chair directly facing the mirror. "Now, then," he went on pleasantly, "we're just going to have a nice chat about some of the different products you use every day." He went on to ask several questions about what brand of toothpaste, laundry detergent, soap, and shampoo I used. I waited for him to get around to Scope. Sure enough:

"What kind of mouthwash do you use?"

"Well," I began, leaning toward him earnestly.

"Don't move the chair!" he shouted, bounding around his desk to shove the chair, with me in it, back to its original position. I smiled, and pretended to see nothing unusual in this bizarre behavior.

"Speak up clearly," he said. "Now, again, what kind of mouthwash do you use?"

"Scope," I chirped obediently.

He sat up and adjusted his tie. "I can't *hear* you. What kind of mouthwash do you use?"

"SCOPE," I bellowed in what I hoped was the direction of the "hidden" microphone.

"Good. Would you mind leaning slightly forward and to the left when you answer? Now," he said, his voice changing to practiced, resonant, pearshaped announcer's tones. "Why do you prefer Scope over the other brands?"

I was prepared. "Why, it leaves my breath so much cleaner and fresher!"

"Repeat that statement using the word *Scope* instead of *it*," he said. "And lean a bit more to the left when you answer."

I did so.

At the end of the interview he announced grandly, "Guess what? Behind that big mirror is a camera. You're being filmed!"

"No!" I said, arranging my features into an expression of shock. "What a surprise!"

"Would you repeat that a little louder and lean to your left?"

As it turns out, this commercial was never aired. I suspect most interviewers are more adept at concealment than the fellow who talked to me. But still, most people know all too well what is really going on during a hidden-camera interview, and they try hard to perform as the producer wishes. Allen Funt says, "There's this enormous desire of people to please an interviewer, to say what a guy hopes you will say because somehow or other that helps him and in some more indirect way it helps you. We've photographed people with cameras stuck down their throats and asked them if they notice a camera and they'll say no. We've shot taste tests with people trying to swallow horrible-tasting food because they think they might get paid for it." He also notes that the decks are usually stacked in favor of the product, and he is angered by "the obscenity of flashing a sign on the TV screen that says HIDDEN-CAMERA COMMERCIAL when they've brought people into a room where they know they're going to get a test and . . . loaded all the factors in their favor."[14]

Take the case of Leonard Olds, a California schoolteacher who did a hidden-camera testimonial for Prell. He explains, "The guy had me put my hands in the two soap dishes and asked me which one feels this way or that way? They didn't say the one on the left was Prell, but when I put my hands in the bowls, it turned out the Prell one was warm and the other was pretty obviously cold. I assumed the warm one was the one to choose. You were kind of led along and you reacted almost exactly the way they wanted you to. You had to be pretty damn dumb not to recognize what was going on."[15]

Stacking the deck in television commercials is tolerated

because it serves a vital need of the Establishment—to keep selling many competitive but almost identical brands and to keep America's mighty production machine going, turning out items that are profitable for corporations but not necessarily useful or beneficial to consumers. The whole concept of "brand loyalty" is a corporate creation, designed to keep consumers from seeking the lowest-priced products. Clorox Bleach, for example, is the nation's number one selling bleach *not* because of its superiority over its competitors (all bleaches have nearly identical ingredients), but because it spends a lot of money in effective advertising promotion. Because of this, consumers are willing to shell out 30 to 50 percent more for Clorox than for any other bleach, though the alternatives would presumably serve them just as well.

Consumers who are not brand-loyal, who seek the best price among competitive items, are considered a threat to corporate interests. Many commercials disparage the "bargain" seeker. Clorox, for example, runs an ad that features a horrified mother chastising her embarrassed daughter for her "betrayal" of Clorox. "Janey," she cries, "you bought that cheap bargain bleach! How could you *do* that!"Buying inexpensive "generic" items, corporate America would have you believe, is un-American. There is currently a commercial for Tetley tea which shows actor Tony Randall helping a neighbor retrieve the contents of her dropped grocery bag. Aghast, he sees that she has bought a box of generic tea. "This isn't Tetley," he scolds her. "This isn't even *a name*!"

There *are* some variations in taste and quality among different brands and their generic counterparts. But these differences are much smaller than most people believe. And often the *least* expensive product actually has the better quality. TV commercials try to make sure you never find this out.

What most people don't know is that even the competition between brands is often phony, for the products are made by the same parent company. White Cloud and Charmin toilet papers for example, are both owned by Procter and

Gamble; Miracle and Parkay margarine are both products of the Kraftco Corporation, as are the Sealtest, Breyers, and Checkerboard ice cream brands; General Foods makes Maxwell House, Maxim, Sanka, and Yuban coffee; and no less than five "different" detergents—Biz, Bold, Cheer, Duz, and Ivory—are all manufactured by Procter and Gamble. The variety of brands gives the consumer an illusion of choice. But, in fact, the products are all but identical. The differences between them are largely cosmetic—and their purchase feeds the profits of the same parent corporation.

Brand-name advertising is now so effective that most people continue to prefer "their" brand, even when they have hard evidence that there is in fact no distinction between it and competing products. One very intelligent friend of mine, for example, admits she knows that Bayer aspirin is identical to the generic product, which sells at one-quarter the cost of Bayer. Yet she cannot bring herself to make the wiser purchase. "It just doesn't *feel* right," she told me. "I know Bayer is no different from any other aspirin, but somehow *I* feel better when I take it." To create this kind of subliminal, stubborn attachment to a brand is every advertiser's ambition.

In his futuristic book, *The Space Merchants*, Frederick Pohl has his adman protagonist explain to his friend Jack how brand loyalties work:

> "You're wearing Starrzelius Verily clothes and shoes, Jack.
>
> It means we got you . . . Smoothly, without your ever being aware that it was happening, you became persuaded that there was something rather nice about Starrzelius clothes and shoes and that there was something rather not-nice about Universal clothes and shoes."
>
> "I never read the ads," he said defiantly.
>
> I grinned. "Our ultimate triumph is wrapped up in that statement," I said.
>
> "I solemnly promise," O'Shea said, "that as soon as I get back to my hotel room I'll send my clothes down the incinera-

tor chute . . . And then I'll pick up the phone and order a complete set of Universal apparel. And you can't stop me."

"I wouldn't dream of stopping you, Jack! It means more business for Starrzelius. Tell you what you're going to do: you'll get your complete set of Universal apparel. You'll wear it for a while with a vague, submerged discontent. It's going to work on your libido, because our ads for Starrzelius—even though you say you don't read them—have convinced you that it isn't quite virile to trade with any other firm. Your self-esteem will suffer; deep down you'll find yourself 'losing' bits of Universal apparel. You'll find yourself 'accidentally' putting your foot through the cuff of your Universal pants . . . You'll walk into stores and in a fit of momentary amnesia regarding this conversation you'll buy Starrzelius, bless you."

O'Shea laughed uncertainly. "And you did it with words?"

"Words and pictures. Sight and sound and smell and taste and touch. And the greatest of these is words."[16]

Pohl's book is fiction, of course, and this conversation may seem an outrageous exaggeration. But brand loyalties are often just that irrational. Can you *really* justify your reasons for preferring your favorite brand of detergent? Of shampoo? Of beer? If so, you're one of a relatively small minority. Take beer, for example. "The fact is," one advertising executive told me, "that with the exception of an occasional taste expert, the overwhelming majority of beer drinkers in this country couldn't recognize their own brand if it wasn't labeled." The results of numerous marketing research tests confirm this assessment. One recent study showed that when a group of over three-hundred confirmed beer drinkers was asked to sample several unlabeled American beers, they were unable to tell their favorite brand from the others, rating *all* the beers they tasted as "not very good." Later, when the very same bottles were labeled and the tasters again sampled them, they found that their own brand was "far superior in taste and quality" to the other brands.[17]

You would think beer advertisers would be distressed by the results of this study. Quite the contrary. They know that what matters is not whether consumers can actually distinguish between one brand and another, but whether they believe that they can. Indeed, one beer ad has managed to use the research on "brand-blindness" to market its own brand. During the 1980 American Football Conference playoffs, and again during the Superbowl, Schlitz ran a 90-second spot that they called a "sudden-death taste-off." In it, one-hundred confirmed Budweiser beer drinkers (in order to qualify, they had to regularly consume at least two six-packs a week) were invited to compare two unmarked mugs of beer, one containing Bud, the other Schlitz. In a live demonstration, they were to drink from both mugs and then indicate their preference by pushing the appropriate button. The result? More than half of the Bud drinkers preferred Schlitz. This was even better than Schlitz had hoped for. But if only 25 percent of the Bud drinkers had indicated a preference for Schlitz, the producers were prepared to turn this to advantage also: The announcer could have said, "Can you believe it? One out of every four Bud drinkers actually prefers Schlitz!"

A brand advertiser tries to create a feeling of strong personal identification with the product. Cigarette manufacturers, in particular, try to build brand loyalty in this way. Take, for example, the following magazine ad for Talls:

> Smokers like the package. People say a cigarette pack is an extension of themselves. Makes a statement about them. Talls' package is simple, contemporary and, according to many smokers, extremely handsome . . .

La cigarette, c'est moi. Another cigarette ad takes the idea one step further: "More cigarettes sit neat in your hand like they were made for it and fit your face like they found a home."

Most of us no longer see anything odd in the equation of

an individual with a mass-produced item, particularly with beer and cigarettes, which are so often marketed in this way. But suppose a banana distributor tried to use the same approach:

> Tropical Island bananas sit neat in your hand like they were made for it, and fit your face like they found a home. A banana is an extension of yourself. Makes a statement about you. About who you are. What you like. How you think. Who you know. What you want out of life.
>
> You're no second banana. You're a Tropical Island banana. Don't you want the world to know? Peel yourself one today.

The overriding message is that the solution to all our problems, our ailments, our guilts, our fears, our social failures, is some corporate-produced *thing*. Most television commercials are in fact little mini-dramas starring three familiar characters: a person with a problem, a friend who is a devoted consumer of product X, and an authoritative salesperson who serves as a kind of Greek chorus, validating the statements of the friend and singing the praises of the product.

The drama begins with the protagonist bemoaning a problem. Along comes the friend who reveals that the solution to this problem is the use of product X. The authoritative salesperson (who is always presented as more intelligent and knowledgeable than either the protagonist or friend) arrives to confirm the truth of this, and to provide additional information about the virtues of the product. Occasionally, this format is altered to include only two characters—the protagonist and the authoritative salesperson, the latter appearing merely as a disembodied voice with a godlike power to read the protagonist's mind:

> A dejected executive sits in his office alone, obviously troubled. Suddenly, a strange voice, not in the room, is heard: "Some-

thing wrong, Mr. Johnson?" The man nods, surprised. "Can't concentrate on your work?" the voice insinuates. He nods again. The voice continues with just a touch of insolence: "It's hemorrhoids, isn't it?"

"Yes," admits Johnson, miserably.

You'd think a person might be a bit put off by having a stranger barge into his privacy to ask embarrassing questions like that, but of course he never is. He's grateful that this salesman/god has appeared to cure his rectal distress and so, by extension, his poor job performance and inability to win a promotion.

Often, there is no logical connection between the problem and the product/solution. Take, for example, the Coast soap commercials. Here, the protagonist's problem is that he feels sleepy and unable to get started in the morning. The solution suggested by the corporate manufacturer is not, of course, to go to bed earlier and get more sleep but to lather up with Coast soap. Within minutes of the first application of Coast, our hero begins to feel chipper and alert and concludes by singing boisterously in the shower. The concept of a soap as a "quicker waker-upper" has proved to be enormously successful.

Other product promises are scarcely less absurd. Is there any reason why L'Eggs pantyhose should make a woman popular with men? Why Duncan Hines cake mix should win a mother the love and respect of her children? Or why a Simmons mattress should help a person get better, longer sleep than a Beautyrest?

Advertising dean Raymond Rubicam, founder of Young and Rubicam, tells how the latter idea was conceived: "Zalmon Simmon, the original head of the Simmons Mattress Company, told me years ago that George Dyer had done more for his business than any other one man. 'What did he do?' I asked. . . 'When Dyer called on me for the first time, he asked me what business I was in. I thought it was a foolish question but I answered making and selling beds.' 'Wrong,' said Mr.

Dyer. 'You are really in the business of selling sleep—good, refreshing, sound sleep.'"[18]

The art of the television commercial is to convince consumers that buying the right things will help them achieve a desired state of mind or social position. Such claims are often indirect and allusive. "Translated" into more overt communication, this is what they are really saying:

> *Soda pop:* Are you lonely? Unpopular? Unloved? Tired? Rundown? Depressed? Drink Bubble-Up and you will find romance, be joyful, energetic, and young at heart.
>
> *Fast-food hamburger chains:* If your husband is a brute and your kids get on your nerves, bring them along to Big Burgerland, where after one bite of a Boggleburger they will be transformed into warm, loving people who cannot do or say enough to express their gratitude for all you do for them.
>
> *Women's "thin" cigarettes:* Smoke our Slimmy-Thin cigarettes and you will weigh 85 pounds. Not only that, but you'll be able to walk roughshod over your formerly repressive spouse.
>
> *Pantyhose:* Wear Gammon stockings and get laid by a gentleman.

Consumers who cannot be coaxed can sometimes be frightened into making the desired purchase. Fear has been a part of commercial advertising ever since ads began. Helen Woodward tells how her ad agency boss had instructed her to write an ad for baby food. He told her:

> Give 'em the figures about the baby death rate—but don't say it flatly. You know if you just put a lot of figures in front of a woman she passes you by. If we only had the nerve to put a hearse in the ad, you couldn't keep the women *away* from the food.[19]

One ad for the product that actually did run showed a pair of empty baby shoes—and left the consumer to draw her own conclusions.

Television has made such terror tactics far more believable and sophisticated. Viewers are threatened not with death and destruction, but with social ostracism or disgrace—the "ring around the collar" school of persuasion. If you do not choose the correct product, commercials tell us, then you can expect to have some or all of the following things happen to you:

- *your husband/wife will refuse to kiss you when you wake up*

- *friends will ridicule you behind your back*

- *strangers will stop you on the street and make disparaging remarks about your dress and appearance*

- *your children will be embarrassed to have their friends come home to meet you*

- *your cat will treat you with disdain and indifference*

From a corporate viewpoint, fear has a salutary effect on society as a whole, since it stampedes people into buying products that will keep the vast industrial machine running smoothly. Former adman Mark O'Dea viewed fear in advertising as a heroic concept. He once argued:

> Since time began, fear has been a regulatory part of humanity—our primitive religion taught the vengeance of the gods, our modern revivalists . . . frightened people with damnation.
>
> Fear of mediocrity drove a little Corsican into becoming Emperor—Europe's fears drove Napoleon into exile. Fear made Patrick Henry a patriot. Fear stalked with Lincoln from his log cabin to his tomb. It was the spur of such men as

Martin Luther, Poe, Peter the Great, Chopin, Julius Ceasar, Balzac, John the Baptist.

So what's a little fear in advertising?

We've a better world with a bit of the proper kind of fear in advertising . . . fear in women of being frumps, fear in men of being duds.[20]

In the world of television commercials, if a woman should fail to choose the appropriate products for her child, she becomes that most despicable of creatures—a "bad mother." As one woman says in a Final Touch fabric softener commercial, "If my little boy is going around with a gray, dirty undershirt, how is that going to look? What kind of *mother* am I?" The implication is clear: one not fit to have a child.

Women—and in particular mothers—are often the targets of appeals to guilt. In the famous Wisk detergent campaign, for example, the man looks accusingly at his wife, who immediately looks shamefaced when he is discovered to have "ring around the collar." Men, by contrast, are seldom appealed to in this way. Ads for office appliances usually directed at male managers who make such purchases, stress how the appliances will ease the employee workload and improve efficiency and economy. There is no effort to motivate a sale through guilt, though such an appeal would be fully as applicable here.

Men are, however, subject to threats of physical reprisal should they fail to purchase the appropriate product. The most famous such ad was the 1977 Schlitz "gusto" spot which pictured a group of Big Lugs standing around a bar carousing and drinking beer. A small timid male voice is heard off-camera—the clear impression is that it represents the viewer—asking meekly if the lugs will consider switching away from Schlitz. Outraged by the question, the lugs advance toward the camera menacingly. "You wanna take away my gusto?" they snarl. One of them adds, "I'm gonna send you out for a pass and you'll never come back." This commercial gave new meaning to the phrase *caveat emptor*, and became known in the trade as the "Drink Schlitz or I'll Kill You" appeal.

Another classic example of physical menace is a commercial for Gleem toothpaste which featured a determined mom hiding behind the bathroom door, holding a toothbrush topped with Gleem and waiting for her unsuspecting young son to appear. When he enters the bathroom she lunges at him. He flees, knocking over laundry and furniture in a desperate scramble to escape. She pursues him and falls flat, recovers and slides demonically down the banister in hot pursuit, toothbrush in hand. She slams right into the piano, her son leaps over her prostrate form and rushes for shelter in the bathroom. Safely inside, he closes the door and leans back with a sigh of relief. When he opens his eyes, however, Mom's there, advancing menacingly. She wrestles him into submission and shoves the toothbrush into his mouth. He resists at first, then he tastes the Gleem, smiles, and begins to brush happily. Mom looks on, triumphant. The voice-over announces, "Nothing makes a kid want to brush more than a toothpaste that tastes good."

Media critic Jonathan Price explains the way this kind of advertising works in the corporate interest: "Having established a world of fear, the admaker can introduce the product as combined parent and genie . . . They could still feed us the milk of paradise if we could just lift our wallet in their direction . . . By watching these spots and by buying the products we can quiet unhappy feelings . . . In this commercial myth, products are like mother's milk—they relieve tense bellies, soothe fevered heads, ease our anger, allay our fears. And at the same time the products keep us in a child's role—dependent and clamoring for more."[21]

Nowhere is this truer than in the television commercials touting over-the-counter drugs. Drug companies spend hundreds of millions of dollars each year trying to persuade Americans that the solution to every ailment from sniffles to sleeplessness can be found in a pill.

Many advertisements directed at mothers equate maternal love with dispensing pills to children. One commercial for a multi-symptom cold medicine shows a young boy in bed, surrounded by literally dozens of medications. He beams, "Whenever I have a cold, my mother spoils me. Look at all these medicines!" Of course, he points out, all he *really* needs is the one multi-symptom pill. But he fondly indulges his mother's foolishness because the purchase of all those medicines proves her love for him. Then his mother appears and says tenderly, "Got everything you need, son?" It's clear she doesn't mean magazines or a back rub or extra pillows—just more medication. When she leaves, the boy turns to the camera and says proudly, "She's terrific, isn't she?"

Television commercials such as these have helped to make Americans the most drug-addicted people in the world. There is some evidence that this equation of love with drugs has also contributed to the rising use of hard drugs. Senator Gaylord Nelson of Wisconsin, who has conducted several hearings into the use of over-the-counter drugs, received the following letter from a doctor at a methadone center set up to help treat heroin addicts:

> TV advertisers are teaching our children to use drugs. It seems to me that any child or emotionally immature adult subjected to the daily and incessant barrage of messages offering "fast, fast, fast" or "instant" relief from every care of life by simply swallowing pills would be tempted to try them—and, finding they do not live up to the glowing promises, would then resort to stronger ones . . . That many arrive at heroin is not surprising. I know of no drug except heroin or morphine which will produce the dramatic relief from all worldly cares TV vividly pictures.[22]

A recent article in *Newsweek* about the alarming rise in heroin addiction among middle-class adolescents says that addicts "offer cheery testimonials to the drug's virtues,

sounding not unlike TV endorsements for an extra-strength
pain-killer."[23]

Many of these advertised medications have questionable
therapeutic value. This is particularly true of the billion-
dollar-a-year cold medication business. Over fifteen years
ago, a Food and Drug Administration panel reported that several cold medications were not only ineffective, but unsafe.
Because of heavy pressure from drug companies, the report
was never released. Another indictment of cold medications
comes from the American Medical Association, which states
flatly, "In most instances, these combination [cold] products
have more sales appeal than actual usefulness. Often they are
irrational or even dangerous."[24]

Having sold you a product that may be irrational or even
dangerous, corporate manufacturers try to convince you that
they did it not for profit, but out of a selfless love for mankind.
Recent magazine ads emphasize the tobacco industry's "dramatic" contribution to the nation's Gross National Product.
One campaign in Virginia announces that "Tobacco means
$1,193,000,000 to Virginia . . . Virginia tobacco helps pave
Virginia roads, build Virginia parks, and support Virginia social programs. Tobacco means 90,000 Virginia jobs."

Tobacco also gives 2,700 Virginians lung cancer each
year—a statistic which the tobacco industry, for obvious reasons, chooses to overlook. As Rodale Press has pointed out,
the industry's reasoning is "roughly akin to the convicted
felon who claims he's helping the economy, because his im-
prisonment creates jobs for judges, jailers, and manufacturers of steel bars." Furthermore, the tobacco industry also
fails to take into account the enormous *costs* of tobacco smoking to the economy. The U.S. Surgeon General has estimated
that the direct cost of treating smoking-related illnesses is
between $5 billion and $8 billion a year. Another $12 to $18
billion is lost because of increased absenteeism and loss of job
productivity—which means we pay more for all kinds of products due to higher manufacturing costs. Fires caused by

smoking cigarettes mean we pay higher fire insurance costs; medical and hospitalization expenses for those with smoking-related diseases mean we pay higher health insurance premiums; and government subsidies to tobacco farmers mean we pay higher taxes. The total cost to us is difficult to determine, but one estimate places it at around $50 billion a year. The money we *get* from the tobacco industry in taxes amounts to about 13 percent of that cost, hardly an economic contribution to America.

Another tobacco industry advertising campaign successfully used this "humanitarian" approach to camouflage its bid for large profits:

> A word to non-smokers about people who build walls. The chances are good that you know a lot of smokers—there are, after all, about 60 million of them—and that you may be related to some of them, work with them, and get along with them very well . . . [This] makes you incredibly important today. Because they mean that yours is the voice—not the smokers and not the anti-smokers—that will determine how much of society's efforts should go into building walls that separate us and how much into the search for solutions that bring us together.
>
> For one tragic result of the emphasis on building walls is the diversion of millions of dollars from scientific research on the causes and cures of diseases which, when all is said and done, still strike the non-smoker as well as the smoker. One prominent health organization, to cite but a single instance, now spends 28¢ of every publicly contributed dollar on "education" (much of it in anti-smoking propaganda)* and only 2¢ on research. But our guess, and certainly our hope, is that you are among the far greater number who know that walls are only temporary at best, and that over the long run, we can serve

---

*The total government expenditure on anti-smoking activities—including school education and stop-smoking clinics—runs to about $2 million a year. Cigarette companies spend over $1 *billion* a year on pro-smoking propaganda called "advertising."

society's interests better by working together in mutual accommodation.

Whatever virtue walls may have, they can never move our society toward fundamental solutions. People who work together on common problems, common solutions, can. There will always be some who want to build walls, who want to separate people from people, and up to a point, even these may serve society. The anti-smoking wall-builders have, to give them their due, helped to make us all more keenly aware of the value of courtesy and of individual freedom of choice.

A common theme in corporate advertising is the appeal to "freedom," a concept which every American will readily endorse. The emotional connotations of the word are profound. But what kind of freedom is really meant? Freedom of the press? Freedom of speech? Freedom to exploit? Freedom to kill? Would the Tobacco Institute support a bill guaranteeing the "freedom" of research institutions to buy airtime for "anti-smoking propaganda"? Or is "freedom" only valuable as a concept that applies to companies with a product to sell?

Television's powerfully suggestive images give such corporate appeals to "freedom" even greater emotional impact. A recent Getty Oil commercial opens with a dramatic shot of a solitary skier making his way down a deserted mountainside. As he dips, turns, and thrusts his way through the virgin snow, an announcer grandly describes the joys of "pursuing our own goals with freedom." But, he goes on to caution viewers, "There are times when neither you nor we can expect such freedom in our daily lives. Not when someone decides the government should protect us from it."

Note the artfully created illusion that what is really under discussion is "individual freedom," when in fact what is meant is freedom for multi-billion-dollar profit-a-year oil companies to charge consumers whatever they like. What *real* connection is there between that skier and an industry whose largest representative, Exxon, has annual sales which exceed the Gross National Product of all but a dozen countries?

The concept of freedom of the marketplace was originated at a time when the relationship between buyer and seller was considerably more direct. Sellers—usually small businesspeople—were free to try to command the best price they could for their products, but buyers were also free to look the seller in the eye when they made their purchase. Television advertising has destroyed such equality between the parties involved in a transaction. The repetition of the same commercial messages over and over again has a powerful subliminal effect on the most resistant of viewers.

The greatest danger is that most of us still believe we are immune from corporate America's propaganda techniques. "When I buy a product," a friend of mine recently assured me, "it's because I think it's the best in quality and price, not because I believe what some television commercial says about it." This attitude makes her an ideal target for the subliminal persuaders. Professor Arthur Asa Berger says, "We frequently have the illusion that we are in complete control of ourselves and the contents of our minds and psyches; and it is this illusion that makes it possible for us to be manipulated all the more successfully."[25] My friend is unaware of how much time and money are spent every year to uncover consumers' deepest desires, to find ways to influence our behavior without our conscious knowledge. Ernest Dichter, who conducts research into people's motivations, states, "Whatever your attitude toward modern psychology or psychoanalysis, it has proved beyond any doubt that many of our daily decisions are governed by motivations over which we have no control and of which we are often unaware."

Here are some things advertisers know about us that we may not even know ourselves:

- Women will buy a round package more often than a square one; men will do just the opposite.

- Women will buy packages with colors of red, blue, and yellow more often than packages with brown, green, or gray; men prefer brown, dark red, and dark blue.

- People like to do a little preparation even with pre-prepared products: A frozen vegetable sells better if a tablespoon of water has to be added when it's in the pan; a cake mix sells better if an egg has to be added before baking.

The art of predicting consumer behavior has become so precise that buyers can now be "sorted" and delivered to sponsors in neatly packaged groups. Organizations such as the Simmons Bureau and the Claritas Corporation specialize in identifying what they call "receptive consumer groups." Working for Colgate-Palmolive, Coca-Cola, Reader's Digest, and even the U.S. Army, Claritas has sorted the entire population in the United States into various consumer groups according to 121 sociodemographic variables. It can pinpoint exactly which people are most likely to buy a luxury car, a life insurance policy, a Book-of-the-Month subscription, a four-year hitch in the U.S. Army.

Claritas and other "consumer research" companies often promote their services in advertising trade journals: advertising for advertisers who wish to advertise to *us*—"ad ads" as they are called in the trade:

> Did you know that men in the north central states are 12% above the national average in heavy cigarette consumption? To light up all the facts about the exact locations, lifestyles, demographics, and media habits of all American consumers, consult SIMMONS . . . The Mirror of the Nation.

Many magazines also run ads in these trade journals offering up their subscribers as profitable "target groups":

> Our subscribers are an active, affluent group. With an average household income of over $44,000, they're the kind of people who refuse to let the future just "happen to them" . . . With us,

you tend not to reach the financially strapped strugglers who have just been stunned by their latest batch of bills. Instead you reach *consumers* who are ready, willing and able to buy . . .

*   *   *

When a young woman says *yes* in 1981, she means business. Totalling 12.6 billion in start-up acquisitions by a record 2.4 million brides . . . Now that she's accepted his proposal, she's open to yours . . . MODERN BRIDE . . . She's determined to *spend* the rest of her life.

*   *   *

Think, if you will, of the volume of business transacted daily in an Epicurean environment. Probably it has to do with the psychology of the senses. Senses that stimulate desire. Desire that motivates people to act . . . The *Cuisine* reader is a leader, entertaining an average of 13.59 guests a month . . .

*   *   *

Over 10 million men are into living in the Ziff-Davis Magazine Network. These men come to our magazines because they offer an environment they know and trust. An environment they're absorbed by. They read everything cover-to-cover. They're wide open to your sales message *because they accept ads and editorial equally.* You can't find a more receptive audience. They're yours in 99 combinations . . . Buy our men and see how they buy you . . . [Italics added.]

This is the ultimate in capitalist endeavor, for people themselves become commodities to be bought and sold. In a devastating indictment of this development, George W.S. Trow wrote a satire on "ad ads" for *The New Yorker*. In it, a fictional market research company called Bobby Bison offers advertisers its "affordable" consumer groups:

Bobby Bison wants to give you Upscale Families. Bobby Bison wants to give you Affluent Purchasers. Bobby Bison wants to give you the best. You want to reach the Young Affordables—

that group of thin-skinned influentials who make 63 percent of all cordial liquor purchases . . .

BUY THE BOBBY BISON AFFORDABLES. Buy them outright. Tell Bobby how many you want. Tell Bobby what you want them to do . . .

LOOK AT THE BOBBY BISON AFFORDABLES. The Bobby Bison Affordables are on the beach. The Bobby Bison Affordables are covering themselves with special unguents and lotions . . . Ninety-two percent of the Bobby Bison Affordables experience some form of anxiety during the day; over 60 percent refuse to talk to their Moms, nearly 40 percent break into unexplained weeping as a matter of habit. And the Bobby Bison Affordables are *twice as likely* to experience a crippling sexual disorder as the viewers of the most popular daytime TV shows.

BOBBY BISON DELIVERS HIS AFFORDABLES . . . Bobby Bison *owns* his Affordables. Outright. If a Bobby Bison Affordable refuses to buy your product you just tell Bobby Bison and that Affordable better watch his or her step. *Bobby Bison Affordables do what they're told* . . .

MAKE THE BOBBY BISON BUY. A Young Affordable will contact you. Call Bobby Bison and he will send a Young Affordable to your office . . . Your Young Affordable will explain the Affordable life-style . . . He'll tell you about the futile impulse purchases that keep each Young Affordable deep in debt. You will agree that you need to reach this fabulous Young Affordable, you'll find him in Bobby Bison's hip pocket—lonely and ready to buy.[26]

Television's broad-based appeal makes this kind of consumer targeting more difficult. But the increasingly sophisticated techniques used to measure audience demographics are beginning to make it possible for networks to offer up specific groups of viewers to prospective commercial sponsors. A CBS brochure titled "Where the Girls Are" has on its cover a revolving disk detailing the age distribution of women who buy ninety-one different products. "And the pages inside," reads the brochure, "show you how you can apply this handy information to Nielson's new audience reports by age of lady viewer."[27]

Motivation researchers are currently exploring how to turn today's children into tomorrow's consumer targets. Research on children begins as early as ages two and three, and uses the full arsenal of psychological techniques: finger sensors, eye-tracking, and brain-wave measurements, as well as detailed questionnaires and observations of children during carefully monitored "play" sessions. The information these studies yield is guarded by advertisers as jealously as gold from Fort Knox. As children's television activist Robert Choate explains, "Industry doesn't want anyone to know about child research. Everything is secret, proprietary. Studies years old are locked away in sponsor and agency files— information that is used to make children into secret agents of big business in the home . . ."[28]

If that last statement seems strong, consider the results of one survey, which revealed that mothers spend an average of $1.66 more on each visit to the grocery store because of their children's demands for specific brand-name products. That means an additional $1.5 *billion* more a year in grocery store sales alone! Since that survey was taken over a decade ago, we can assume that this figure has more than doubled with inflation. With that much money at stake, advertisers do not regard children through the misty eyes of sentiment: Children are a market to be profitably exploited. An Oscar Mayer advertising executive comments, "When you sell a kid on your product, if he can't get it, he will throw himself on the floor, stamp his feet, and cry. You can't get a reaction like that out of an adult."[29]

Children are fledgling consumers who must be "educated" in the rituals of purchase. Advertising to children is corporate America's bid to shape the consumers of tomorrow. Jonathan Price comments:

> . . . commercials give children the superficial markings of our nation, the tags of our tribe, the secret handshakes that show *we are all middle-class Americans* . . . Children eventually learn, like their parents, to expect that a gadget will cure them, cheer them up, calm them down, and clean house like magic. And commercials raise children to "participate" in this adult ritual, the economy, by sending in premiums, getting Mom to buy something for them, by quoting from commercials at school . . .[30] [Italics added.]

Advertising both creates and preserves the myths of the corporate Establishment. Of these, the most important is the belief that "the good life" consists of having better products, and more of them, than our neighbors.

"Things," Emerson once said, "are in the saddle and ride mankind." Americans now spend over $20 billion a year just on "personal care" items such as mouthwash, cosmetics, shampoo, deodorant, sleeping pills, and stomach settlers. Though we constitute less than 5 percent of the world's population, we consume at a rate equal to the rest of the world combined. We consume out of the conviction, gained from the endlessly repeated messages of television advertising, that consumption is a valuable and important goal *in itself*. Economist John Kenneth Galbraith says, "In one area the industrial system is uniquely powerful . . . This is . . . television broadcasting [which is] essential for effective management of demand and thus for industrial planning. The process by which this management is accomplished, the iterated and reiterated emphasis on the real and assumed virtues of goods, is powerful propaganda for the values and goals of the system. It reaches to all cultural levels. In the United States there is no satisfactory non-commercial alternative. It would be good if there were."[31]

Television commercials sustain the illusion of freedom of choice. But whether we buy Contac or Dristan, Scope or Listerine, a Chevrolet or a Ford, we are expressing our unity of belief that corporate-produced *things* can solve our problems, soothe our fears, fill our emptiness. Which brand we buy is secondary to the primary ritual of purchase, nourished and sustained by the language of television advertising.

Nowhere do the illusions of our affluent society become more apparent than at Christmas time. In a brilliant illumination of the impact of advertising on the American soul, Art Buchwald wrote the following "Holiday Greeting":

> May you never have iron-poor blood or an Excedrin headache. May your breath be always fresh, and may you never perspire in case someone in the family has made away with the deodorant. God grant that you have the wisdom to choose the right toothpaste. I pray that your soap will give you twenty-four-hour protection, and that you never develop dishpan hands.

> May you get more shaves with your blade than with any other brand. May your cigarettes always be mild and their tar content low. May your beer always be cold. May the wax stay on your floors, and the stains on your linen disappear in seconds. May your peanut butter never stick to the roof of your mouth.

> May your bank be ever ready with a loan to tide you over the rough places in life, and may you never get stuck in the mud because you used the wrong gasoline. May your spark plugs spark, and your battery never run down. And may you win thousands of dollars at gas station sweepstakes.

> Finally, I wish each and every one of you instant tuning, a clear, ghost-free picture, and on this holiday may all your TV tubes be bright.[32]

Amen.

2
All the News That Fits

What ails the truth is that it is mainly uncomfortable and often dull. The human mind seeks something more amusing and more caressing.
                                        H.L. Mencken

What the American people don't know can kill them.
                                        Fred Friendly

Recently, one of my freshman college students remarked to me, "Well, you know you can't believe anything that the Russians say."

"What about *us*?" I asked the student. "Can you believe what *we* say?"

He looked shocked. "Well, of course! We're a free country. We get to hear what's really going on."

His feelings are typical of what most people believe about the kind of information we receive from our "free press" in America. It's certainly true that no government agency exercises a formal right of censorship over our press, and that articles embarrassing and even harmful to Establishment interests can and do appear on news programs. Yet despite a steadily worsening economy and growing social inequities, the American electorate remains overwhelmingly pro-Establishment—in favor of keeping our social and economic frameworks essentially unchanged. Is this because contemporary American society really is "the best of all possible worlds"? Or are Americans simply made to feel that way? How much of what we believe we know is the result of a deliberate attempt to direct our thinking in a particular way?

Probably a great deal more than most of us would like to admit.

There are forms of propaganda far subtler than the kind we associate with Moscow-style government repression. In *Brave New World Revisited*, Aldous Huxley describes just such a form:

> In regard to propaganda the early advocates of universal literacy and a free press envisaged only two possibilities: that propaganda might be good or it might be false. They did not foresee what in fact has happened above all in our Western capitalistic democracies—the development of a vast communications industry, concerned in the main neither with the true nor the false but the . . . more or less totally irrelevant. In a word, they failed to take into account man's almost infinite appetite for distractions.[1]

Television news promotes the status quo by directing our attention toward a daily series of diverting but unrelated events, and away from deeper social problems that might lead us to question or challenge the current system of doing things. The very name "television news *show*" reveals its main purpose: to entertain, not to inform. Like other television programs, news shows even have theme music to put us in the mood for what we are about to hear, and the musical accompaniment to these shows is usually intended to convey an impression of brisk efficiency; the tunes themselves are unremittingly cheerful and upbeat. The melodies of most local and network news shows would not be inappropriate in a

Broadway musical. The same music is played whether the story that follows is on a Middle East war or a royal marriage. Neil Postman thinks that the underlying message being communicated is this: "By using the same music each night, in the same spots, as an accompaniment to a different set of events, TV news shows contribute toward the development of their leitmotif: namely, that there are no important differences between one day and another, that the same emotions that were called for yesterday are called for today . . ."[2]

A further source of distraction is that news shows promote the messenger above the message. The word "anchorman" derives from sports, referring to the last runner of a relay team, the one whose final effort decides the race. "Today's anchormen, particularly at local news stations," says one cynical network reporter, "are engaged not in delivering or interpreting the meaning of the news, but in helping to distract viewers *from* the meaning."

TV anchorpeople (now called "news presenters") are persons who, as Ron Powers has said, "by their very dress and manner and sense of fulsome consumer well-being speak a new national language of comfort and assurance, of a peace that passeth for understanding."[3]

An ad for NBC news pictured a viewer saying, "I don't want anyone but Jim Hartz to break the news to me . . . These days, nothing could make the news easy to swallow. But when you're hearing about all the horrible things that are happening—there's something comfortable about Jim Hartz. You can tell he cares about it—but he gives it to you straight. When you see him calm and cool like that you feel it can't be all that bad. I guess to me he's the voice of sanity. And besides, I like his smile!"

"The job of the anchorman is to distract viewers from the disturbing parade of images that constitutes the news," says one acerbic newspaper critic. "He reassures them that despite appearances, all is well. One reason why Cronkite was so much loved is that he somehow had the situation firmly under control, that the right way, the competent way to do things is known."

Art Buchwald also remarked on this quality of Cronkite:

> I remember once when the astronauts were in trouble and I was worried, my wife said, "Don't worry, Walter will solve the problem." Twenty minutes later Walter came back on the air . . . and fixed it. Dan Rather will never be able to do anything like that.[4]

One New England newscaster, displeased with the way the news broadcast was developing that day, complained to the program manager during a commercial break: "You've got to get the camera closer to me. I have to make love to that camera. That's what I do—*make love* to those women right through that lens."[5] And a former anchorwoman for WABC-TV in New York was hired even though her only previous job experience was as a California fashion model. (She recently admitted she once interviewed Henry Kissinger without even knowing who he was!)

Russell Baker filed this bill of complaint about TV anchorwomen:

> The faces of television newswomen are never wrinkled . . . The faces of television newswomen always seem to have arrived fresh from the presser two seconds ahead of the camera.
>
> Several years ago, to be sure, there was a woman with a wrinkled face on the networks, but they put her aside. "That woman is wrinkled," said a vital executive, and they cut the juice to her camera.
>
> I still miss that woman. She was evidence that women who had undergone human experience grew faces like everybody else in spite of being on television . . . After that, news could be emitted from women only if they were unwrinkled. It also helped to be blond and to have a name like Portia or

Melanie . . . No Mabels were allowed to stand under the spreading White House elms at twilight and say "Meanwhile, the Presidency continued as usual today . . ."

How this was decided I cannot say for sure. My guess is that when it was proposed some vital executive said: "Mabel! You want to have a woman named Mabel standing under those beautiful White House elms?"

"Well, she is pretty good at getting a story."

"This country will never go for any woman named Mabel standing under the beautiful White House elms at twilight. Get me a class act. Get me a Portia. Get me a Melanie. We're talking class, for God's sake! We're talking White House, we're not talking chicken liver.[6]

Not long after Baker's article appeared in the *New York Times*, an undaunted CBS News announced that it was considering actresses Candice Bergen and Marlo Thomas as anchors for a new 4:00 P.M. news show. The ascendancy of messenger over message is now so complete, in fact, that no one saw anything amiss when one Baltimore station devoted segments of five separate newscasts to reporting the secret fantasies of its own anchor team. One anchorman who had had a childhood dream of being a subway motorman was filmed flying home (at company expense) to drive a hometown subway train. And when CBS took out a full-page advertisement for its coverage of the 1980 Iowa caucuses, the top half of the page was occupied by a picture of Walter Cronkite; ten other CBS newsmen appeared in smaller photos at the bottom. None of the candidates running for President was shown or mentioned.

Cronkite himself has decried the promotion of "personalities" in TV news. "I think," he said, "that it would be absolutely splendid if you got rid of the anchorperson entirely and found some other way—subtitles or voice-over—to do the broadcast. The reason I say that is because of what has happened to the anchorman, this over-glorification. There are a lot of reasons that is a mistake but one is the mere suggestion that a person, because he anchors an evening broadcast, might be qualified to run for office. That terrifies me. There's no relation between those two things. It shows how skewed our values have become."[7] Yet during Cronkite's tenure as anchorman, CBS continued to bill itself as "Cronkite and Co."

One man whose business was to sign up celebrities for endorsements couldn't wait for Cronkite to retire so he could line him up to endorse products. "For him, we'll take the rubber band off the bankroll," he said. "People *believe* what Cronkite says—and they'll believe him about any product he endorses." So far, Mr. Cronkite has resisted the blandishments of the advertising fraternity.

Yet Cronkite remains such an object of veneration by the American people that when he retired, one UPI editor wrote, "It can be said of three men that, in their time as communicators, this nation hung on their words, waited in eager anticipation of what they were going to observe and report and treat in their special way—Mark Twain, Will Rogers, and Walter Cronkite." This is a perfect example of the confusion of messenger with message. If a TV news program had existed in Mark Twain's day, no "continuity acceptance" chief would have allowed Twain's savagely anti-Establishment messages to go on the air. Imagine tuning in to these barbs:

> —"He was always the champion of vigorous reform before he became President. He talks fairness and justice noisily but evidently has no fixed idea of what they are. He is ready to sacrifice them to expedience at any time."
>
> —"Congress is a body of men with tongues so handy and information so uncertain that they could talk for a week without getting rid of an idea."
>
> —"If you don't want to work, become a newspaper reporter . . . That awful power, the public opinion of the nation, is created by a horde of ignorant, self-complaisant simpletons who failed at ditches and shoe making and fetched up in journalism on the way to the poorhouse."

Few of history's great men could have passed muster on the network news. If their commentary was not deemed too offensive, their personal appearance might have been. One can only guess at what a news consultant would have had to say about Samuel Johnson as an anchorman:

> Personal appearance—unkempt. Nose too bulbous and eyes too heavy-lidded. Tell makeup to get on the ball about this. Voice gravelly and difficult to hear. Got to do something about all that off-camera spitting and wheezing—newsboys near the anchor desk are beginning to complain.
>
> With a lot of work, we could get Johnson to improve, though he's very difficult to work with and keeps insisting that our suggestions are "lacking in decorum." *My* advice is that he's hopeless and should be replaced as soon as possible. Have we looked into the possibility of getting Eric Estrada, now that "CHiPS" has been canceled?

The distraction from real information reached its apex in the Happy News format, so popular on many local programs. Happy News consists of cheerful interplay among the broadcasters to fill time between news stories:

> Tom: Hurricane Martha raged through the tiny town of Fall River, Massachusetts, today, leaving in its wake millions of dollars' worth of property damage. At least twelve people have been found dead, and the death toll is expected to rise as rescue operations continue. Over to you, John.
>
> John: Thanks, Tom. Gee, that's too bad about Fall River. But at least we're having wonderful weather here, eh?
>
> Tom: Oh, you bet. (Cheerily) It's been just beautiful. We're planning on going out to the lake to take the kids sailing this weekend.
>
> John: Great idea. Nothing like being near the water in springtime, I always say. Well, Tom, here's a late-breaking story about the drowning death of a twenty-eight-year-old Springfield housewife . . .

Much Happy News banter centers around the weatherman. On the "Today" show, for instance, the anchors get a lot of mileage out of jokes about weatherman Willard Scott's obesity. (Gene Shalit: "If you step on his foot, his mouth opens.") And most news programs maintain a running gag—by now slowed down to a walk or even a crawl—about the weatherman somehow being responsible for the weather:

> Anchor: Slacking off on the job again, eh, Tom? When do you plan to do something about all this rain we've been getting?
> Weatherman: Well, *excuuuuuuse me*! You win some and you lose some, you know, Jim.

Former ABC weatherman Tex Antoine was responsible for Happy News' darkest moment when he came on, after anchorman Bill Beutel's story about a rape attack on an eight-year-old girl, with this remark: "With rape so predominant in the news lately, it is well to remember the words of Confucius: 'If rape is inevitable, lie back and enjoy it.'" After hundreds of outraged phone calls were clocked in at the station, Antoine was fired. But on such shows rape is often taken very lightly. One report called an attempted gang rape of a seventeen-year-old girl a "frolic" in the woods. Another story on the rape of a twenty-four-year-old woman by a masked intruder wielding a knife stated simply, "The woman was not harmed." (A remark which won it a Columbia Review of Journalism Award for "pachydermatous journalism.")

To liven things up on station WTBS, anchorman Bill Tush used to bring on a German Shepherd outfitted with shirt and tie as his "co-anchor." During "slow" news segments, Tush would start tossing lemon-meringue pies at the staff and cameramen.

Happy News also tried to end on a "happy" note. Cute animal stories are very popular as closers, like the one about a "watchpig" who guards a local junkyard. And in case you missed the point, the fadeout shows an image of a smiling or chuckling anchorman whose reaction is needed to emphasize that this is a "fun" finale. This format has proved so successful that it has now infiltrated network news:

> Max Robinson: Finally tonight, in the tradition of Killer Kowalski, Gorgeous George, and Haystacks Calhoun, there's Victor. Hughes Rudd reports.
>
> Hughes Rudd: Victor is an Alaskan brown bear, 650 pounds, 8 feet, 5 inches in his bare feet. Trainer George Allen has taught Victor to wrestle human beings for a living. The Athletic Commission has barred Victor from wrestling in Virginia on the grounds that he is mentally incompetent and has too much facial hair.
>
> Bear's Trainer: If they say he has too much facial hair, they should check their own wrestlers, because they have a Russian team with full beards.
>
> Hughes Rudd: Victor knows eighteen classic wrestling holds, which is more than most athletic commissioners probably know. The young fellows who wrestle Victor don't get a test for mental competency; maybe that's just as well . . . Between bouts Victor keeps his strength up with big slugs of Kool-Aid. After all, wrestling is a hairy business. This is Hughes Rudd, ABC News, Fairmont, West Virginia.
>
> Frank Reynolds (smiling): And that's the news for tonight. Thank you, and good night.

The philosophy behind Happy News is to keep the viewer from being too upset by the news reports he is hearing. The language is meant to soothe and to pacify. The underlying message is that, despite appearances, all is still *wunderbar* in America. As anchorwoman Kelly Lange of Los Angeles explains, "Look, you've got your boredom. You've got your misery. You've got your tragedy. You've got to have your laughs, too. You've got to have your chuckles. Otherwise, you're just asking too much of viewers who've been hassled all day long."[8]

Chicago TV weatherman John Coleman pictures Happy News as a form of community service, saying, "Unless you give the viewer a framework of humanity, the perspective that day-to-day life will go on, that people are still drinking beer and laughing, I think you've done a disservice to the community."[9]

No one would argue that people have a right to be entertained. But the light-hearted assurances of Happy News are not presented as entertainment—and, in the process, real information is crowded out. Recent polls show that despite the fact that more Americans are getting more news than ever before, they are actually less well informed. Over half the population doesn't know who their senators or congressmen are and almost as many don't even know how many senators there are from their own state. Half of all the seventeen-year-olds in the country think the President can appoint members of Congress. One survey revealed that almost 70% of the people surveyed could not identify the three branches of government or the Bill of Rights, and could not say what important event happened in America in 1776. Other surveys reveal that substantial sections of the voting public do not know who current political candidates are, what they stand for, how Presidential candidates are nominated, nor do they understand such basic concepts as price supports or monopolies.[10]

Television news shows don't seek to remedy such ignorance; instead, they play to it. A sign posted on the wall of a CBS affiliate station reads, "Remember, the vast majority of our viewers hold blue-collar jobs. The vast majority of our viewers have never seen a copy of *The New York Times*. The vast majority of our viewers do not read the same books and magazines that you read . . . In fact, many of them never read anything."[11]

News consultant Frank Magid explains, "It is not surprising . . . that research indicates ratings rise when the broadcaster is successful in exposing the listener to what he *wants* to hear, in the very personal way he wants to hear it. In terms of news, this means ratings are improved not when listeners are told what they *should* know, but what they want to hear." The "news value" of a story is determined not by its intrinsic importance, but by how many people can be expected to "buy" it. This turns information into a commercial product, like soap. Says media historian Eric Barnouw:

> Producers and editors generally feel they are responding to "news value" in their selections. They may not be aware that they are responding to some extent to "news value" *they have helped to create.* [Italics added.] When they explain an omission by saying, "People are not very interested in that," they may in effect be saying, "We have never mentioned that before." What they decide to mention, to show, tends to become "the" news, "the" subject of interest.[12]

TV news trades in "safe" disasters. At the local level, stories on fires, burglaries, rapes, and muggings abound. The inevitability of these stories is such that one hee-haw program led off with a mock anchorman whose entire broadcast was confined to the statement, "The news was pretty much the same today, only it happened to different people." Reports on fires and robberies play upon childhood fears and help distract viewers from more adult worries. As children, we worry that our house will burn down, or that a bad man will break into our home to harm us. We do not fear a deteriorating standard of living, or the lack of opportunity for decent major medical care, or the demands of society's disenchanted and disenfranchised. Events like fires and burglaries are random occurrences; there is little we can do to protect ourselves against them, and anyway, the chances of one of these things actually happening to us are relatively slim. The kinds of things adults fear are all too predictable and real—and they happen all too frequently.

Media critic Edwin Diamond comments, "Press-guide-line values . . . may work against the basic task of getting at, and facing 'the facts.' This is especially so when 'the facts' involve the circumstances of black Americans—a story that many white Americans in the audience may not want to dwell upon too long, out of fear, or doubt, or guilt, or a combination of largely unexamined emotions . . . the black story is too fraught."[13]

The job of TV news is to distract us from disquieting thoughts while preserving the excitement provided by an illusion of danger and fear. Dr. Robert Dupont, a psychiatrist who has made an extensive study of the fears television news plays to, says that most reporting is more concerned with "what if" rather than "what is." He describes the ultimate news broadcast as a camera shot of a placid swimming pool in front of which a TV newsman urgently announces, "Do you realize that there's enough water in this pool to drown 100,000 people?*

There is a growing body of evidence that long-term exposure to the language of TV news is detrimental to a person's thought processes. Seven out of ten people now get their information about the world exclusively from TV. Yet one recent study revealed that these people can no longer give even one reason to justify their choice of a particular political candidate or policy. The study concludes, "TV news reporting does little to develop our potential to analyze, think independently, or learn from grasping overall patterns in the unfolding of events."[14]

Marshall McLuhan made famous the concept that "the medium is the message," and there is no doubt that modern technology provides its own distraction on news broadcasts. TV news watchers are distracted by flashy sets and gadgetry. One Chicago news station actually introduced a program

---

*Newspapers also indulge in manufactured disasters. A friend told me that once as he approached a newsstand he saw that a popular tabloid had a full-page headline. He feared that a headline set in such type might herald the end of the world. It consisted of only one word: FOG!

called "Heart of the News" in which a toothsome anchorwoman delivered headlines while ensconced in a heart-shaped bed—provided free by the bedding company sponsoring the show. A brilliant wedding of manufactured news and manufactured product! Perhaps in future, we may see other such pairings: a "Top of the News" program broadcast from the cockpit of a plane—provided by Boeing? An anchorwoman in a pair of tight Calvin Kleins starring in "Behind the News"?

Devices with space-age names like Quantel can mold electronic images into any shape a TV news director desires. There are stop-action, slow-motion and freeze-frame shots. A different scene can be inserted into each corner of a picture, and at the touch of a button, one can be zoomed up to fill the entire screen—or zoomed down to catch an image the size of a postage stamp. Another device called a Chyron 4 can produce charts, graphs, and printed texts in any one of sixty-four brilliant colors, alone or in combination. The texts can be made to appear to move with "page wipes" which provide the illusion of swiftly turning book pages. The profusion of such sophisticated devices calls to mind Fred Allen's comment (made before such things were even dreamed of) that "Television is a triumph of equipment over people and the minds who control it are so small you could put them in the navel of a flea and still have room beside them for a network vice-president's heart."

Gadgetry helps create the illusion that what is being said is of great importance and interest. Surround the weatherman with enough maps, flashing arrows, electronic indicators, radar scans, and satellite photos to launch a Voyager mission and few people notice that the actual information he gives can be found in the upper right-hand corner of any daily newspaper. Fly a reporter to the scene of an ordinary story in a helicopter and the story automatically assumes heightened importance. In fact, "Live in the Sky" coverage is often the sole determinant of a story's news value. Phoenix, Arizona, newsman Jerry Foster comments, "Many times in the helicopter I've caught a car actually going off the road. A minor accident isn't really news, but when you catch the car actually going over the side of the road, then it changes the whole perspective on the story. Even though no one's injured and there isn't a lot of news value, it still makes a good story because it's action. People like to see things that are happening."[15]

WNEW news director Mark Monsky explains the overuse of gadgets on the news as "television's moronic attempt to understand human beings through toys." He adds, "It's insulting to the audience to call attention to the device itself. It's the ends of reporting that are significant, not the means."[16] Dressed in a diver's suit and flippers, Monsky once ridiculed the rival WCBS "Eye in the Sky" helicopter service by sending a reporter to do a story on a submarine patroling off the New Jersey shore. The reporter emerged dripping from the river to announce that he was WNEW's new "Reporter in the Water."

Perhaps this trend may also make it to network news. In that event we will see Dan Rather broadcasting from aboard a military vessel, as CBS "Anchor in a Tanker." Or Charles Kuralt may give his opinions on national events while shuttling between floors of the World Trade Center, thereby becoming TV's first "Commentator on an Elevator." The first seeds of this trend are evident in the predilection of newscasters for tossing a story around among themselves before throwing it out to the viewer:

> Anchor No. 1: Good evening. Once again, a terrorist action is precipitating a major crisis in the Middle East. Here's Peter with the story.
> Anchor No. 2: Thanks, Frank. Tonight Palestinian terrorists raided an Israeli commune, taking twelve civilians hostage, including two children. Here's Tom with the story.
> Correspondent: Thanks, Peter. There's a highly charged atmosphere of tension and open anger here in Haifa today.

People talk openly of a punitive strike against Jordan if the hostages aren't released unharmed. Here's Marilyn with details . . .

Reporter: Thanks, Tom.

Mere movement from place to place and from commentator to commentator replaces genuine information. And an air of importance is created simply because so many people are covering a single news story.

Viewers are often denied information if it doesn't meet entertainment standards. Stories without a strong visual appeal, for instance, are rarely given more than cursory attention. One former NBC producer proposed to do a story on Washington lobbyists, that enormously powerful group whose activities affect how the rest of us eat, drink, get paid, get taxed, have children, etc. But the story was killed before it even started. "We just couldn't show how lobbying goes on," says the producer. "Congress has rules that forbid filming in corridors, so we couldn't follow a lobbyist on his rounds. And although we could have used artists' renderings, it wouldn't have been very effective."[17] Another reporter was very excited when she was assigned to cover the workings of the Department of Health, Education and Welfare (now retitled the Department of Health and Human Services). "More than any other arm of government," she said, "[HEW] affects Americans on a day-to-day basis. You are talking about health care, Social Security, schools, child immunizations—the things that touch us all." But reports on such topics are not considered to have good "news value"; one news executive titles them "D.G.S.N.W."—"Dull Government Shit Nobody Watches." Because the information this reporter gathered could not be condensed into a single televisable happening, she rarely got on the air. "People thought I had disappeared from the face of the earth," she says, adding, "I think we are missing the boat, and that the American people are being denied important information."[18]

The late newsman Chet Huntley commented, "In our zeal for shooting film with interesting facades and lovely landscapes, and in our fear of dullness and the low rating, we arbitrarily rule out a long and imposing list of awesome subjects and conclude they were just not meant for television."[19] Stories on corporate crime, consumer fraud, and price fixing rarely get the attention that street crime does, even though those crimes are far more serious and affect many more people. The reason is simple: Stories about banks robbing people cannot be made as "entertaining" as shots of people robbing banks.

Newspeople frame the messages they speak. Most TV news stories are framed like miniature playlets, with clearly defined beginnings, middles, and ends (Aristotle would have called these Incitement, Complication, and Resolution.) Before the play starts we're given the "tease," a three- to ten-second advertisement for the entertainment ahead: "Coming up next . . . the amazing story of the eleven-year-old who brought a dead man back to life!" or "Still ahead . . . one hundred seven dogs, two cats, and a monkey!" (One tease that appears on network gag reels features the anchor seated behind the desk, saying, "I'm not wearing any pants! Film at eleven!") The idea of a tease, of course, is to keep the viewer tuned to the channel through the commercial. "Teaseologist" David Saltman describes his education writing teases at WABC's Eyewitness News:

> I had written, "Next on Eyewitness News . . . the cost of living dips . . . plus a special report on designer jeans . . . including a profile of Calvin Klein."
>
> "It's dull," [executive producer Howard] Doyle said. "Who gives a bleep about the cost of living or Calvin Klein?"
>
> I returned to my typewriter. I thought over what Kris had taught me in Teaseology School: Be unpredictable! Use words that stick in the viewer's mind! Personalize! I wrote: "Coming up next . . . the holes in your pockets and the patches on your

pants" . . . I took it back to Doyle. He would not elaborate beyond saying, "Sell that story—it's still too dull."

. . . the tease that passed muster that night was "Still ahead on Eyewitness News . . . some good news about your money. For once, you might even have enough left to buy a pair of those snappy new designer jeans. We'll show you the man behind the behinds!"[20]

After the commercial break, you get the story/playlet, which generally begins with a strong attention-grabber. To help promote the impression that the viewer is getting his news hot off the presses, the opening lines of a story are written in the present tense—even if the actual events took place some time before. It's not "Three firemen died this morning"; it's "Three firemen dead tonight." In mockery of this practice, a "Saturday Night Live" "news" broadcast led off with "Franco . . . still dead tonight."

The ideal opening line catches viewer interest without revealing what actually happened. News consultant Frank Magid offers this advice to reporters who want to write a good "narrative hook": "Avoid starting a newscast with a stark fact. Begin instead with an evocative line which will catch the ear of the listener, arouse his curiosity, and begin to 'pull' him into the newscast* . . . For example, instead of beginning with the words 'Ralph Botts has been fined $10,000 for his part in an alleged . . .' you might begin with 'Is the FBI nosing in on Chicago?' or, 'He'll have to cough it up . . .' or, 'Ten thousand dollars and the poor guy is penniless . . .' The whole idea is to set the listener up so that he becomes interested and must listen for more."[21]

After the hook, or incitement, comes the story, which ideally features some kind of dramatic conflict: blacks against

---

*When James Thurber was advised by his newspaper editor to write short catchy leads to his stories, he filed one report that began "Dead. That's what the man was when they found him with a knife in his back at 4:00 P.M. in front of Riley's Saloon at the corner of 52nd and 12th streets."

whites, police against criminals, school boards against teachers, FAA against striking air controllers, Congress against President. The promise or actuality of violence is highlighted to help intensify the theatrical effect. In *News from Nowhere*, Edward Jay Epstein wrote: "The one ingredient most producers interviewed claimed was necessary for a good action story was visually identifiable opponents clashing violently. This, in turn, requires some form of stereotype . . ." Other kinds of stories are less desirable since, as one CBS producer put it, "It would be hard to tell the good guys from the bad guys."[22]

Stories that do not fit this dramatic framework are often ignored by reporters who simply do not know what to do with them. Gaye Tuchman cites the example of one reporter who filed no story on an important feminist conference because, as he explained, "There were a lot of interesting things going on, but I couldn't nail things down. There was formless talk, I could see things changing, but it was hard to put my finger on it and say . . . 'this is what's happening.'"[23] The lack of a clear-cut dramatic peg on which to hang the story rendered the information "unnewsworthy."

Newswriters generally try to wrap up their brief story-dramas with a "snapper closer." A snapper closer provides a sense of resolution so viewers can relax and stop worrying, at least for one day, about *that* problem. After reporting the American boycott of the Moscow Olympic games, for example, one newscaster concluded, "Is an American boycott of the Moscow games the answer? For many Americans, the answer appears to be yes." That conclusion was based on film interviews with a grand total of four people.

If the newscaster's closer can communicate a sense of optimism, so much the better. A CBS report on school-children who were fed leftovers to keep them from going hungry because of cutbacks in the school lunch program concluded cheerfully, "Old rolls, new rolls. It appears that one way or another, kids here are going to get their lunch." What is being communicated is the feeling that nothing more need be done—or thought—about the problem, that there are simple solutions that will resolve it. Yet, as H.L. Mencken says, "For every complex problem, there is an answer that is short, simple—and wrong."

Compare the kind of "snapper closer" that characterizes network news with this closing statement by Robert MacNeil to his guest panelists on "The MacNeil-Lehrer Report": "Gentlemen, we're not going to solve this argument, which has gone on for weeks, and which will probably continue. We've heard your charge and your reply to it. Thank you very much for joining us. Good night." By avoiding a tidy conclusion, by leaving things unresolved, MacNeil is, in effect, inviting the viewer to think, to form judgments, protest, perhaps, even, take action. As MacNeil explains, "We make each viewer his own pundit—in a sense, his own reporter—looking over our shoulders as we interview leading sources . . . We don't wrap it up in a tidy package. We let the viewer do that. And we know of many families and some large groups of people where the debate continues when we go off the air."[24] The language communicates a sense of possibility rather than finality. This is a closer reflection of reality than the artificial resolutions of network news.

The bias toward dramatic storytelling means that viewers get a distorted view of the world. School busing to achieve integration, for example, rarely gets coverage unless it is the cause of community unrest and protest. There have been myriad broadcasts on the troubled busing controversy in Boston, while the majority of communities, in which busing has been widely accepted, have been all but ignored. Minority groups in general are invisible on TV news except in moments of crisis, such as the rioting in Watts and in Miami. "Burning ghettos makes good television," says Edwin Diamond, "but they don't advance the story of race in America significantly."[25] The Kerner Commission report states flatly, "The media have failed to report accurately on the causes . . .

of civil disorders and the underlying problems of race relations . . . The media have never . . . even glimpsed what it is
like in a racial ghetto and the reasons for unrest there."[26]

In the movie *Medium Cool*, a black ghetto dweller tells a
television news crew, "You people don't know. You don't
want to know. You don't know the people. You don't *show* the
people. Sometime when some poor cat who's nobody—some
cat who wakes up and says 'I'm going to die and nobody but
my old lady will even know that I ever lived' . . . when this cat
throws a brick through Charlie's window . . . and *shoots*
[points finger as with a gun], then he lives. He lives on
the tube. A hundred million people know that the former
invisible man *lives*. The whole world knows where he went to
school . . . The tube is life, man—life. And you make him the
TV star, the Emmy man of the hour . . . Why don't you find
out what *really* is? Why do you wait till somebody gets killed,
man?"

Black perspectives are equally absent in foreign affairs
reporting. During the war in Zaire, Africa, Katangese insur-
gents killed hundreds of civilians—whites *and* blacks. Walter
Cronkite opened the story by saying, "Good evening. The
worst fears in the rebel invasion of Zaire's Shaba Province
reportedly have been realized. Rebels being routed from the
mining town of Kolwezi are reported to have killed a number
of Europeans." The next night, the story added that "One
hundred white civilians were killed by the rebels, among
them women and children." Not until the end of the third
night's report did anyone mention that "the number of African dead is also placed at about one hundred fifty." CBS
correspondent Randy Daniels, who covered the story, says,
"There was a preoccupation with the deaths of Europeans,
when more than a thousand Africans had died, and thousands more became refugees." He adds, "The preponderance
of news from Africa is clearly from a white point of view and
deals primarily with whites."[27] "TV news executives figure
that the American population cares less and less about what

happens to people the darker their skin is," comments another network news reporter.[28]

A story's "newsworthiness" is often determined by geography. Journalist Thomas Griffith describes how he and his colleagues used to argue over "how many people would have to be killed where to make news—three people in an auto wreck in your own town? Ten people drowning in a shipwreck in the English channel; twenty-five in an avalanche in the Alps—and now the numbers increase sharply—one hundred in an earthquake in Turkey; three hundred in the collapse of a bridge in Bolivia; one thousand in a typhoon off Calcutta; fifteen hundred in a fire in China?"[29] News, it appears, is what happens in your own backyard.

This kind of reporting helps to magnify our provincialism. The average American, asked to draw a map of the world, would probably show the U.S.A. occupying half of the land surface, with Europe and Russia and China and Africa tucked off in some untidy, insignificant corner of the globe.*

Television news dissolves meaning in a wash of flashy images. The takeover of Afghanistan is summed up with a close-up view of a weeping widow, the problem of inflation with an image of the interior of a supermarket with a tight shot of the price of hamburger, the importance of gold price fluctuations with footage of gold traders frantically jostling each other to get their orders in. A typical half-hour news broadcast has fifteen to twenty stories. Allowing time for commercial interruptions, that leaves an average of one minute per story. Congressman Michael Synar says this makes for a simple-minded electorate: "When I go home I have to deal with people, and all they know of a four-hundred-page bill is one paragraph in the Sunday paper or a thirty-second TV

---

*A similar parochialism is seen in newspaper reporting. On the average, foreign affairs stories constitute only 11 percent of the news reported. In contrast, such stories constitute 17 percent of the space in Russian newspapers, 23 percent in Third World countries, 24 percent in Western European countries, and 38 percent in Eastern European countries. An elite newspaper, the German *Die Welt*, gives about 44 percent of its space to foreign affairs news.

spot. Issues don't break that way, but people just don't grasp the complexity."[30]

The criterion for how much time a story gets, or whether it appears at all, is not its relative importance in world affairs. "We like stories that have wiggle," one network executive says. "Sexy stories. Iran has wiggle. Defectors from the Bolshoi have wiggle. Stories about government agencies have *no wiggle*."

In the mind of many network news executives, the difference between a good news story and Marilyn Monroe's posterior is undetectable. Reporters are told to go after the human interest angle to a story—the "people factor"—rather than to explore the how or why of a particular event. Researcher David Altheide once accompanied a reporter assigned to do a story on proposed alternatives to achieve racial integration. As they left the studio, the reporter explained how he planned to do the story: "Just barely give a background as to what these alternatives are. Explain the story over film of kids, bless their little hearts, who have no say in the matter whatsoever, caught in a game of politics between their parents and the school board."[31] The dramatic peg for the story was thus determined before the reporter had even arrived at the scene!

In selling a human interest peg, reporters rely on "how do you feel" questions to get at "the emotional heart" of a story: "How do you feel now that your husband is taken hostage/your home is destroyed/your dog is run over/your boy has eaten 250 bananas?" The background and context of an event are ignored in the scramble to get "on the scene" testimony from participants.

The language of TV news is fragmented, patchwork, ahistorical. Viewers are not encouraged to make connections or form hypotheses. One story has no connection to the stories before or after it—except for gimmicky "lead-ins" born of a broadcaster's desire to weave the entertainment into a seamless continuity. One reporter was told by his producer to conclude a story about an alternate theory of creation with a reference to bibles, even though the theory did *not* represent the biblical view and bibles had nothing to do with what the story was about. The reason? The following story began with a line about "welfare cheaters swearing on a stack of bibles."[32]

Apart from such artificial transitions, each news story is individual and unrelated to others. Viewers are presented with a series of discrete, unrelated facts—a surface mosaic of events. No linkages are suggested or even looked for. As *New York Times* correspondent James Reston says, "We are fascinated by events but not by the things that cause the events. We will send five hundred correspondents to Vietnam after the war breaks out, and fill the front pages with their reports, meanwhile ignoring the rest of the world, but we will not send five reporters there when the danger of war is developing."[33]

The coverage of the hostage crisis in Iran is another case in point. The seizure of the American embassy by Iranian militants in October 1979 took most Americans entirely by surprise. Few Americans knew anything about the Islamic revolution that had taken place nine months before—and even fewer knew anything about America's role thirty years before in deposing the democratically elected Mossadegh and replacing him with the Shah. One *New York Times* editorial said, "The embassy seizure broke over much of the United States like a freakish autumn storm, its origins unseen, its course wild and menacing." Subsequent coverage almost entirely overlooked the roots of Iranian grievances against the United States, concentrating instead on repeated images of angry Iranians shouting epithets in the direction of the American embassy. Later, we learned that the demonstrations were often stage-managed solely for the benefit of TV cameras. At one point, the well-rehearsed chants of "Death to the Shah! Death to Carter!" were repeated in Persian, English, and French to accommodate the respective TV crews present.

Wall Street Journal correspondent Ray Vicker, who was on the scene at the American embassy during one such demonstration, wrote, "You must be at the center of this crowd, complete with its hot-dog stands, peanut vendors and soda merchants to appreciate what can only be called a carnival atmosphere—a *bonhomie* without signs of hatred. Then a camera man appears. Fists are waved. The mood changes. Fierce expressions are adopted."[34] Though many newsmen knew the demonstrations were being choreographed for their benefit, they could not resist reporting an event so perfectly fashioned to fit the demands of American TV news entertainment standards.

Night after night Americans were witness to Walter Cronkite's obvious indignation over Iran's action. Columnist James Reston believes that a great deal of the reason for the abortive raid on Iran was the continual "drum roll" of Cronkite's closing words each day: "And that's the way it is, Thursday, May 6th, the 169th day of captivity for the American hostages in Iran." But the prize for incendiary journalism goes to the Cleveland anchorman who concluded the eleven o'clock report with an on-screen burning of the Iranian flag.

Another angle to the Iranian story which got a lot of play was the travails of the families of the hostages. Hardly a night went by without a "How do you feel" interview with at least one family member. TV crews stayed so close to some families that they became good friends. CBS news helped hostage wife Dorothea Morefield keep track of her sons by providing them with electronic beepers. The crew also took turns chauffeuring her to the hairdresser. Newsmen were allowed to enter the house without knocking and to help themselves to whatever they wanted from the refrigerator. On the day of the hostages' release, Mrs. Morefield said, "These people have become my friends. They cried with us, they laughed with us—now they can celebrate with us."

Former Under Secretary of State George Ball comments, "In 1968, when the *Pueblo* hostages were taken, it was not made into one of the great events of our time . . . [the cover-age of the Iranian crisis] is absolutely childish. If it were not for the importance of Iran itself . . . it would be a relatively minor incident . . . This deep public obsession with the issue is largely because we live in a country where people are ac-customed to soap operas and when a foreign policy is trans-lated into that idiom, they react accordingly."[35] Newscaster Robert MacNeil agrees that TV news coverage served to in-flame, not enlighten, the public, pointing out that "On stories with a very high factor of audience emotion or anxiety built in, news reporting should de-emotionalize them, so people can get at them. News shows should drain the emotional charge from an atmosphere rather than augment it."[36] After the return of the hostages, the "information" we got from the news became pure chauvinistic tub-thumping. The hostages, of course, could be expected to be full of praise for America after over a year of captivity, but just in case they didn't fully understand what was expected of them, newsmen gave them a nudge in the right direction. Take this leading question from ABC newsman Roger Caras to Kathryn Koob: "Kate, you and your fifty-one fellow former hostages came home to more than your native land. You came to an outpouring of love that is unprecedented for persons other than war heroes. It's Val-entine's Day. What's your message to America?" Not sur-prisingly, she responded in kind:

I would say, first of all, a Valentine message for you, you're beautiful. Remember your strength and your resilience. You came through a crisis that lasted four hundred and forty-one days. But your coming through this didn't just happen because fifty-three of us were taken captive in Iran. It goes back to your growing, to all of our growing, growing through a Civil Rights movement that is unlike any that's taken place anywhere in the world . . . It got us through Watergate. These were all times that weren't very good. And then something happened, and I happened to be part of it. And all I can say is you grew;

you grew through Civil Rights; we all grew through Watergate, through Vietnam, and we could stand up proud and . . . we can't ever forget that. And my Valentine message to you is I love you, America . . .

Later, Caras added this epilogue: "If the result of the ordeal is to draw people close, to make them more at home in their own land, to give them a greater appreciation of what is theirs, then who is to say, it is all bad, all, all for nothing."

The rhythms here belong to fiction rather than fact, evoking Sydney Carton's memorable final words in Dickens' *A Tale of Two Cities*: "It is a far, far better thing I do than I have ever done . . ." The emotions aroused by that kind of reporting were somewhat less noble in sentiment, however. Witness an ABC broadcast featuring hostage Sam Gillete saying, "The most marvelous letters we received were from little kids . . . There was Tom Daly in New York who wrote me a beautiful little letter. He's in fourth grade, but it came out and said, 'I think we ought to bomb the bastards.' [Laughter.] 'Bomb' was misspelled. 'Bastards' was misspelled. It was, oh, it brought tears to my eyes, it was so beautiful."

ABC coverage of the hostage parade in Washington was titled "America Celebrates: A Salute to Freedom." The program was a binge of patriotism, including "man-on-the-street" interviews which featured comments like this: "We're the only nation in the world that puts human life above everything . . . We can show the world we're the leaders of the free world . . . These are fifty-two of the greatest people in the world . . . in the greatest city in the greatest country in the world." One might suspect this young man of having a limited vocabulary, but ABC's Frank Reynolds entertained no such objective view. His approving comment: "That was a patriotic and eloquent young man . . . He was right." Meantime, on NBC, Eric Sevareid was informing viewers that "What we have here is proof of the goodness of the American people—and of their patience . . . The great strength of America is that we recognize there is goodness in the world."

The "objectivity" of that program was displayed even in its title: "Home Are the Brave." A listener from a country not involved might have experienced some difficulty in distinguishing such "news reporting" from the propaganda purveyed in countries that do not enjoy the privilege of having an independent press, free from the responsibility of carrying out government directives.

Walter Lippmann noted that in times of crisis, "there seems to operate a kind of Gresham's Law of the emotions, in which leadership passes by a swift degeneration . . . from a high-minded statesmanship to the depths of virulent, hating jingoism." Why does this happen? "The cardinal fact is the loss of contact with objective information. Public as well as private reason depends on it. Not what somebody says, not what somebody wishes were true, but what is beyond all our opining, constitutes the touchstone of our sanity."[37]

One of the great myths of modern America is that of the objectivity of the press. In fact, to be "objective" in a news report usually means to conform to traditional ways of thinking. *New York Times* columnist Tom Wicker calls the practice of objectivity "an act of advocacy for the status quo." The following remarks made by Harry Reasoner during an appearance on "The Dick Cavett Show" are revealing:

Reasoner: Lyndon Johnson said the [Vietnam] War was lost after Walter [Cronkite] came out against it.

Cavett: Mr. Johnson's assumption, then, was that he'd been for it before that?

Reasoner: He *had* been for it, in the sense that he was objective, *his inclination was to believe in and support the United States military*—which was all our inclinations.* [Italics added.]

---

*On the same Cavett program, Ted Koppel remarked, "I'm sure he [Cronkite] felt he was being objective. I've seen some old films of Walter in Vietnam in the early and mid-sixties. Looking at those reports now . . . he was *so* supportive of the war effort that now I'm sure he'd be embarrassed by those films."

*   *   *

Objectivity appears to be equated here with an instinctive, almost reflexive allegiance to the military establishment. Journalist Philip Meyer comments, "We reporters tend to be conventional people with conventional ways of looking at things. So our interpretations seldom do more than reinforce conventional wisdom."[38] Former FCC Commissioner E. William Henry adds, "The middle position isn't *no* position; it *is* a position."[39]

Since pro-Establishment reporting builds on conventional wisdom—that is, on the things most people already more or less agree upon—it seems more plausible than other forms of propaganda. Its values seem praiseworthy, "correct," "normal." Perhaps they are. But how can we judge reliably? One of the greatest propagandists of all time, Joseph Goebbels, declared that what people regard as truth is the "information" with which they are most familiar.

On the night of the Massachusetts presidential primaries, ABC correspondent James Wooten bypassed any comment on the candidates and their positions to file this report while standing in front of the statue of Paul Revere in Boston:

> "These are the times," wrote Tom Paine, "that try men's souls," and men like Paul Revere understood. All those many years ago when that silversmith closed his shop and clattered off into history; when those lanterns in the spire burned a hole in the night; when Boston was bursting with the noise of politics, the noise of the American process handed down from one generation to the next. Different times than these, certainly. Yet in this place, in this Boston, all those names and faces and places don't seem that long ago, not that far removed, not on a Massachusetts election day, which is a genuine celebration of those times that tried men's souls.
>
> We clock our history by leap years, with presidential campaigns coming and going and setting one moment apart from

another, and perhaps that's as it should be. For all those noisy ideas and all those noisy times are never better remembered than on a day like this, an election day. It's a part of history, too.

This kind of reporting goes considerably beyond the "facts" of the occasion. Yet most broadcasters would probably regard it as "objective," because there is no directly stated opinion. "Opinion" is supposedly reserved for news segments clearly labeled "commentary" or "analysis," the implication being that all other news stories present facts without making value judgments. In reality, "straight" news reporting often contains hidden statements of opinion. After Ted Kennedy's loss to Carter in the 1980 Iowa straw poll, reporter Cassie Mackin announced, "This was the most serious defeat that any candidate has ever had." And wrapping up a report on inferior medical care for minority groups, one NBC correspondent commented, "The problem of bad and expensive medical care cannot be cured quickly by some big government program."

Despite such blatant editorializing, many people continue to believe television news shows are neutral and value-free. NBC Vice Chairman Richard Salant certainly feels that way. "Our reporters do not cover stories from their point of view," he says. "They are presenting them from nobody's point of view." Semanticists know that is impossible. Any kind of communication requires making decisions about what information to include, what to omit, what to stress, what to play down, what to put first, etc. Such decisions inevitably involve value judgments.

Our press regularly assails the Soviet press for its lack of objectivity. A recent article in *Time* magazine, for example, pointed out:

[Soviet news] stories about the West almost invariably emphasize doom and gloom, with such headlines as SOCIETY OF VIOLATED RIGHTS or WORLD OF CAPITAL: SOCIAL PROBLEMS. Correspondents overseas do not deny that their primary duty is to promote socialism . . . Says Thomas Kolesnichenko, *Pravda* correspondent in New York: "We try to give people a story that is true, but in terms of a historical perspective, in terms of our understanding of world events."

The clear implication is that our reporting of Soviet affairs is free from such self-serving interest. But historian George Kennan, a specialist in Soviet affairs, says our television news reports on the U.S.S.R. are filled with "endless series of distortions and oversimplifications, systematic dehumanization of the leadership . . . routine exaggeration of Moscow's military capabilities and the supposed iniquity of its intentions." He warns, "If we insist on demonizing these Soviet leaders— on viewing them as total and incorrigible enemies consumed only with their fear or hatred of us and dedicated to nothing other than our destruction—that, in the end, is the way we shall assuredly have them, if for no other reason than that our view of them allows for nothing else, either for us or for them."[40]

The same bias exists in reports of almost any country in the Soviet bloc. To take just one example, look at how television news handled the story of the emigrants from Castro's Cuba. Stepping off the boat, they were met with a barrage of "how do you feel" questions. When some of the emigrants did not wax sufficiently eloquent, the questions were refined to elicit a more satisfying answer: "After all the years of oppression, of fear, and the hazards of your journey, how would you describe the kind of hospitality you've encountered here?" Or, another example: "What would they do to you if you were sent back to Havana?" To which the emigrant answered dutifully, "Oh, they'd kill me." What else could he have been expected to answer except "I don't know"—in which case the interview would never appear on the air. If he said "Nothing," he would be encouraging the U.S. to send him back.

News coverage of the Cuban emigration emphasized that this "flight to liberty" was an escape from the "oppression" of Castro's communism. Perhaps in some, or most, cases it was, but it is fair to ask: What Caribbean nation, with years-long waiting lists for emigration to the United States, would not have at least 100,000 or more people ready to seize an opportunity for instant departure? Would our press have had so much of the "flight to liberty" if the emigrants had flocked to us from Jamaica or Haiti, from Honduras or Guatemala? The biased news reporting left most Americans completely unaware that the Cuban emigrants amounted to less than 2 percent of the entire population. It would have been as "objective" to report that, offered a chance for free emigration from their country, over 98 percent of Cubans elected to stay in their homeland.

"TV . . . does not enjoy rocking the boat, politically or commercially," says newsman Robert MacNeil. "It enjoys the status quo. It identifies with the Establishment nationally or locally."[41] Partly, this is because of media reliance on government information. The bulk of our news stories comes from prepared statements and press releases by government officials and agencies. Reporters, anxious to preserve their special beats, do not like to challenge officials on whose good graces future stories may depend.

Then, too, TV stations are understandably reluctant to bite the hand that licenses them. No network has actually been denied a license because the Administration didn't like the way it was being reported. But the idea has been suggested, and the threat remains. During his presidency, Richard Nixon attempted to "punish" the *Washington Post* for its role in exposing Watergate by challenging the license for a profitable television station held by the *Post*'s mother corporation. He also established a White House "communications" office to put pressure on the owners of television stations. The result, as NBC bureau chief William Monroe says, is that "An increasing number of people are getting their news from a medium which is intrinsically nervous about government."[42] Looking back on his years with CBS, Fred

Friendly comments, "I suppose I was subtly influenced to do controversial subjects in a non-controversial manner." He adds, "I must confess that in my almost two years as CBS News President, I tempered my news judgment and tailored my conscience more than once."[43]*

Even without the draconian threat of license revocation, which amounts to simple expropriation of property, the government can do a lot to discourage stations from tackling stories which are not in its best interests. NBC News President Reuven Frank explains: "Every time you undertake something that is just not quite as bland as all the other things you do, you worry about—will I be cited by the FCC? Will I have to testify to an examiner? Will I have to turn out my papers for them to look at? Will I be called by that House committee or that Senate committee?"[44] After enough of this kind of harassment, it's a miracle that *any* stories unfavorable to the government appear. Another NBC executive adds, "If you are operating in the newsroom of a local broadcast station and you are doing your job and one day three lawyers walk in with an FCC inquiry about something you've treated and you spend eighteen hours going through your files, maybe next time you have an issue you want to treat you'll think, 'Jesus Christ, do I have to go through all that?' and you may not do it the same way."[45]

Defenders of TV news often point to the coverage of Watergate as proof that reporting is free of government influence. This argument fails to take note of the fact that TV news did not pursue the story until it was already a well-established matter of discussion in the press and among politicians. During the time when Americans might have profited most from a full exploration of the scandal—before a

---

* If this was true of Friendly, a man who was known for his staunch news integrity (he resigned in protest when CBS chose to ignore the Congressional hearings on Vietnam and broadcast "I Love Lucy" reruns instead), one can only guess how many more such concessions may be made by network executives whose sense of civic responsibility may be somewhat less acute.

national election—TV news was still presenting the story as the Administration billed it: a "second-rate burglary." And that's where it would have been left if it weren't for the efforts of the print media, who kept the story alive for months while TV news ignored it. It was only after the full implications of the Watergate affair were published in the *Washington Post* and became public knowledge that TV news coverage joined the chorus of recrimination against the Nixon Administration. "Television," says Robert MacNeil, "is a cheerleader for the team that has already won."[46]

Newspapers and newsmagazines, directed at far more select and limited audiences, can often afford to take the kind of controversial stand that TV news dares not take. And the much greater volume of information in printed news sources (the content of an average half-hour television news show would fit easily into three newspaper columns) increases the likelihood that a controversial story will get a chance to surface. A story that appears on page 32 one week may draw enough attention to warrant page 1 coverage the next.

But television news programs must obey the same imperative as any other kind of television show—to attract the largest possible number of viewers and to keep them watching until the commercial break. Audience research reveals that viewers' anxieties are heightened by news stories that challenge their basic assumptions—and that anxious viewers are twice as likely to change the channel. It's not surprising that television news executives are reluctant to broadcast a story that will cost them ratings points, and, it must follow as the night the day, millions of dollars in lost advertising revenues. The most profitable course is to steer news broadcasts into safe pro-Establishment harbors.

Thanks to the advanced technology of television news, even our last thoughts on this earth will be carefully guided along the "correct" lines. Ted Turner, who owns the Cable News Network, has prepared a special news videotape to be shown in the earth's last moments. The apocalyptic tape is locked in the office of the executive vice president of the news station, along with handwritten instructions from Turner should he already have perished. Thanks to such entrepreneurial thoughtfulness, we may now all vanish into oblivion to the accompaniment of the musical strains of "God Bless America" and "The Stars and Stripes Forever."

Our survival as a species may well depend on the nature of the information we get from our news media. Of these, none is more important than television news, which reaches all social classes, all educational levels, and influences the thinking of more people than any other single social institution. The accuracy of its messages seems crucial. As has been shrewdly pointed out, we should never underestimate the intelligence of the American people—nor should we overestimate the amount of information they have.

II

The Hidden Persuaders

3

Let Me Entertain You. . . .

Television is a machine to manufacture reassurance for troubled Americans. Not confined to commercials, reassurance is part of the entertainment . . . the object is to disconnect the audience from uncomfortable realities, to lull it on a sea of gentle inconsequence—and then to sell it deodorant.

Robert MacNeil

One central myth dominates the world of fabricated fantasy: the idea that entertainment and recreation are value-free, have no point of view, and exist outside . . . the social order.

Herbert Schiller

One night, a friend and I sat watching "Too Close for Comfort," a popular situation comedy about the trials of a father trying to protect the virtue (i.e., virginity) of his two nubile young daughters. Most of the jokes revolved around Daddy's alternating consternation and relief about the girls' presumed sexual activities. For example:

Mother: Is Jackie in bed?
Father: I hope not. She's not home yet.

*   *   *

93

Father: Where's Jackie and Monroe?
Daughter: They're at a beach party.
Father: Hope they don't get cold.
Daughter: No, they brought lots of blankets.
Father: Blankets. . . ? Oh, no! (starts crying)

Daughter Jackie returns home later, still chaste, and hastens to reassure her worried father:

Jackie: Daddy! You thought me and Monroe. . . ? Oh! What kind of girl do you think I am! (starts crying)

A secondary plot line concerned a young male acquaintance of the family who is unhappy because he's still a virgin. After a lot of pat talk about "double standards," the family decided that the best course of action was to hire a professional sexual surrogate to initiate the young man into the wonderful world of intercourse.

That's when I got angry. "Listen to that!" I said to my friend. "They pay lip service to the unfairness of a double standard, but it's perfectly clear that they accept that standard as 'normal' and correct! Feminists should really have the right to demand equal time to counter this kind of programming."

My friend was amused. "Don't you think you're taking this too seriously?" she asked. "It's not a documentary on women's rights; it's just harmless entertainment."

That started me wondering. Is entertainment *really* harmless? Is it possible for people to remain unaffected by the basic premises of such a program because they know its purpose is not to educate but to divert?

Broadcasters uniformly deny that entertainment programs have any direct influence on how people think and behave. They argue, for example, that televised violence has no connection with the aggressiveness and violent behavior among children who are heavy viewers. Yet broadcasters will readily take credit for "public interest" messages which they occasionally insert into entertainment programs. Garry Marshall points proudly to the way shows such as "Happy Days" and "Laverne and Shirley" have helped push the idea of energy conservation: "We are not saying buy this or do that. It's subliminal. . . . We tie energy up with sex so viewers will listen." Producer Norman Lear says, "A half-hour documentary on seat belts will make only so many converts, but have Archie Bunker or Fonzie strap themselves in with a seat belt and there will be a run on seat belts everywhere."[1] Broadcasters also like to boast of how children's programs such as "Fat Albert" and "Ark II" teach pro-social messages about international brotherhood and the dangers of smoking and drugs. Herbert Schlosser comments, "Television is a powerful educational medium even when it isn't trying to be, even when it's only trying to entertain. There must be millions of people who have learned, simply by watching crime dramas in the past few years, that they have the right to remain silent when arrested."[2]

If this is true, then one must ask: What *else* may they have learned? Broadcasters cannot simultaneously take credit for "pro-social messages" and declare that any other messages have no impact because they are merely part of the "entertainment."

If we believe entertainment to be "harmless," it becomes all the more effective as a carrier of propaganda. If we think we are merely "passing the time," we are less inclined to question or challenge—even to recognize—the basic ideas and attitudes being transmitted. As media critic Robert Cirino says, "Bias that is the hardest to detect or explain is the most effective bias in the long run; people absorb it unknowingly. . . . Obvious bias puts readers or listeners on guard . . . [but] people tend to forget about political bias when it comes in the form of entertainment . . . At the same time they are enjoying the entertainment, people unknowingly absorb the political, social, and economic messages that are assumed in the program."[3]

Who determines what "lessons" are appropriate for television to teach the American people? By and large, these decisions rest with three social groups of enormous power: the networks, the government, and the sponsors. Of these, the sponsors are probably the most important. By agreeing or refusing to support certain kinds of programs, sponsors exercise great influence over television programming. The programs they prefer, not surprisingly, are those which best serve their own selling needs.

Not content with confining their messages to commercial breaks, some sponsors have actually inserted their advertising right into the entertainment. When tobacco advertising was still permitted on television, tobacco company sponsors sometimes insisted on program scripts that helped "create positive product feelings." In testimony before a Senate committee, one advertising agency executive explained how this was done:

> I can give you what I hope will not be an indiscreet example. . . . Last year two tobacco companies had similar programming. Each issued a tobacco policy for his show. These were on two separate shows. One company manufactured a filter cigarette, and his policy indicated that the heavy must smoke non-filter cigarettes.
> Q.: The heavies are villains?
> A.: Yes, villains. Whereas the manufacturer of the non-filter cigarette insisted that the heavy smoke a filtered cigarette. It sounds ridiculous, but it's not at all. . . . The association of the product that might be recognized as the client's product with a villain, a murderer, or whatever, is certainly something to be avoided.[4]

Other kinds of script adjustments were made to please tobacco sponsors. Characters on a tobacco-sponsored program were not allowed to light up a cigarette to "calm their nerves," since this might be suggestive of a narcotic, addictive effect. Cigarettes could not be smoked in short rapid puffs, but always gracefully, elegantly, with poise and assurance. Characters were never to cough. Villains could shoot, stab, rob, rape, kill, and commit all manner of mayhem *except* arson, because that might call to mind fires started by cigarettes.

A wide variety of sponsors successfully manages to insert commercial messages into entertainment programs.* General Motors donated seven Chevrolet Camaros to the long-running show "Mannix" on condition that none would ever be driven by a heavy, and that when two crashed, the Chevy would never be the car that gets totaled.

Chrysler had a similar promotion agreement with the "Mod Squad" producers, and car company executives monitored each program carefully to make sure it delivered "good product identification." A Chrysler executive explains, "Door handles and windshields don't mean anything. We want exposure that's meaningful, such as the side or the entire car, or the car driving into the camera with the nameplate on the screen." He adds, "If the show does not come through, you may have to reduce the number of vehicles they have."[5]

Sponsors have also demanded changes in scripts that they determine to be in any way "detrimental" to their product. A rival motor company once insisted that a shot of the New York skyline be taken out of a script it was sponsoring because it showed the Chrysler Building. Another automobile manufacturer wanted all mention of President Lincoln deleted from a script on the Andersonville Trials, presumably to avoid favorable associations with their production rival, the Lincoln. A breakfast-food manufacturer made a writer take out a line "She eats too much" because, in the opinion of the multimillion-dollar-a-year company, *nobody* could ever eat too much. And a gas company sponsoring a TV version of *Judgment at Nuremburg* got the producers to blip the word

---

* The simple mention of a product has a dramatic effect on sales. After the host of one variety show jokingly said, "Look that up in your Funk and Wagnall's," the dictionary had to go into a new printing to accommodate a 20 percent rise in sales.

"gas" out of the accounts of the horrors of Nazi concentration camps.

This kind of direct product propaganda is less common today. But television entertainment is still expected to accommodate corporate sponsors by promoting the ideal of ever greater and better consumption as a desirable way of life. Critics often bemoan the scarcity of lower-class people and settings on television programs—though they neglect to explain why this is so: Lower-class settings do not put people in the mood to buy. Indeed, they often make the glamorous promises of commercials seem fraudulent by contrast. As Eric Barnouw explains: "Sponsors prefer beautiful people in mouth-watering decor, to convey what it means to climb the socio-economic ladder . . . Commercials look out of place in Bronx settings . . . the drama undermines the message."[6]

The Pulitzer Prize-winning play *Street Scene* was turned down by sponsors for reasons best articulated in a letter the playwright, Elmer Rice, received from an advertising agency executive: "We know of not one advertiser or advertising agency of any importance in this country who would knowingly allow the products which he is trying to advertise to the public to become associated with the squalor . . . and general 'down' character . . . of *Street Scene* . . . On the contrary, it is the general policy of advertisers to glamorize their products, the people who buy them, and the whole American social and economic scene . . . The American consuming public *as presented by the advertising industry today* is middle class, not lower class; happy in general, not miserable or frustrated. . ." [Italics added.]

Frank Stanton, Vice Chairman of ABC, openly admits, "We must take into account the general objectives and desires of advertisers as a whole. An advertiser . . . is spending a very large amount of money—often many millions of dollars—to increase his sales, to strengthen his distribution and to win public favor. And so . . . it seems perfectly obvious that advertisers cannot and should not be forced into programs incompatible with their objectives."[8]

What every sponsor ideally wants is programming that teaches the joys and benefits of consumer buying—a program like, say, "Hart to Hart." That show features Jonathan and Jennifer Hart, a married couple whose fabulous wealth buys them plenty of free time to indulge their passion for unofficial detective work (the blurb for the show announces, "Murder is their hobby"). Though ostensibly a murder-mystery show, the demands of plot are of relatively little concern. One recent episode, for example, required viewers to swallow the following:

> 1. A jewel thief aboard a cruise ship dresses up like a cat burglar (black tights, sweater, gloves, and hood) in plain daylight in order to gain entry to a passenger's compartment.
> 2. After removing a diamond necklace from the safe, the thief walks to the mirror in the passenger's room, pulls off her black hood, and holds the necklace up to her neck to admire it. (isn't she just a bit worried that the passenger might return? And since the hood has eyeholes, why does she have to take it off to view the necklace?)
> 3. An ignorant houseboy successfully plays the role of an important Italian industrialist throughout a five-day cruise— without being able to speak a word of Italian.
> 4. Professional detectives forget to get fake IDs before assuming new aliases.
> 5. Jonathan Hart, a middle-aged man who apparently spends most of his time dining, drinking, and making love, out-karate-chops a trained karate expert.

Such plot loopholes do not bother the writers or producers, who know that the success of "Hart to Hart" depends not on its qualifications as a good mystery story, but on the visions it provides of all the beautiful possessions of its two beautiful protagonists. The Harts are constantly presented in settings of luxury: they discuss the latest case over breakfast, elegantly served to them in bed by their manservant on fine china and crystal; they rush to the scene of the crime in matching his-and-hers Rolls-Royces; they pursue elusive witnesses to Caribbean hideaways in their private jet; they corner culprits at society parties after sipping champagne and caviar. The plots and dialogue are merely background accompaniment for the attractive images paraded in front of us.

Such a program fits a sponsor's needs so perfectly one almost suspects it was designed by one. But sponsors rarely need to become directly involved in program development any more, since network programmers have come to understand and accept their unstated wishes so well. Eric Barnouw says, "Sponsorship has become so essential, so crucial to the whole scheme of things, that interference of the old sort is no longer necessary. A vast industry has grown up around the needs and wishes of sponsors. Its program formulas, business practices, ratings, demographic surveys have all evolved in ways to satisfy sponsor requirements. He has reached the ultimate status: most decision making swirls at levels below him, requiring only his occasional benediction at this or that selected point. He is a potentate of our time."[9]

Networks themselves are vast corporate enterprises whose needs are becoming increasingly indistinguishable from those of the sponsor. NBC, for instance, is part of the even vaster RCA empire, which manufactures and sells everything from radios, television sets, stereos, carpeting, and frozen food to satellites and defense equipment.

To provide the best possible environment for their product messages, both networks and sponsors try to steer clear of "controversial" topics. Controversy is avoided for two reasons: viewers who do not agree with the message might boycott the sponsor's product; and viewers who are deeply moved or politically aroused are less likely to be receptive to deodorant soap commercials. One advertising agency executive explains,

"The impact of the sponsor's message must not be diminished by the program content."[10]* ABC Vice President Bob Shanks adds, "Program makers are supposed to devise and produce shows that will attract mass audiences without unduly offending those audiences or too deeply moving them emotionally. Such ruffling, it is thought, will interfere with their ability to receive, recall, and respond to the commercial message."[11] This state of affairs is simply not permissible in a broadcasting system grounded firmly in the principles of the marketplace.

So television entertainment is rigorously censored. All programs are screened for "offensive" material by "broadcast standards departments," whose decisions are often so wildly irrational that one television producer describes handing in a script as an experience akin to "delivering a Stradivarius into the hands of a gorilla." A typical example of censoring whimsy: In an episode of "Three's Company," Jack's two female roommates conspire with him to keep his visiting mother from discovering that he lives with two women. At one point, roommate Janet says, "I did my best . . . I put the toilet seat up." After Jack's mother leaves, she announces, "I put the toilet seat down." The first line was judged to be acceptable; the second was censored. Presumably, as far as the top brass was concerned, toilet seat descent is more "offensive" than toilet seat ascent.

Decisions such as these help explain why network censors are known in the trade as "profit-prevention engineers." In their book *Stay Tuned*, television writers Richard Levinson and William Link describe a typical censorship meeting: "Grown men sit pleasantly over coffee and argue about the potentially offensive nature of words. Producers alternate be-

---

*On the rare occasions when powerful drama does make it on the air, this effect on the surrounding advertising is observable. After *Roots* was first broadcast, *Variety* remarked on the ridiculousness of cutting "from the anguished screams of a mother whose son has just been enslaved to a blurb for Ben-Gay, for use 'when pain is at its worst.'"

tween rage and cajolery; they often insert profane expressions into a script, with no intention of using them, so they have bargaining chips for trading . . ."[12]

Of far greater concern than censorship of "bad" words is censorship of ideas. Freedom of speech is one of our most cherished Constitutional guarantees, yet the fact is that many ideas are not permitted to be aired on the nation's most influential medium of communication. Doubtless the Founding Fathers believed when they wrote, in the First Amendment, "Congress shall make no law abridging the freedom of speech" that only Congress would ever be a powerful enough body to curb free speech. They could not possibly have foreseen the enormous power television sponsors would acquire over the people's access to information. Jerome Barron comments, "A realistic view of the First Amendment requires recognition that a right of expression is somewhat thin if it can be exercised only at the sufferance of the managers of mass communications."

Former FCC Chairman Nicholas Johnson states flatly, "Censorship is a serious problem in this country," and this view is confirmed in a poll of the 3,000 members of the Writers Guild of America: 86 percent of the writers queried said that they had found, from personal experience, that censorship exists on "entertainment" programs. Many added that they had never written a script that had not been censored. The majority also said that they believed such censorship was depriving Americans of important information: 81 percent stated flatly that the vision of America presented on entertainment programs is seriously distorted—"politically, economically, and racially." Many reported proposing shows about the elderly, mental disease, politics, business, labor, students and minorities, and "being chased out of the studios."[13] Christopher Knopf, a television scriptwriter and past president of the Writers Guild, says, "In documentaries and in news, certain truths can be told, but you can't tell them in commercial drama. You can't take up real problems seriously

. . . We're feeding middle America all the pap we know as lies and nonsense; we are feeding things we personally resent, which have no resemblance to real life."[14] Mason Williams, a writer for the heavily censored—and eventually canceled—"Smothers Brothers" show, penned a bitter piece of verse about "The Censor," who

> Snips out
> The rough talk
> The unpopular opinion
> Or anything with teeth
> And renders
> A pattern of ideas
> Full of holes
> A doily
> For your mind

If a controversial story is presented, it is usually "killed" before it can be written. Those that survive often emerge from the censor's pen rather remarkably transformed. Perhaps the most famous case of "story evolution" occurred with a script called "Noon at Doomsday" by Rod Serling. Initially, the story was based on the story of Emmett Till, a fourteen-year-old Mississippi youth who was killed by two white men after he whistled at a white woman. A local jury later acquitted the two men despite overwhelming evidence of their guilt. Rod Serling's story was accepted—on condition that "the racial factor" be removed. So the murder victim was changed from a black youth to an elderly white pawnbroker. This, of course, meant that the motive for murder also had to be changed, since the old man was unlikely to have been whistling at *any* woman, black or white. The revised story called for him to be killed by a disturbed young man seeking a scapegoat for his own failures.

With these changes, the script was approved and production begun. But then Serling mentioned to a reporter in an interview that the story had originally been suggested to him by the Emmett Till case. The program sponsor worried that this revelation might cause its Southern customers to "take offense" (i.e., stage a boycott). It was decided that the story would take place in New England, to avoid any possible slur on Southerners. Further plot changes were made to accommodate this change in locale. And to leave no possible doubt in anyone's mind, the film opened with a long camera shot of a white church spire.

By then any resemblence to the original story was purely coincidental. If television had existed in Shakespeare's day, *Othello* might have turned out to be a story about a Scandinavian priest who, driven by the evil promptings of his prelate, Iago, comes to distrust and finally excommunicate his favorite altarboy, Desmond.

The same kind of censorship that Serling experienced exists today, though the topics considered too "controversial" for broadcast have changed. Richard Levinson and William Link describe some of their many battles with network censors over the years. The difficulties they encountered with a script called "That Certain Summer" are typical. They wanted to tell the story of a middle-aged, middle-class man who has divorced his wife and "come out" as a homosexual. His teenage son, who doesn't know about his father's homosexuality, arrives for a summer visit, and the father must face the problem of telling the boy the truth. Their idea was to portray a homosexual as a full human being and not a ridiculous caricature. NBC immediately turned down the story, saying, "We wouldn't touch anything like that with a ten-foot pole." Link and Levinson comment, "It was perfectly acceptable for Bob Hope or Johnny Carson to mince about the screen doing broad parodies of homosexual behavior, but anything else, anything not derisive or played for laughs, was out of the question."[15] (That view was shared by many actors, who were unwilling to play the role of the homosexual father. "My fans wouldn't accept it," one actor stated. When asked if he would consider playing the role of Hitler in a televised drama, the same actor replied, "Of course.")

Eventually, ABC did approve the story. But when the network representatives saw the final script, they told Link and Levinson such a treatment would be perceived as "pro-homosexual" and thus in opposition to "the prevailing climate of public opinion."* A rewrite was demanded. The writers describe their response:

> We countered that the script was neither pro- nor anti-gay and we suggested that a much larger issue was involved: the question of the writer's rights to use the public air for the expression of opinions, popular or otherwise. Was controversy to be denied anyone who wrote for television? . . . If a writer dared to take a position, must the countervailing view always be incorporated in the script? . . . And by giving weight to opposing opinions, didn't the writer risk eviscerating his material to the point of all-things-to-all-men blandness?[16]

In the end, Link and Levinson were forced to make changes which they felt seriously undermined the script. In the final scene between father and son, for example, the father originally says, "A lot of people—most people, I guess—think it's wrong . . . They say it's a sickness . . . They say it's something that has to be cured . . ." The writers were required to add the following lines: "Maybe they're right, I don't know . . . I *do* know that it's not easy. If I had a choice, it's not

---

* Apparently, networks believe that the simple appearance, on-screen, of a homosexual who is not a villain or a clown constitutes a "pro-homosexual" stand. The pilot movie for "Love, Sidney," a story about a reclusive bachelor who takes a young woman into his apartment and helps her raise her illegitimate daughter, portrayed Sidney as a homosexual. The references to his sex life (at his age, largely in the past) were few and subtle: a photograph of a former lover, a line of dialogue—"You mean . . . you're. . . ? "Yes." Even that proved to be too much for NBC, however, which went to great lengths to publicize, before the series debut, the fact that Sidney was no longer to be a homosexual—indeed, he was no longer to display any sexual preference at all.

something I'd pick for myself." This, it was felt, helped "balance" the scales more equitably.

This concern for "balance" is not, however, in evidence with scripts that ridicule homosexuals. The following exchange, from "Three's Company Too" is typical of the way homosexuals are portrayed on most television programs:

> Girl: Goodbye, honey. (kisses Jack)
> Jack: (wiping kiss off cheek in disgust) Oooooh, yuuck!
> Mr. Roper: Who's that?
> Jack: Oh, just a pal.
> Roper: Does she know that you're . . . (lifts up pinky in an effeminate gesture and wiggles across room)
> Jack: Yes, she knows.

Such scripts are not considered "unbalanced" because they reflect the views of the social majority. The values and habits of white middle-class America are seldom questioned and never ridiculed, while those of minority groups such as Hispanics, Indians, blacks, and the elderly often are. After analyzing three years of sitcoms and other television entertainment programming, one research group made the following report on the portrayal of Hispanic-Americans:

> 1. They're hard to find. If you watched three hundred different television characters, you'd find less than a handful of Hispanics.
> 2. They're males, of dark complexion, with dark hair, most often with heavy accents. Women are absent and insignificant.
> 3. They're gregarious and pleasant, with strong family ties . . . half are lazy, and very few show much concern for their futures. Most have had very little education, and their jobs reflect that fact.[17]

Minority groups are made to appear laughable apparently so they will seem less threatening to the established social order. After "Welcome Back, Kotter" had been on the air for just a few weeks, audience surveys revealed that middle-class viewers were disturbed by the tough talk and wild manners of the ghetto teenagers. Fred Silverman ordered the writers to make the "sweathogs" goofier so their actions would appear funny, not frightening.

Network and sponsor censorship seeks to eliminate ideas with which the social majority is not comfortable.* The result is a virtual blackout of differing points of view. As Nicholas Johnson says, "The ideas and life-styles endorsed and purveyed by American television are truly 'popular' only with those Americans fortunate enough to be native-born-white-Anglo-Saxon-Protestant-suburban-dwelling-middle-class-and-over-thirty."[18]

Television executives defend this state of affairs by saying that programming decisions are based on a "democratic" system in which people get to vote for or against programs by switching channels or turning off their sets. But as Cornell professor Rose Goldsen points out, such "voting" takes place "in a system that disenfranchises minorities who have no way to mobilize public support for converting themselves into majorities."[19] This is why censorship inevitably results in reinforcing the social status quo.

The same bias is evident in censorship of political messages. This was particularly obvious during the Vietnam War. Once, for example, CBS censored part of Carol Burnett's appearance on the Merv Griffin show in which she appealed to viewers to write supporting world peace. Several weeks later, Bob Hope appeared in an *un*censored hour-long special in which he appealed to viewers to support the Vietnam War effort. Similarly, ABC once blacked out a performance by a college band during halftime in a televised football game

---

* An old Procter & Gamble censorship code read, "If there is any attack on American custom, it must be rebutted completely on the same show."

because, as Sports President Roone Arledge said, it was deemed "too political in nature." The act, called "Give Peace a Chance," was critical of the war. Yet a few weeks later ABC broadcast a halftime tribute to American prisoners of war. It was later revealed that the "show" had been organized by the Nixon Administration as a piece of pro-war public relations. In the eyes of network censors, opinions are "too political in nature" only if they do not agree with established government policy.

Often, censorship of political opinion results from government pressure, either real or anticipated. A CBS producer describes how government intimidation works: "The administration has two techniques for manipulating the networks. One is the 'early warning letter' . . . It says something like, 'We understand you are planning to do a program on [such-and-such] a topic. We trust you will be checking with so-and-so at the Pentagon to get all the facts you need . . ." [The network president] sends the letter on to [the vice-president] who sends it to the executive producer . . . Each executive scribbles on the buck slip 'What's up?'—and promptly puts the matter out of his mind . . . The guy at the end of the line is all shook up. He's the lowest man on the totem pole and he knows if he goes ahead with the project and there's a complaint, he is the one in trouble since everyone else had, in effect, called it to his attention. So you damn well call so-and-so at the Pentagon and wrap your item in a lot of bland cotton. . . The second technique is the 'eleventh-hour telegram.' Again, it goes right to [the network president]. It may come from a Cabinet officer and it warns of 'the great danger in putting out a biased account.' This last-minute appeal is intended to shake them up so much that the project doesn't get on the air." He adds, "I've seen it happen."[20]

Another way that the government can influence television programming is by withholding assistance for programs that are "not in the national interest." This is particularly effective with dramas having anything to do with the military. In order to film military bases and rent military equipment, producers of such programs need to get clearance from the Defense Department. Without such clearance, the costs of producing any story about military matters would be prohibitively high. This, in effect, gives the Defense Department the right of censorship over such programs. When, for example, the script of "Enola Gay," a story about the men on the plane that bombed Hiroshima, was submitted to the Defense Department for approval, it was turned down because the Department judged it to be "far to sympathetic to the Japanese." The producers were denied access to any military bases, men, and equipment until the script was rewritten by a retired Navy man. The revised script had a more pro-American stance, stressing the fact that faced with such a fanatical enemy, dropping the bomb was the only reasonable alternative. This version was approved by the Defense Department and eventually broadcast.

Another story, called "Winter Soldier," was judged "inappropriate" by the Defense Department because it portrayed the all-volunteer army as inefficient and unprepared. At this writing, the script is being rewritten to win approval. Still a third story about the life of Dwight Eisenhower was censored by the Defense Department in order to whitewash the romance between Eisenhower and his secretary, Kay Summersby.

In contrast, stories with messages supportive of the American military can expect a great deal of assistance and cooperation. When CBS decided to do a story on the Air Force flyers who train new fighter pilots by staging dangerous midair dogfights, the Air Force provided the producers with planes and pilots at very low rental costs, gave permission for camera-carrying helicopters to fly over the base, and even provided accommodations for the stars of the show at the VIP suite on base. The Air Force was happy to help out because, as its spokesman said, the story left viewers "with a warm, fuzzy feeling toward the Air Force."21 *

Of course, it's only natural for the military to behave this way. All social groups welcome the broadcast of stories favorable to them, and try to censor or prevent those that are unfavorable. The difference is that the Defense Department has the power to ensure that most of the time its wishes will prevail. This is not true of groups outside the established social and political order, and as a result their wishes are often ignored. Their only recourse then, as Rose Goldsen points out, is "the negative power of the boycott—in this case, simultaneous blackout of millions of television screens." She adds, "In the political sphere such acts would be called plebiscite, general strike, or insurrection. A political system that offers only these alternatives for making the public will known is called totalitarian. We do not yet have a similarly familiar term for our television system."22

The most dangerous kind of censorship is invisible. It occurs when writers give up trying to write about ideas they know will not be acceptable. As one television screenwriter says, "After you get burned enough times, you learn to stay away from the fire. What's the point of submitting a script you know will not be touched—or one that will be so altered it loses all its impact anyway?" Another writer adds, "You can't write scripts for a number of years without coming to know exactly what is acceptable and what isn't. In fact, after a while you find you can't even *think* of an idea that would have no chance of acceptance because it might cause controversy. You succeed in totally censoring out your own imagination."

Testifying before the Senate, a vice president of one of

---

* The same situation exists in the production of full-length feature movies. The army provided a huge number of troops and military equipment at very low prices to the producer of John Wayne's film *The Green Berets*, which glorified the Vietnam War. The navy offered similar help to Darryl Zanuck for his film *Tora! Tora! Tora!* about the Navy's heroic performance in World War II.

the major advertising agencies said:

> Actually, there have been very few cases where it has been necessary (for the sponsor) to exercise a veto, because the producers involved and the writers involved are normally pretty well aware of what might not be acceptable.
>
> Q.: In other words, they know already before they start writing and producing what the limitations are, the subject matter limitations, that you will accept and your client will accept— is that correct?
>
> A.: That is correct.[23]

What, then, is left? After the sponsors, the networks, the government, and writers themselves get through censoring entertainment programs, what is left? Generally the ideas that survive are those with which the majority of viewers feel comfortable. A major television sponsor sees the ideal television program as "interesting but not intrusive, exciting but not offensive, provocative but not antagonistic." Newton Minow translates this to mean that what most sponsors want are "provocative programs that don't provoke anybody."

Most entertainment programs follow what is known in the trade as the principle of Least Objectionable Programming, or LOP, an idea best explained by its originator, NBC executive Paul Klein:

> A very old law has become more and more useful in figuring our program popularity . . . Sir Isaac Newton's First Law of Motion, the one that says that a body at rest tends to stay at rest. Once a viewer chooses his program, he may have to fiddle with a lot of knobs should he decide to switch channels, especially if it's an older color set . . . So a viewer in a chair tends to stay in his chair.[24]

In other words, viewers don't watch specific programs;

they watch television. After an initial period of flicking the dial around to sample what's available, viewers tend to choose one channel and stay with it *unless they hear something that offends or upsets them.* Thus, a "hit" show often is the one least objectionable to its viewers. Or, as Klein explains, a program's success is really determined by "75 million thresholds of pain plus the law of inertia." A network executive adds, "Our goals will be whatever they have to be to avoid being labeled whatever the label may be."[25]

This programming principle results in an overwhelming bias toward the status quo because viewers are less likely to be disturbed by ideas that are familiar to them and do not challenge their settled convictions. This also accounts for the poor quality of much television programming. Actor Jack Lemmon comments, "Ninety percent of [television entertainment] stinks because it's a multi-billion-dollar-per-year industry, which is understandably occupied with selling something else—but not the show. They are appealing to the lowest common denominator—'Don't offend anybody!'—and nothing of real artistic worth can be made that isn't going to offend *somebody.* That's been my experience, because you have a point of view—*all* art has a point of view, all *good* art, that is, art of substance. Not everybody's going to like it, but those that do appreciate it are going to be terribly enlightened, and you don't get enlightened on television very often."[26]

Many television programs are pretested at research facilities that measure viewers' "galvanic skin responses"—variations in the amount of sweat in the palm. Such measurements clearly seek to determine the level of agitation, not enlightenment. At the Preview House in Los Angeles, viewers are invited to express their opinions of entertainment programs by indicating their degree of approval on a dial installed at their seats. To determine whether the audience is "normal" or standard in its preferences, the group is first shown a Mr. Magoo cartoon. If the audience responds in an unusual way, the results are adjusted up or down accordingly. The rating a previewing show gets is measured in points called "Magoos," and it is judged successful if it gets a score of between 5.1 and 6.3 Magoos.

Anything new or unfamiliar scores very low on Magoos. As writers Link and Levinson observe, television has "a conservative way of doing business . . . Instincts and gut reactions give way to research. Risk is minimized as much as possible."[27] A recent cartoon by Schochet shows a network executive with a script in his hand, saying to a writer, "I must admit, it's quite a unique and funny premise—why don't you try us again when one of the other networks has done something similar?" This is, as they say in the trade, joking on the square: more and more time is being given over to fewer and fewer program types. A recent University of Georgia study revealed that since 1955 there has been a steady decline in the diversity of entertainment programs.

Most television entertainment is crafted according to "proven" (i.e., previously successful) formulas. There are crime shows, sitcoms, variety shows, family dramas. Each provides a set of readily identifiable character types and plot situations, usually organized into simplistic bad guy/good guy conflicts. "Bad" characters inevitably meet a "bad" end, unmourned because they have no redeeming human qualities. "Good" characters can be trusted to behave in equally predictable ways, displaying courage, honesty, unselfishness, kindness, or warmth, as the situation may require.*

The stereotypical, mechanistic formulas of most television entertainment programs make them extremely effective vehicles for pro-Establishment propaganda. Eric Barnouw has done a fascinating analysis of how, for example, the "spy story" dramas of the 1960s helped justify America's involvement in the Vietnam War—and cold war politics in general.

---

* They, of course, are expected to be rewarded for their "goodness." When "good guy" Henry Blake, played by McLean Stevenson, left the series "M*A*S*H," the writers had him die in a helicopter crash. In reruns, networks cut off the ending announcing his death.

Programs like "Mission: Impossible," "I Spy," and "The Man from U.N.C.L.E." showed "good" American agents battling against "bad" Iron Curtain villains. Sometimes the enemy countries backing the villains were referred to only vaguely as "People's Republics" to avoid diplomatic protests. But Cuba, East Germany, and Red China, which had no diplomatic ties with the United States, were often directly specified as the engineers of devilishly ingenious plots to destroy America. One "I Spy" episode concerned the efforts of the Red Chinese to poison the water supply of a large American city by dumping bubonic plague bacteria. A "Man From U.N.C.L.E." plot dealt with another Red Chinese plan to "program" the daughters of prominent American political leaders to kill their fathers. Barnouw comments: "At a time when the Administration was justifying the Vietnam War as necessary to contain Chinese hordes who would otherwise sweep down from the north, and was picturing the North Vietnamese as Chinese puppets, such inventive plots made their contribution to paranoia. Paranoia was, indeed, the underlying theme of [such programs]. Americans seemed to be surrounded, at home and abroad and even in outer space, by fiendish enemies who must be combated by the weapons and tactics they were expected to use on us, if given the chance."[28]

More recently, there is the example of crime dramas like "CHiPS," "Shannon," "McClain's Law," "Strike Force," and "Today's FBI," whose underlying messages admirably serve the prevailing political order. Their familiar formulas invariably portray dedicated, heroic, selfless law enforcers. On such programs, unlike what we all know to be happening in real life, justice is invariably served—and it is dealt with an even hand. Rich villains fare no better than poor ones; whites get no better treatment than blacks. The statistics showing that this is contrary to fact are simply ignored in favor of what might, in other countries, be classified as propaganda. A black policeman tells a group of young recruits on one show:

I wanted to do something for my country. I wanted to do something for my own people . . . And I'll tell you something else. Some of our own people talk about "white man's law." There's no such thing, not when black men like you and me wear this uniform . . . It's *everybody's* law.

The crimes committed in such programs have no identifiable social causes. Crime occurs randomly, without background or context; criminals spring out of nowhere to wreak havoc on innocent and defenseless victims. One program based on the true experience of a Los Angeles schoolteacher who was raped in her own classroom completely avoided any suggestion of the political and economic roots of violence in inner-city schools. The teacher on whose experience the story was based believes that this seriously distorted the real significance of the event. She comments, "I had something a little more political in mind, not so sensational."[29]

Such omissions and distortions of reality are typical of these programs, which prefer to emphasize that the only barrier standing between us and such random inexplicable violence is the Forces of Law and Order. Many crime shows are blatant promotional devices for law enforcement agencies. On an episode of "Today's FBI," a worshipful young friend tells an FBI agent, "Do you have any idea what kind of celebrity you are back home—just being in the FBI?" Such admiration is never "balanced" by any dramatizations or even references to news reports of FBI activities that violate citizens' rights and harass minority groups. *

Law enforcers are always portrayed as brave, tough-but-kind, and extraordinarily dedicated, willing to work

---

* For example, the now-famous episode in which the FBI bugged Dr. Martin Luther King's hotel room to obtain potentially embarrassing information and later sent him an "anonymous" letter which read: "There is only one thing left to do. You are done. There is but one way out for you. You better take it before your filthy, abnormal, fraudulent self is bared to the nation."

overtime—indeed, *all* the time—to "see justice done." The following exchange was heard on a recent crime drama:

> Woman: (to cop) You're missing your son's fifth birthday party? Why aren't you there?
>
> Policeman: (ruefully) That's what my wife says. I told her, I'm here because I want him to grow up to be six.

Crime drama heroes—this includes *ex officio* law enforcers like private detectives and bounty hunters—are sturdily incorruptible. Witness this conversation between bounty hunter Colt Seevers and the bank robber he has just apprehended:

> Bank robber: You catch a man who stole five million dollars and all you get is ten thousand dollars? You didn't work out a very good deal for yourself.
>
> Colt: I don't like putting a large price on a man's head.
>
> Bank robber: Maybe you would be interested in my offer?
>
> Colt: Sure I would. If you're thinking of returning the money in return for plea bargaining, I'm interested.
>
> Bank robber: That's not what I meant. I'll let you in for part of the take.
>
> Colt: No way, Sam.

When law enforcers are shown to have such unswerving integrity, only the most churlish among us would question the methods they use to "get their man," though these methods often involve violation of citizens' constitutional rights. A University of Massachusetts study of crime programs revealed law enforcers routinely breaking and entering illegally, failing to inform suspects of their rights, terrorizing and coercing witnesses, and committing bribery. Professors Katsch and Arons, who conducted the study, found that almost every episode of most crime dramas contained one or more violations of the Fourth, Fifth, or Sixth Amendments. The professors conclude: "The message was pretty clear. The right to privacy, the integrity of the individual and the right to due process of law do not seem to be observed by successful police whose activities always subdue evil."[30] Law enforcement and law breaking are separated by a very thin, almost invisible line.

Constitutional guarantees are regarded as bothersome "technicalities" that impede honest law enforcers in the performance of their duties. Consider the pilot show for "Mc-Clain's Law," a drama about a retired cop who returns to the force when his best friend is murdered. The program was billed as "a cop show with a difference . . . the difference between the law and what's right." At one point, a police chief tells McClain, "Police work has changed, you know. It's not like it used to be. They have new laws, new rules." McClain responds, "I've heard that. Maybe the old laws were better." The police chief agrees, "Yeah, maybe. But we've gotta live with them." Later in the show, we learn exactly what they mean. McClain apprehends a robber; then, obviously disgusted, reads him his rights. But as he does, he shoves the point of his gun into the man's ear. The man later complains about this rough treatment, and the police chief questions McClain's partner: "The suspect says while McClain was reading him his rights, McClain was screwing his gun into his ear. Did you see anything like that?" Though he did, in fact, witness the whole episode, the partner replies, "No, sir, I didn't." Yet we are not distressed by this bit of police brutality or by its coverup since the suspect is not only undeniably guilty, but brazenly unrepentant—a "bad guy" who deserves anything he gets. The "correct" way to interpret the episode is demonstrated in a later scene between McClain and his partner:

McClain: Well, he sure learned the lesson of his ways. He learned it in a flash. (chuckle)
Partner: Yeah (chuckle). Right in the ear. (chuckle)

*   *   *

If such methods are shown to be acceptable police procedure, what safeguards are left for someone who is not undeniably guilty but actually innocent?

Rose Goldsen comments: "The violence an established order exercises in maintaining itself is more easily condoned—even approved—than the same or lesser degree of violence unleashed by those who threaten authority. Most societies—ours is no exception—even define violence and crime one way for the powerful, another way for the powerless . . . Such unequal definitions can be maintained as legitimate only as long as there are strong social supports assuring and reassuring the public that the selective angle of vision is 'normal' . . . that, after all, this *is* the right way to look at things."[31]

Crime shows do not teach viewers why such "technicalities" as informing suspects that they have the right to remain silent and the right to have an attorney are important: to keep police from extracting a confession by force or threat of force—perhaps from the wrong man. As a British police officer stationed in India once said, "It is easier to throw hot pepper in some poor beggar's face than to go out into the hot sun looking for evidence."

But of course, if law enforcers always get the right man, this makes Bill of Rights protections not only unnecessary but actually harmful. On television, these hard-won democratic rights do not protect anyone, but only permit dangerous criminals to escape punishment. To return to McClain (the cop who prefers the "old laws"), one program shows him preparing to beat the truth out of an uncooperative villain. "I think I can get it out of him," he says. His partner stops him, not because he is concerned about the man's constitutional rights, but because he knows the ramifications of dispensing with these "technicalities." "Look, McClain. You got away with the gun-in-the-ear stunt once. A judge could throw the case out of court 'cause you weren't patient." *

Professors Katsch and Arons comment: "Police shows seem to reduce the ordinary citizen's awareness of constitutional rights and responsibilities. Many people engrossed in the drama of rapid-fire action or preoccupied with violence fail even to notice blatant police-state tactics." Katsch and Arons believe the end result of such programs is to erode popular support for Bill of Rights protections. Noting that recent Supreme Court decisions have legalized "outrageous police conduct, enacting into law principles much like those projected in the television crime shows," they argue that "What started off as merely fictional entertainment has now begun to have the political effect of 'softening up' public opinion."[32]

This argument may help explain the wide popular support for Ronald Reagan's "anti-crime" campaign. Announcing that violent crime is "an American epidemic," Reagan recently proposed abolishing the so-called "exclusionary rule," which forbids the use of illegally seized evidence at criminal trials, and denying bail to federal offenders. These proposals were applauded by the public, though many criminal justice officials, including those in the Reagan administration, knew they would have little actual effect on crime. One reason is that federal offenders do not, as a rule, skip bail. Another reason is that studies by the Reagan administration's own General Accounting Office reveal that the exclusionary rule is used to throw out evidence in less than .4 percent of all cases. On the other hand, as a spokesman for the American Civil Liberties Union pointed out, Reagan's proposals would "encourage police misconduct and undermine the constitutional presumption of innocence *without reducing crime.*"[33]

---

* "Bad" lawyers often try to get their criminal clients freed on such "technicalities." "Good" lawyers never do: they establish their client's innocence by uncovering fresh evidence or tracking down new witnesses.

ACLU Executive Director Ira Glasser adds, "These proposals are a public relations fraud. They propose to make the Constitution a scapegoat for the fear of crime that all of us have. Crime is a serious issue. These proposals do not address that issue seriously."[34]

Reagan's own Task Force on Violent Crime agreed that the proposals would have little effect. Reagan neatly sidestepped two other recommendations that his Task Force considered far more crucial: stricter gun controls, and federal subsidies to build more prisons. These suggestions were less likely to be popular with an electorate that has grown up watching "entertainment" in which the gun is a symbol of virility, and only "bleeding hearts" concern themselves with the social causes of crime. Crime shows offer a simpler solution: the extermination of the criminal offender before the final commercial break.

Newsman and publisher Roy Larson says, "There is considerable evidence that millions of people—especially many of our youth—have become inclined toward simplistic solutions to complicated problems, because for years they have seen problems dramatically presented and neatly solved on television within a thirty-minute period. Millions have been tempted to the fantasy that reality is something either black or white, good or bad, desirable or reprehensible—never anything in between."

Of course, crime shows cannot be held entirely responsible for Americans' attitudes about crime and law enforcement, and to a certain extent these attitudes are based on reality: some criminals do commit further crimes while out on bail, and courts do allow some guilty criminals to go free because of infringement of their legal rights. Until fairly recently, this was a price we were willing to pay in order to protect the rights of all citizens against illegal search and seizure.

What crime shows do is magnify the importance of such occurrences and thereby reinforce the idea that the solution to the problem lies in the sacrifice of democratic liberties. "The preservation of society and social order finally may require that we subordinate charity and sometimes even justice to punish most severely what most endangers society and the social order, even when there is little guilt or none," says a recent book on crime.[35]

Public attention is directed by "entertainment" shows toward certain kinds of criminal activities and away from others. Most people, for example, grossly overestimate the actual incidence of violent crime in America. This isn't surprising, since the American Medical Association calculates that the average American child now watches 18,000 murders on television before he reaches the age of eighteen! University of Pennsylvania researcher George Gerbner says that the emphasis on murder and other violent crimes has given Americans a "victim mentality." During Senate testimony, former FCC commissioner Newton Minow, quoted from a letter he had received from a mother who said that when she told her four-year-old son that his grandfather had died, the child responded, "Who shot him?" Another woman whose husband was murdered by his business partner was shocked to discover, when she broke the news to her children, that they had suspected what had happened from the first moment their father disappeared. "It never occurred to me that such things can happen," she said later, "but my kids watch things like that every night and evidently thought such murders are a normal part of life."[36]

When people living in rural Wisconsin, Oregon, and Nebraska were asked by pollster Patrick Caddell what they thought were the most serious problems facing America today, the majority replied "crime on the streets." Yet the crime rate was almost nonexistent in their communities, many of which didn't even have streets.

Television deals almost exclusively with "crimes that are the easiest for the poor and disadvantaged to commit," says Nicholas Johnson, former FCC Chairman. He adds, "What we haven't been told is that much of the crime in the United States is 'white collar' crime; that the rich steal as much or more than the poor . . . A *single* recent price-fixing case involved a 'robbery' from the American people of more money than was taken in *all* the country's robberies, burglaries and larcenies during the year of that criminal price-fixing."[37] Media critic Robert Cirino adds, "Even though the violence and death caused by individual crime affects thousands, it is on a smaller scale than the silent and unseen violence inflicted on Americans by the illegal disposal of poisonous pollutants, poor auto safety design, uninspected meat, contaminated food, overuse of pesticides, misleading advertisements and violations of work-safety standards."[38]

Recently, I watched a "Donahue" show which dealt, in part, with illegal bribery and price-fixing by large oil companies. The guest, Senator Howard Metzenbaum, spoke feelingly of how such practices steal millions of dollars a year from the people and undermine democratic processes. The studio audience was undismayed. "Why don't you people *care* about this?" Donahue said at one point. "I am really surprised at what I perceive to be a considerable lack of interest in these issues in this audience." A few audience members helpfully suggested that they felt the problem was just "too big."

Somehow, that didn't seem the right explanation. A few weeks earlier, a similar audience had been quite outraged by the accounts of families who had relatives kidnapped and murdered. Surely, the problems involved in putting an end to crimes such as these are just as "big" as those of "establishment" crime.

I believe that audience didn't care about oil company crime because they didn't really think it was a problem worth worrying about. Years of television entertainment had subtly indoctrinated them as to where the "real" problems of American society lay. As every good propagandist can tell you, once a person forms an opinion, even one based on illusions and lies, he becomes extremely unreceptive to ideas that do not fit in with that opinion. Though most people are willing to admit that Establishment crime is "bad," they don't become angry about it because it doesn't fit comfortably with their world view—a view formed, at least in part, by the six hours of television that most Americans watch *every day*.

The stories that we hear shape our thoughts. Television's storytellers are people who are, by and large, satisfied with the existing social order. As a group, they are quite affluent— often, particularly the movers and shakers—among the top 1 percent in annual income. Quite understandably, they support the political and economic system that created and continues to support their wealth and privileged status. As Robert Cirino says, "It is the ownership of the mass media by the wealthy . . . rather than a conspiracy of any kind, that explains why the important decisions usually favor viewpoints that support things as they are rather than viewpoints that support fundamental changes in society . . ."[39]

Television entertainment is more than just a way to pass an idle hour; as Eric Barnouw says, it is "basically, propaganda for the status quo." From the vantage point of another culture, it would be clearly seen as propaganda. But the messages of such entertainment, endlessly repeated, are so familiar to most of us that they seem perfectly natural and correct. They are perceived as truth, not propaganda. This makes them all the more effective. Herbert Schiller comments: "For manipulation to be most effective, evidence of its presence should be nonexistent. When the manipulated believe things are the way they are naturally and inevitably, manipulation is successful."[40]

4

Sin, Suffer, and Repent

Soap operas reverse Tolstoy's famous assertion in *Anna Karenina* that "Happy families are all alike; every unhappy family is unhappy in its own way." On soaps, *every* family is unhappy, and each is unhappy in more or less the same way.
                                                            Marjorie Perloff

It is the hope of every advertiser to habituate the housewife to an engrossing narrative whose optimum length is forever and at the same time to saturate all levels of her consciousness with the miracle of a given product, so she will be aware of it all the days of her life and mutter its name in her sleep.
                                                            James Thurber

In July 1969, when the entire nation was glued to television sets watching the first man walk on the moon, an irate woman called a Wausau, Wisconsin, TV station to complain that her favorite soap opera was not being shown that day and why was that. The station manager replied, "This is probably the most important news story of the century, something you may never again see the equal of." Unimpressed, the lady replied, "Well, I hope they crash."[1]

124

One can hardly blame her. For weeks, she had been worrying that Audrey might be going blind, that Alice would marry that scoundrel Michael, and that Dr. Hardy might not discover his patient Peter to be his long-lost natural son before the boy died of a brain tumor. Suddenly, in the heat of all these crises, she was cut off from all information about these people and forced to watch the comings and goings of men in rubber suits whom she had never met. It was enough to unhinge anybody.

Dedicated watchers of soap operas often confuse fact with fiction.* Sometimes this can be endearing, sometimes ludicrous. During the Senate Watergate hearings (which were broadcast on daytime television), viewers whose favorite soap operas were preempted simply adopted the hearings as substitute soaps. Daniel Shorr reports that the listeners began "telephoning the networks to criticize slow-moving sequences, suggesting script changes and asking for the return of favorite witnesses, like 'that nice John Dean.'"[2]

Stars of soap operas tell hair-raising stories of their encounters with fans suffering from this affliction. Susan Lucci, who plays the promiscuous Erica Kane on "All My Children," tells of a time she was riding in a parade: "We were in a crowd of about 250,000, traveling in an antique open car moving ver-r-ry slowly. At that time in the series I was involved with a character named Nick. Some man broke through, came right up to the car and said to me, 'Why don't you give *me* a little bit of what you've been giving Nick?'" The man hung onto the car, menacingly, until she was rescued by the police. Another time, when she was in church, the reverent silence was bro-

*Contrary to popular belief, soap operas are not the harmless pastime of lonely housewives only. Recent surveys show that many high school and college students, as well as many working and professional people, are addicted to soaps. A sizable chunk of the audience is men. Such well-known people as Sammy Davis, Jr., Van Cliburn, John Connally, and Supreme Court Justice Thurgood Marshall admit to being fans of one or more soap operas.

ken by a woman's astonished remark, "Oh my god, Erica prays!"[3] Margaret Mason, who plays the villainous Lisa Anderson in "Days of Our Lives," was accosted by a woman who poured a carton of milk all over her in the supermarket. And once a woman actually tried to force her car off the Ventura Freeway.

Just as viewers come to confuse the actors with their roles, so too they see the soap opera image of life in America as real. The National Institute of Mental Health reported that a majority of Americans actually adopt what they see in soap operas to handle their own life problems. The images are not only "true to life"; they are a guide for living.

What, then, is the image of life on soap operas? For one thing, marriage is touted as the *ne plus ultra* of a woman's existence. Living together is not a respectable condition and is tolerated only as long as one of the partners (usually the woman) is bucking for eventual marriage. Casual sex is out; only the most despicable villains engage in it: "Diane has no respect for marriage or any of the values we were brought up with. She's a vicious, immoral woman." Occasionally, a woman will speak out against marriage, but it's clear that in her heart of hearts she really wants it. Women who are genuinely not interested in marriage do not appear on soap operas except as occasional caricatures, misguided and immature in their thinking. Reporter Martha McGee appeared on "Ryan's Hope" just long enough to titillate the leading man with remarks like, "I don't know if you're my heart's desire, but you're sexy as hell." Punished for this kind of heretical remark, she was last seen sobbing brokenly in a telephone booth.

No, love and marriage still go together like a horse and carriage in soap operas, though many marriages don't last long enough for the couple to put away all the wedding gifts. As Cornell professor Rose Goldsen says, this is a world of "fly-apart marriages, throwaway husbands, throwaway wives."[4]

There is rarely any clear logic behind the dissolution of these relationships; indeed, the TV formula seems to be: the happier the marriage, the more perilous the couple's future. A blissful marriage is the kiss of death: "I just can't believe it about Alice and Steve. I mean, they were the *perfect* couple, the absolute *perfect* couple!"

Most marriages are not pulled apart by internal flaws but by external tampering—often by a jealous rival: "C'mon, Peter. Stay for just one more drink. Jan won't mind. And anyway, the night's still young. Isn't it nice to be together all nice and cozy like this?"

Often the wife has willfully brought this state of affairs on herself by committing that most heinous of all offenses: neglecting her man. "NHM" almost always occurs when the woman becomes too wrapped up in her career. Every time Rachel Corey went to New York City for a weekend to further her career as a sculptress, her marriage tottered. At this writing, Ellen Dalton's marriage to Mark appears to be headed for big trouble as a result of her business trip to Chicago:

Erica: I warned you, Ellen, not to let your job interfere with your marriage.
Ellen: I have tried to do my best for my marriage *and* my job . . . Mark had no right to stomp out of here just now.
Erica: Don't you understand? He just couldn't take anymore.
Ellen: What do you mean?
Erica: It's not just the trip to Chicago that Mark resents. It's your putting your job before having a family.
Ellen: I demand the right to be treated as an equal. I don't have to apologize because I don't agree to have a child the minute my husband snaps his fingers. I'm going to Chicago like a big girl and I'm going to do the job I was hired to do. (stalks out the door)
Erica: (musing, to herself) Well, I may be old-fashioned, but that's no way to hold onto your man.

Career women do appear frequently on soap operas, but the ones who are romantically successful treat their careers as a kind of sideline. Female cardiologists devote fifteen years of their lives to advanced medical training, then spend most of their time in the hospital coffee shop. One man remarked to a career woman who was about to leave her job, "Oh, Kate, you'll miss working. Those long lunches, those intimate cocktail hours!" Women residents apparently schedule all their medical emergencies before dinnertime, because if they should have to stay late at the hospital, it's the beginning of the end for their marriages. It's interesting to speculate how they might work this out:

> Nurse: Oh my God, Dr. Peterson, the patient's hemorrhaging!
> Dr. Peterson: Sorry, nurse, it'll just have to wait. If I don't get my meat loaf in by a quarter to six, it'll never be ready before my husband gets home.

Husbands, weak-minded souls, cannot be expected to hold out against the advances of any attractive woman, even one for whom they have contempt, if their wives aren't around. Meatloafless, they are very easily seduced. The clear suggestion is that they could hardly have been expected to do otherwise:

> "Well, after all, Karen, you weren't around very much during that time. It's not surprising that Michael turned to Pat for a little comfort and understanding."

If, in the brief span of time allotted to them, a couple manage to have intercourse, the woman is certain to become pregnant. Contraception on soap operas is such a sometime thing that even the Pope could scarcely object to it. The birth rate on soaps is eight times as high as the United States birthrate; indeed it's higher than the birthrate of any underdeveloped nation in the world. This rabbitlike reproduction is fraught with peril. One recent study revealed that out of nineteen soap opera pregnancies, eight resulted in miscarriages and three in death for the mother. Rose Goldsen has estimated that the odds are 7 to 10 against any fetus making it to full term, worse if you include getting through the birth canal. Women on soap operas miscarry at the drop of a pin. And, of course, miscarriages are rarely caused by any defect with mother or baby: again, external forces are to blame. Often, miscarriage is brought on by an unappreciative or unfaithful mate. For example, on "Another World," Alice, the heroine, suffered a miscarriage when her husband visited his ex-wife Rachel. One woman lost her baby because her husband came home drunk. This plot twist is no doubt particularly appealing to women viewers because of the instant revenge visited upon the transgressing mate. They can fantasize about similar punishment for husbandly malfeasance in their own lives— and about his inevitable guilt and repentance:

Husband: (stonily) Jennifer, these potatoes are too gluey. I can't eat this!

Wife: (clutches her belly) Oh no!

Husband: What? What is it?

Wife: It's the baby! Something's wrong—call the doctor!

Husband: Oh my God, what have I done?

Later, at the hospital:

Doctor: I'm sorry, Mr. Henson, but your wife has lost the baby.

Husband: (brokenly) I didn't know, I didn't know. How could I have attacked her potatoes so viciously with her in such a delicate condition!

Doctor: Now, now. You mustn't blame yourself. We still don't know exactly what causes miscarriages except that they happen for a complicated set of physical and emotional reasons.

Husband: Oh, thank you, Doctor.

Doctor: Of course, carping about the potatoes couldn't have *helped.*

*   *   *

Miscarriage is effective as a punishment because it is one of the very worst things than can happen to a woman on a soap opera. In the world of soaps, the one thing every good and worthwhile woman wants is a baby. Soap operas never depict childless women as admirable. These "real people" do not include women like Katharine Hepburn, who once announced that she never wanted to have children because "the first time the kid said no to me, I'd kill it!" Childless women are either to be pitied, if there are physical reasons that prevent them from getting pregnant, or condemned, if they are childless by choice.

Second only to neglecting her man in her hierarchy of female crime is having an abortion. No admirable character *ever* gets an abortion on a soap opera. Occasionally, however, a virtuous woman will consider it, usually for one of two reasons: she doesn't want the man she loves to feel "trapped" into marrying her; or she has been "violated" by her husband's best friend, a member of the underworld, or her delivery boy, who may also be her long-lost half brother. But she always "comes around" in the end, her love for "the new life growing inside me" conquering her misgivings. If the baby should happen to survive the perilous journey through the birth canal (illegitimate babies get miscarried at a far higher rate than legitimate ones), she never has any regrets. Why should she? Babies on soap operas never drool, spit up, or throw scrambled eggs in their mothers' faces. Babyhood (and its inevitable counterpart, motherhood) is "sold" to American women as slickly as soap. Kimberly, of "Ryan's Hope," is so distressed when she finds out she is pregnant that she runs away from home. She has the baby, prematurely, while alone and unattended on a deserted houseboat. It is a difficult and dangerous birth. But once the baby is born, Kimberly is all maternal affection. "Where is she?" she shouts. "Why won't they let me see my little girl?" By the end of the day, she announces, "If anything happens to this baby, I don't know what I'll do!"

Mothers are never tired, sleepless, or discouraged. Radiant, they boast about the baby's virtues:

> Well, he's just the smartest, best little baby in the whole wide world!

> He looks just like his daddy—those big blue eyes, that enchanting smile!

> Look at her little hands and feet. Have you ever seen anything more adorable! And she's good as gold—really, no trouble at all. She's Mommy's precious little princess, aren't you, darling?

One producer of a (now defunct) soap opera actually wanted, as a promotion gimmick for one of the plotlines, to give away one baby a week as a prize! The idea was abandoned only because of the lack of cooperation from adoption agencies.

After the age of about ten months, children are of no interest in soap operas unless they are hit by a car or contract a fever of unknown origin, in which case they occasion a lot of hand-wringing and pious sentiments from all the adults. If the producers cannot arrange any such misfortune, the rule is that children are not to be seen or heard. Having a young child around would interrupt the endless raveling of the sleeve of romance. It won't do to have little Bobby need to go on the potty or have his nose blown in the middle of the adults' complicated lives, which have, as one critic says, "all the immediacy of a toothache and the urgency of a telegram."[5]

You may hear a good deal of pious talk about a young child's need for stability and love, but usually only when a couple's marriage is on the rocks. Children on soap operas still go to sleep at night having no idea whether one or both of their parents will be around in the morning—a situation which brings to mind Lady Bracknell's remark in *The Importance of Being Earnest:* "Losing one parent might be regarded as a misfortune; losing two seems like carelessness."

Children on soap operas are secondary. Because they serve largely as foils for the adult characters, their development does not follow the slow, steady pattern of the rest of the action.* Their growth is marked by a series of sudden and unsettling metamorphoses as new and older juvenile actors assume the role. On Tuesday, little Terence is cooing in his cradle. On Monday next, he is the terror of the Little League. By Thursday, his voice begins to change. Friday night is his first date. He wakes up on Monday a drug-crazed teenager, ready to be put to use creating heartbreak and grief for his devoted mother and her new husband. He stays fifteen years old for about two to five years (more if he manages to get into lots of scrapes), and then one day he again emerges from the off-camera cocoon transformed into a full-fledged adult, with all the rights, privileges, pain, and perfidy of that elite corps. And so the cycle continues.

Under the surface of romantic complications, soap operas sell a vision of morality and American family life, of a society where marriage is the highest good, sex the greatest evil, where babies are worshiped and abortion condemned, where motherhood is exalted and children ignored. It is a

---

* The pace of many soap operas has picked up considerably in the last few years, as audience surveys have revealed a strong viewer interest in action-and-adventure stories. Before 1980, however, plot movement on the soaps was glacierlike, and on the earliest soaps, almost imperceptible. James Thurber claimed that it took one male character in a soap three days to get an answer to the simple question, "Where have you been?" He wrote, "If . . . you missed an automobile accident that occurred on a Monday broadcast, you could pick it up the following Thursday and find the leading woman character still unconscious and her husband still moaning over her beside the wrecked car. In one program . . . [a character] said, 'It doesn't seem possible to me that Ralph Wilde arrived here only yesterday.' It should not have seemed possible to anyone else, either, since Ralph Wilde had arrived, as mortal time goes, thirteen days before."[6]

vision of a world devoid of social conflict. There are hardly any short-order cooks, bus drivers, mechanics, construction workers, or farmers on soap operas. Blue-collar problems do not enter these immaculate homes. No one suffers from flat feet or derrière spread from long hours spent at an unrewarding or frustrating job. The upwardly mobile professionals who populate soap operas love their work, probably because they are hardly ever at it—one lawyer clocked in at his office exactly once in three months. Their problems are those of people with time on their hands to covet the neighbor's wife, track down villains, betray friends, and enjoy what one observer has called "the perils of Country Club Place."

It is a world largely devoid of black people and black viewpoints. When black characters do appear, they are doctors or lawyers whose problems, ambitions, and anxieties are identical to those of their white colleagues.* Racial discrimination and inequality do not exist, and the black romantic plotlines are indistinguishable from white—though, of course, the two *never* mix. Once, it is true, in a daring departure from the straight and narrow, "All My Children" showed a black–white romance which shocked a lot of viewers. But it wasn't really a romance in the usual sense. At least, it was perfectly clear that black Dr. Nancy Grant had turned to her white boyfriend Owen solely for comfort after the breakup of her marriage to black Dr. Frank Grant. They were not—gasp!—sleeping together. Anyway, the whole mess was resolved when Owen considerately died just minutes after marrying Nancy to save her from disgrace because she was pregnant with black Dr. Frank Grant's baby. Another experiment with a black–white flirtation was abruptly ended when the black family moved to another town. Still another such

---

* "All My Children" has recently introduced a "lower-class" black character—a streetwise teenager named Jesse, who is the despair of his black aunt and uncle, both doctors. It is clear, however, that Jesse's scorn for Establishment values is merely a defense against rejection, and his eventual conversion and admittance to Pine Valley society seems inevitable.

plotline was resolved when it turned out that the white woman in an interracial relationship was actually a light-skinned black woman who had been "ashamed" of her heritage.

The world of soap operas is without doubt white,* upper middle-class—and decidedly small-town. Emerging out of the mists of the American heartland as mysteriously as Brigadoon are towns like Oakdale, Pine Valley, Rosehill. On soap operas, towns never have real-life names like Secaucus or Weedsport. The great American myth of the Good, Clean, Safe Small Town, which some thought had been laid to rest by the likes of Sinclair Lewis and Sherwood Anderson, has been resurrected on the soaps. Only in small towns, the daily message is, can one find true happiness and fulfillment:

> Carol: I've wondered sometimes if you don't get bored living in Oakdale? Living in New York or on the Coast can be so much more exciting.
> Sandy: Excitement is one thing. Real feelings are another.

One half expects her to add, "Oh, Auntie Em, there's no place like home!"

Everyone knows everyone else in these close-knit little communities, and they are always knocking on each other's doors. Rarely does anyone phone; they just "stop by"—a custom which would be rude and unnerving in real life, but which soap opera characters never seem to mind. Indeed, they must expect it, since they keep themselves in a constant state of readiness for the ring of the doorbell. No soap opera character is ever caught wearing a ratty old robe when friends come to call.

Good characters on soap operas never feel the urge to

---

*One study revealed that of 333 characters listed in the *Afternoon TV Yearbook*, only 21 had names that indicated they were not Anglo-Saxon.

take in a Broadway play, go to an art museum, or dine at a fancy French restaurant. Journeying to the Big City is an undertaking equivalent in peril only to a safari among savage African head-hunting tribes. When Erica of "All My Children" first went to New York, she was seduced by a married man and abandoned, then subsequently lost her husband. An even worse fate awaited Leslie of "Another World," who had her purse stolen, got amnesia, and was confined to a mental hospital. *

Even those wise enough to stay home amidst the smell of honeysuckle are not safe, for villainous emigrés are always pouring out of the Big City's melting pot and invading the peaceful groves of the small town. In matters of morality, the difference between residents of the Big City and residents of Sing Sing is not great. Gangsters, scheming fortune-hunters, pimps, child beaters, power-hungry rich folk all hail from New York, Chicago, or the less clearly defined but somehow more ominous "Center City." Recently, there has been a surge of villains from foreign countries. In sinister accents, they hatch nefarious and improbable plots to destroy small-town folk. One European doctor transformed a popular soap hero into his reluctant slave by implanting an electronic device in his brain which made it impossible for the hero to resist his commands. A Greek tycoon plotted to destroy an entire soap town by altering its weather and freezing the inhabitants to death.

Such villains are convenient, because the source of good characters' woes can again be chalked up to external causes, not any defect in themselves or their way of life, which are never open to question. Good people endure, and the Small Town eventually triumphs over Evil, all ending in a reaffirma-

* "Ryan's Hope" is actually set in New York City, but the intimate, friendly neighborhood the characters inhabit is indistinguishable from a small town. It is only when characters venture beyond the confines of Ryan's restaurant and environs that they encounter evil.

tion of the power of faith, simplicity, and the American Way:

> Didn't I tell you that if you simply had faith, everything would turn out all right? Heaven has a way of smiling on us just when things seem darkest, you know.

You are more likely to find an atheist in a foxhole than on a soap opera.* The following conversation from "Days of Our Lives" is typical:

> "I can't believe it. Scott and Nora—alive and laughing one minute—"
> "—and in Heaven the next."
> "Yes, I believe that."
> "You know, for Christians the only pain in death is for those who are left behind."
> "Yes, I feel that."

When one young man's mother had a drinking problem, he brought her around with a rousing rendition of "The Battle Hymn of the Republic": "Mine eyes have seen the glory of the coming of the Lord/He is trampling on the vineyards where the grapes of wrath are stored." Occasionally, a character, already in deep moral and emotional trouble, may admit to having a few doubts about the existence of God, but always just prior to his eventual redemption through restoration of faith. No sympathetic person in a soap opera has ever failed to express a deep and abiding faith in God when the moment called for it.

The characters in soap operas have good reason to put their faith in the Establishment. If they get into legal trouble,

---

* This is, of course, true of television broadcasting in general. There are numerous programs that promote the Christian view of matters religious, scientific, and political, but the FCC has consistently denied the requests of atheists who ask to buy air time to offer their views. Minority religious groups and cults are similarly excluded from using television to promote their beliefs.

the local lawyer will handle everything from divorce to a murder trial; if they have a nervous breakdown, the local psychiatrist will give them all the time they need to talk about it; if they get sick, the local doctor will come to their home to treat them and even perform surgery on the spot if necessary. No one on a soap opera need ever worry about legal or medical bills (they are never mentioned), which is fortunate because these people do not suffer from the same diseases as the rest of us. They may develop multiple personalities, and they often need brain surgery, but they never catch colds or suffer from hemorrhoids. As Philip Wander notes, "There are no diseases resulting from smog or bad working conditions, a sudden increase in the work load, unemployment, or the insane pace of social change. Problems are rooted in personalities."[7]

There are no working-class diseases on soap operas. Characters develop mysterious and romantic-sounding ailments—syringomyelia, myasthenia gravis, subacute bacterial endocarditis. Death is accompanied by little suffering; if the character suffers, he almost always survives. The most common afflictions are going blind and losing the use of both legs, useful tragedies because they render the victim helpless and thus more vulnerable to attack from external forces. One recent episode in a popular soap saw the heroine, half blind and hallucinating, groping her way along a rope strung across a six-hundred-foot waterfall while trying to escape the evil Big City doctor who was pursuing her. She eventually was rescued and then recovered; in soap operas, blindness, like acne, is a temporary condition that usually clears up in six to eight weeks.

All soap operas avoid having characters perish of common, real-life diseases—especially diseases that viewers fear. Cancer is the second leading cause of death in America, yet one recent study showed that out of almost one-hundred-twenty-five different diseases on soap operas, only two cases were cancer—and *both* the victims made a full recovery.[8] The same study revealed that almost 80 percent of the sickness and death on soaps resulted from violence and accidents. One grandmother died not of the terminal cancer from which she was suffering, nor from the complications of carrying and delivering a baby so late in life: She survived all these hazards only to be run over by a truck. Murders alone account for over one quarter of all the deaths on soap operas. Anne Martin of "All My Children" survived five years of drug therapy in a mental institution—and was killed shortly after she was released when her car was blown up by an underworld mobster. Mary Kennicott had her leukemia go into remission but was murdered by an out-of-town gunman she let into her home in a moment of distraction.

In the world of the soaps, grief over the loss of a loved one may be intense, but it doesn't last long. Loneliness does not come with widowhood, which is, anyhow, an extremely short-term condition. Usually, a woman acquires a new love interest before her husband has even given up the ghost: No one experiences any serious mental distress as the result of the death of a spouse.

Mental illness on soap operas takes one of two forms: a nervous breakdown temporarily brought on by personal or career strains, or amnesia, which strikes on soap operas about as often as the common cold in the real world. Mental hospitals are pastoral refuges staffed by trained, sympathetic, tolerant personnel. There are no chronically ill mental patients, and confinement to an "institution" is short-lived, designed to get the character out of the way for a while, so her love interest (almost always it's a woman who cracks up) can develop a new romantic entanglement and thereby provide a fresh source of plot convolutions when the patient returns a few weeks later, fully cured.

After a steady diet of soap operas, one's view of the world begins to be affected. A recent study of soap opera addicts at the University of Kentucky found that they grossly overestimate the incidence of mental illness and divorce. Another

Michigan State study revealed that teenagers who watch soaps are likely to conclude that married people rarely have intercourse, while single people do almost nothing else.

Television researcher George Gerbner has studied the attitudes of heavy viewers and found them to be similarly distorted. His survey included questions like:

• *What are your chances of being the victim of a serious crime this year?*

(a) 1 in a million; (b) 1 in fifty; (c) 1 in ten

Heavy viewers almost always overestimate their chances and choose (c). The correct answer is (b).

• *What percentage of the world's population lives in the United States?*

(a) 5 percent; (b) 12 percent; (c) 20 percent

Again, heavy viewers choose answer (c) over the correct answer, (a).

• *What percentage of workers in the United States is employed in managerial or professional jobs?*

(a) 5 percent; (b) 15 percent; (c) 25 percent

Only 5 percent—one out of twenty—are professionals (i.e., doctors, lawyers, etc.), though heavy viewers often choose answer (c)—one out of every four people!

Semanticists call this kind of discrepancy between what one believes and what really is true having a false "map" to the actual "territory." In the topsy-turvsy world of soap operas, characters worry more about amnesia than about nuclear armament, more about murder than Medicare. The problems presented on soap operas distract viewers from *real* problems and lead them away from exploration of genuine sources of unhappiness. The effect of constant exposure to the soaps thus constitutes propaganda by distraction.

Consider the unlikelihood of any of the following story lines appearing on a soap opera:

—A black woman steals five dollars' worth of groceries and is sentenced to five years in jail. Meanwhile, a white woman shoots her unfaithful husband and is given a probated sentence, meaning she will serve only one year in jail.

—Three policemen beat up a young Hispanic man, suspected of car robbery, so badly that he later dies of his injuries. They are acquitted by a sympathetic home-town jury.

—Local authorities discover the town's large papermill is dumping carcinogenic waste products that pollute and destroy the river. When the company threatens to move to another town if legislation is passed preventing the pollution, it is allowed to stay and continue dumping its waste.

Certainly stories like these have as much potential for heart-wringing drama as those appearing in soap operas. But they never appear on the soaps because they have the uncomfortable ring of the truth—they were culled from recent news stories. These people's problems do not stem from the cruel and whimsical fancies of external villains, but from predictable social ills, which soap operas cannot recognize because they might raise questions about the unchallengeable perfection of the American Way.

In sum, soap operas sell us more than laundry detergent and leak-proof baby diapers. They sell an idealized vision of American life. In this familiar and reassuring world, there are no minority groups, no air pollution, no diminishing energy supplies, no old people struggling to survive on a fixed income, no poverty, no crime on the streets (only in the living room). There is equal justice for all, rich or poor, black or white—and equal opportunities for health care, education, and law protection. Problems arise not from the social structure but from individual perversity which strikes and subsides as inexplicably as a summer storm. In this morally simplified universe, faith is the answer to life's vicissitudes. There is always an unambivalent "right" thing to do.

The stock phrases which characterize the language of soap operas are dedicated to the perpetuation of ancient American myths and to maintenance of the status quo. Soap operas propagandize not by taking an overt political stand but, as Philip Wander says, by making "modern life appear coherent and relatively secure.* The old religion of love, family life, and God enters the symbolic world of the soaps and is rejuvenated. We see the consequences of violating tradition . . . Soap operas implicitly make the best of the upper-class, honest, hard-working professional stand for a system which has changed America from a land of family farmers and shopkeepers into a vast factory for the production of military hardware and consumer goods. In a society troubled with real problems, the soaps resurrect the nineteenth-century romantic novel and fill it with characters struggling to keep things the way they were."9

Every indication is that the folks of Oakdale, Pine Valley, and Rosehill will keep right on struggling, up until Doomsday. As Thurber said, "The characters in Soapland and their unsolvable perplexities will be marking time on the air long after you and I are gone, for we must grow old and die, whereas the people of Soapland have a magic immunity to age, like Peter Pan . . . When you and I are in Heaven with the angels, the troubled people of Crisco Corners, forever young or forever middle-aged, will still be up to their ears in inner struggle, soul-searching, and everlasting frustration."10

---

*Though, on occasion, characters will utter "safe" political opinions. After the exposure of a corrupt state governor on one soap, a character commented, "I think I feel about him the way I feel about Richard Nixon. Having absolutely no political future might just be bad enough."

5

Being Somebody

Farrah's hair is magic. It makes her the fantastic person she is. A fantastic person means you can be a major symbol in today's society . . .

Hugh York, Farrah Fawcett's hairdresser

Results of a nationwide survey asking young people to name their favorite heroes:
1. Abraham Lincoln
2. Alan Alda

One hundred years ago, people became famous for what they had achieved. Some of their achievements might be questioned in the hard Sophoclean light of today's ethical standards, but men like J.P. Morgan, E.H. Harriman, Jay Gould, and Jim Fisk were indisputably notable achievers. So were Thomas Edison, Mark Twain, and Susan B. Anthony.

Their accomplishments are still evident in our own day. But today's celebrities often do not become known for any enduring achievement. The people we most admire are invariably those who are most highly publicized by the media.

In 1981, a Gallup poll revealed Nancy Reagan to be the nation's "most admired woman." The year before, that distinction went to Rosalynn Carter. Three years before that, it went to Betty Ford. In fact, the wife of the incumbent President is always one of the nation's "Ten Most Admired Women." Today's celebrities, as Daniel Boorstin says, are "people well known for their well-knownness."

To become such a celebrity, one needs luck, not accomplishment. As Boorstin says, "The hero was distinguished by his achievement; the celebrity by his image or trademark. The hero created himself; the celebrity is created by the media. The hero was a big man; the celebrity is a big name."[1]

There is another distinction: heroes inspire respect; celebrities inspire envy. Few of us believe we could be another Jonas Salk or Eleanor Roosevelt, but we could be another Telly Savalas or Suzanne Somers. Except for the attention they get from the media, these people are exactly like us. We even speak of them with raffish familiarity, as the following headlines from gossip magazines reveal:

BO DEREK GOES APE OVER HUNKY *TARZAN* CO-STAR

CALVIN KLEIN SAYS "BOTTOMS UP" TO BROOKE SHIELDS IN SUCCESSFUL AD CAMPAIGN

SALLY FIELDS: ONCE BURT [REYNOLDS], TWICE SHY

Such irreverence would have been unthinkable in a previous era, when people became well known for more than just their well-knownness. Imagine the absurdity of headlines such as these:

A PERFECT "10": MOSES RATES WITH HIS PEOPLE ON RETURN FROM MOUNT SINAI

MARIE ANTOINETTE'S SWEET TOOTH GIVES HER A PAIN IN THE NECK

HIGH STAKES: BOYISH FRENCH MAID RISKS ALL FOR GOD AND COUNTRY

The world still has heroes, of course—but the glare of celebrity often casts them into the shadows. The shift from hero- to celebrity-worship occurred around the turn of the century and was closely tied to the rise of new forms of media—first photography, and later moving pictures, radio, and television. These media gave fame in America an entirely new dimension—physical recognition. Previously, men like Gould, Harriman, and Stanford White, whose names were all household words, could easily have passed through a crowd without being recognized. The invention of the halftone process, which reproduced photographs for newspapers, turned famous people into celebrities whose dress, appearance, and personal habits were widely commented upon. Slowly, the focus of public attention began to shift away from knowing what such people did to knowing what they looked like.

The shift was accelerated by the arrival of moving pictures, which created an entirely new kind of celebrity—the movie star. Mary Pickford, Douglas Fairbanks, Clara Bow, Lillian Gish, Rudolph Valentino became objects of near-worship, all with readily identifiable images: Fairbanks was the "dashing adventurer," Clara Bow the "It girl," Pickford "America's sweetheart," Theda Bara the "vamp," Valentino the "lover." These stars dominated public attention—and in the process frequently crowded out the kind of achievers who had previously been admired. One study of the nation's major magazines showed that whereas between 1901 and 1914, 74 percent of the subjects of biographical articles were political leaders, inventors, pioneering professionals, and businessmen, after 1922 most articles were about movie stars.

Since the new stars were media creations, they had to have continued media attention to maintain their celebrity status. Gossip columnists like Walter Winchell, Ed Sullivan, Dorothy Kilgallen, Sidney Skolsky, and, most strikingly, Hollywood columnists Louella Parsons and Hedda Hopper were believed to be able to make and unmake stars merely by promoting or withholding their names.* Most stars paid them court, or paid the price. "That," Hedda Hopper used to say of her expensive home in Beverly Hills, "is the house that fear built." Stars Hedda took a disliking to were often subjected to vituperative and unrelenting attack in her column. Writer Donald Zec once remarked of her, "Take a black widow spider, cross it with a scorpion, wean their poisonous offspring on a mixture of prussic acid and treacle and you'll get the honeyed sting of Hedda Hopper."[2] Louella Parsons was equally famous for the viciousness of her attacks on Orson Welles, among others.

Actually, being attacked by a gossip columnist was often far preferable to being ignored. *What* is said about a media celebrity is usually less important than *how many* people know it has been said. Many careers even flourished as a result of negative publicity. Once, for example, Louella Parsons embarked on a series of attacks on comedian Benny Rubin, accusing him, among other things, of getting drunk and breaking a violin over his wife's head. In fact, she had confused him with a musician who had a similar name. But Rubin didn't complain; as a result of the column, he began getting more and more job offers. Finally, one day, he and Miss Parsons met, and she repeated her accusation to his face. "Look," he told her, "I never drink. And I never hit a woman with a fiddle because I don't play one."

"Oh, my God!" Louella said, suddenly recognizing her mistake. "It was Jan *Rubini!* Oh, how can I make it up to you?"

---

* And, in the process, the columnists became celebrities themselves. In their heyday, Louella Parsons and Hedda Hopper claimed a combined readership of 75 million readers. Parsons' column alone ran in over six hundred newspapers. Walter Winchell's column ran in over four hundred newspapers, and his radio show, "Jergen's Journal," was practically required listening for most of America. Ed Sullivan's rise from *Daily News* columnist and radio personality to full-fledged television star is perhaps the best example of how strong a glow is cast from the reflected light of celebrity.

"I can't get better than you've been giving me all over the country," said Rubin. "Just keep printing my name. Make it a mock feud."[3]

In the 1930s radio brought its own kind of media celebrity—the broadcast "personality." People listened to the radio not so much to get the news or hear a good story as simply to spend time with Jack Benny, Burns and Allen, Groucho Marx, Rudy Vallee, Joe Penner, Fred Allen, Milton Berle, Fibber McGee and Molly. Radio celebrities were less glamorous than movie stars and less remote; people could feel they knew them as they could never know their movie idols. It was possible to imagine having dinner with George Burns, but not with Douglas Fairbanks.

But the biggest boost to celebrity status was yet to come. People were accustomed to seeing their favorite stars pictured in fan magazines, but television showed them in action. For the first time, the faces of the stars became as familiar as those we saw across the breakfast table. We came to know more about the lives of the celebrities than we did about most of the people we know personally. Less than seventy years after the appearance of the first moving pictures, the advance of celebrity was complete.

Television also made popular the *sine qua non* of modern celebrityhood: the talk show. At first, talk shows were simply comedy vehicles for celebrity hosts like Arthur Godfrey, Steve Allen, and Jack Paar—occasions for them to tell jokes and exchange wisecracks with a sidekick.

Probably the best-known early talk show joke is the following, which created a national furor when Jack Paar quit as host of "The Tonight Show" because NBC would not let him tell it on the air: An English lady, while visiting Switzerland, was looking for a room, and she asked the schoolmaster if he could recommend any to her. He took her to see several rooms and when everything was settled, the lady returned to her home to make the final preparations to move. When she arrived home, the thought suddenly occurred to her that she had not seen a W.C. (water closet) around the place. So she immediately wrote a note to the schoolmaster asking if there was a W.C. around. The schoolmaster was a very poor student of English, so he asked the parish priest if he could help in the matter. Together they tried to discover the meaning of the letters W.C., and the only solution they could find for the letters was a Wayside Chapel. The schoolmaster then wrote to the English lady the following note:

Dear Madam:

I take great pleasure in informing you that the W.C. is situated nine miles from the house you occupy, in the center of a beautiful grove of pine trees surrounded by lovely grounds.

It is capable of holding 229 people and it is open on Sunday and Thursday only. As there are a great number of people and they are expected during the summer months, I would suggest that you come early, although there is plenty of standing room as a rule.

You will no doubt be glad to hear that a good number of people bring their lunch and make a day of it. While others who can afford to go by car arrive just in time. I would especially recommend that your ladyship go on Thursday when there is a musical accompaniment.

It may interest you to know that my daughter was married in the W.C., and it was there that she met her husband. I can remember the rush there was for seats. There were ten people to a seat ordinarily occupied by one. It was wonderful to see the expression on their faces.

The newest attraction is a bell donated by a wealthy resident of the district. It rings every time a person enters. A bazaar is to be held to provide plush seats for all the people, since they feel it is a long-felt need. My wife is rather delicate, so she can't attend regularly.

I shall be delighted to reserve the best seat for you if you wish, where you will be seen by all. For the children, there is a special time and place so that they will not disturb the elders. Hoping to have been of service to you, I remain,

Sincerely,

The Schoolmaster[4]

Despite the great popularity of a host like Paar, it was clear that a single celebrity couldn't carry such a show alone. Other celebrities were invited on to talk, and soon such invitations began to be regarded as a measure of the degree of one's celebrity. "Making the rounds" on the talk show circuit became a required part of maintaining one's celebrity status.

Today, of course, an appearance on a television talk show is the ultimate certification of "making it" in America. Actually, the term "talk show" is a misnomer, for celebrities do not appear on such a program because of an actual desire—or ability—to converse, but simply to gain recognition, to prove, merely by showing up, that they are "somebody."

"Guesting" on a talk show does not require qualities of wit, eloquence, brilliance, insight, or intelligence. Craig Tennis, a former talent coordinator for "The Tonight Show," says that when he would ask a scheduled guest, "What would you like to talk to Johnny about?", the reply he got most often was "Have him ask me anything." This, he says, could usually be translated to mean, "I am a typical Hollywood actor, so I have never had an original thought and I have nothing to say of any interest to anyone anywhere."[5] He adds, "Most performers are either limited in intellectual scope and therefore dull, or they're unable to really *talk*—that is, converse outside of a role."

Some celebrities are so inept they appear to have difficulty even following the minimum requirements of Dick Cavett's ten tongue-in-cheek "Rules for Being a Good Conversationalist":

l. Do not place yourself in such a way that your back is to the person with whom you are speaking.

2. Be within hearing distance of the other person.

3. Do not leave the room while the other person is speaking.

4. Have at least one language in common.

5. Do not attempt to conduct the conversation in an inappropriate place, such as the center of a busy highway.

6. Do not use the word "albeit" more than four times.

7. Make an effort to be wearing clothing during the conversation.

8. Do not address letters or repair a diathermy machine during the conversation.

9. Do not light firecrackers or attempt to fish during the conversation.

10. Do not take hold of a wart on the person's face and go "beep-beep."[6]

Most hosts are grateful just to get someone who will fill the room with sound. One talk show booker comments, "We look for the guest who is sure to talk no matter what. Ten seconds of silence appears very awkward on television; thirty seconds is disastrous. A guest who's got to stop to think about everything he says before he opens his mouth is a ratings nightmare." A different booker adds, "Yes, we look for a good-looking astronomer who can talk over someone who hesitates before every answer—what he is talking *about* isn't that important."

This kind of attitude rewards glibness, and makes hesitancy look like stupidity. As critic Gilbert Seldes says, it puts "a premium on speed . . . on the quickness rather than the quality of wit and has somehow equated the process of contemplation—the painstaking working out of a judgment, the careful consideration of what has been said before replying—with slow-wittedness, with the stooge for the popular comedian's brightness."[7]

"Even as an ex-president," says one talent coordinator, "we wouldn't have used George Washington on our show. Mr. Dullsville in person. He might have been first in the hearts of his countrymen, but today he'd be dragging his bottom in the ratings."

Glibness is what talk shows treasure. The give-and-take of real conversation would only distract viewers from the real message being communicated: *Look at me. Admire me. Be like me.* Accordingly, the show's content often centers around the pleasures of carefree consumerism:

> "You look gorgeous. Is that mink?"
> "Of course, darling. Is there anything else?"

> "Hold up your hand so the camera can get a better shot of that. Will you look at the size of that rock, ladies and gentlemen?"

On one recent talk show, Burt Reynolds revealed that he had received five million dollars for doing his last movie. "Isn't that obscene?" asked the laughing host, obviously disclaiming any serious intent to classify the sum as obscene. "Sure it is," Reynolds readily agreed. "Paying anybody five million dollars to act in a movie is obscene. The only thing more obscene would be not to take it!"

Talk shows usually try to avoid "serious" topics, particularly if the times are serious. One talk show guest told me that he was forbidden to tell a joke about the United Nations ambassador who once mixed his metaphors so badly he ended up telling the Arabs and the Jews to calm down and settle their differences "like good Christians." The show was scheduled to be broadcast just after the taking of the hostages in Iran, and the show's talent coordinator told the guest they had to avoid any remark that might seem to be related to that crisis. "But this doesn't have anything to do with the Iranian hostages," the guest said. "Doesn't matter," the coordinator replied. "But the Iranians aren't even Arabs," the guest protested further. "No difference," said the coordinator. "We just have to steer very clear of the whole topic. We don't want to get everyone all stirred up."

The limited list of permissible topics has led to a numbingly narrow range of conversations. Flicking the TV dial on a typical weekday morning is likely to yield results such as this:

> . . . so, Doctor, according to your survey, the sexual position men most prefer is *beneath* the . . .
>
> CLICK
>
> . . . Western omelette, which is quick to prepare, high in vitamin content, and very good for your . . .
>
> CLICK
>
> . . . eyebrows. Lashes, on the other hand, should be gently lifted and separated like this, creating the illusion that the eye is actually . . .
>
> CLICK
>
> . . . jumping up and touching the other one three times. John, perhaps you'd like to join me as I demonstrate this exercise. *One,* two, three, four. *One,* two, three, four . . . Notice that after just two repetitions, you begin to feel that you're . . .
>
> CLICK
>
> . . . missing a left breast. She is here to discuss her terrifying ordeal with us, and with her is the person to whose pioneering efforts she owes her life . . .
>
> CLICK
>
> . . . Zsa Zsa Gabor! Let's give her a great big hand!

On the rare occasions when a "controversial" topic is permitted, discussion is generally brief (most talk show conversations are about ten minutes long, allowing for commercial breaks) and pointedly superficial. One observer remarks that talk shows are like conversational clinics where serious issues get treated and released. Blandness is beautiful. Saul

Braun satirized "serious" talk show discussions in an article for *Esquire,* using the now-defunct "Joey Bishop Show" as an example:

> Joey was very serious tonight, with an edifying discussion of capital punishment. Sammy Davis, Jr., and Ben Gazzara were with him. Ben is against it. Joey handled the topic with typical thoughtfulness and puzzlement: "Now, what do you do with someone, a cold-blooded killer? . . ."
>
> Ben said he thought we should turn our prisons into hospitals and Sammy said, "Most of the psychopathic murderers, when you look back into their case history, there has been a need for psychiatric help."
>
> Then they talked about the conditions in the prisons. Ben said, "The homosexuality, the cruelty, it's incredible." "It's frightening," Joey said. "It really is." At least with capital punishment, I felt like saying, you don't have any of that, but there was a commercial then.
>
> After it, Sammy explained the reason for capital punishment. "It's all part of our society's emotional—now please don't think I'm being frivolous when I say this—hang-up." Ben agreed. "They never lay on 'turn the other cheek.'"
>
> . . . Joey represented the other view: "What I'm talking about is, should they be analyzed, right? Do you honestly think we could reach a point where we could categorize these people . . . Well, I must say, in all honesty that I can agree . . . but somehow, you know . . ."[8]

The effect of talk such as this, says newsman Thomas Griffith, is to "trivialize subjects so that millions feel superior to ideas they haven't really taken the measure of because they got them in such oversimplified form. It teaches us to bear the misfortunes of others lightly; we don't have to look at it long; on to the commercial . . ."[9]

It has been persuasively argued that talk shows are not in the business of educating the public. That's not their intent, nor is it what people want. As one talk show producer explains, "Viewers have been shoved, jostled, insulted, robbed, unappreciated and unloved all day long. What they need—and want—is a little comfort like a pretty girl singing to them and a little relaxation like a few jokes to take the raw edges off their nerves. The thinkers, the second-guessers, the sidelines players say we should turn our programs over to discussions of the Mideast crisis, or school busing problems, or the decay in our prisons or the insanities in our asylums . . . Hell, ninety minutes of enlightened discourse on unemployment wouldn't help the problem but only add to it—by adding our employee list to the unemployment lines."[10]

He's quite right. But this argument implies that "entertainment" programs have no social significance. In fact, such programs do an excellent job of communicating well-defined social—even political—messages. Chiefly, they present lifestyles of material acquisition and consumption in a favorable light. The heavy emphasis on people who are wealthy and beautiful is powerful propaganda for the notion that wealth and beauty are what matter most, just as an emphasis on social workers, conservationists, and philosophers would support the notion that social service, conservation, and knowledge are what matter most.

Of course, people aspire to beauty and wealth without any prodding at all, but television's message of approval helps to persuade them that such aspirations are the highest possible good. This is quite contrary in spirit to the Judeo-Christian ethic to which our society supposedly adheres. But the values of the marketplace have rarely had much in common with that ethical system anyway. When Jesus threw the moneychangers out of the temple, they just moved their place of business elsewhere for a while.

It is fair to say that the messages communicated by the media establish moneychanger values in the public consciousness as "correct," "good," "normal." As Robert Shayon, Professor of Communications at the Annenberg School, says,

"Entertainment programs give audiences cues as to what is valued in our society and how to behave. They're really forms of education, of indoctrination."[11] Media critic James Monaco adds, "What the talk show celebrates isn't the accomplishment or the talent or the intelligence of the guests, despite all pretense to the contrary: what it celebrates is the star and the certifying medium." He adds, "This may be the ultimate end of those millions of conversations. Television talk teaches that everything outside the view of the cameras is worthless. The camera is everything."[12]

This is why many people will do almost anything to get on television and prove they are somebody. Talent coordinators of the major talk shows tell hilarious stories of being cornered by determined young hopefuls. The following account by Craig Tennis is typical:

> I was in the housewares section of Bullock's department store one day, minding my own business and making a few humble purchases. I gave the girl at the counter my charge card, and as she ran it through she glanced at the name and said, "Oh! It's very nice to meet you—how do I audition for 'The Tonight Show'?" I was stunned. I couldn't imagine how anyone who didn't know me personally could possibly be familiar with my name, but before I could recover and escape through a side door into the toy department, three other saleswomen were at the girl's elbow, cornering and badgering me about what a great singer this girl was, and how I should really put her on the show. I tried to explain that I was no longer *with* the show, but to no avail. I ended up backing out the door with my pots and pans, mumbling incoherently and staring while the girl wailed out "Feelings" right there in the middle of the housewares section.[13]

Some people, lacking "celebrity talent," will offer to reveal intimate and embarrassing secrets about their personal lives in order to gain entree to the validating eye of the television camera. Recent talk show confessionals include: a father who talked frankly about his seduction of his daughter, a married couple who talked frankly about their affairs with other people, a polygamist who talked frankly about his relationship with his seventeen wives, a victim of bladder cancer who talked frankly about the open bladder sac she must wear externally and how it interferes with her sex life. Often such guests are clumsily prodded into displays of emotion. Host Tom Cottle once told a mastectomy victim, "I'm sitting here wondering if I could get into bed with a woman like you, knowing you're missing a breast." At the conclusion of the show, he said, "I feel a little part of me is still gawking at you."

Offered a chance to "be somebody," most people will share with millions things they would hesitate to tell their best friends. A fascinating experiment conducted by novelist Jerzy Kosinski offers startling testimony to this. Kosinski interviewed a group of ten- to fourteen-year-old schoolchildren individually, asking them very personal questions, such as "Do you masturbate?" and "Have you ever stolen anything?" Embarrassed, the kids mumbled, hedged, and wouldn't answer completely. Kosinski describes what he did next:

> I said, "Now, I'll tell you why I asked you all these questions. You see, I would like to film the interview and show it on television . . . Your parents, your friends, strangers, the whole country would see it . . ." All the students assured me they were willing "to try harder" to answer the same questions . . .
>
> Once the equipment was installed, I started the video camera and it was time to address my first "guest." "Now tell me," I asked . . . "do you masturbate? If you do, tell our audience how and when you do it." The boy, suddenly poised and blasé, leaned toward me. "Well, yes, occasionally I do. Of course, I'm not sure I can describe it. But I can try . . ." An inviting smile stolen from the "Mike Douglas Show" . . .

> After the boy described all, leaving nothing to the public's imagination, I changed the subject. I said, "Everyone will be interested in your experiences as a thief. Have you ever stolen anything?" Pensively, as if recalling a pleasant childhood incident, the boy said, "Every once in a while when I go to the Five and Ten, you know, I like to pick up something . . ."[14]

Most of the other children performed similarly. Kosinski says that in contrast to the first off-camera interviews, the children were willing—even eager—to talk on-camera "about the most incriminating subjects, ranging from less common sexual experiences to acts of violence, the very betrayal of one's family, friends, etc." He adds, "Often I pretended to be embarrassed by what they said. But trained in the best talk show tradition, the guests were not put off by their host."

In a recent television interview with Barbara Walters, Patty Hearst spoke quite openly about being raped and sexually humiliated while held prisoner by the Symbionese Liberation Army. Before an audience of millions she also described her sexual encounters with her former captors, both male and female, after she became a member of the group. At the end of the interview Barbara Walters asked Miss Hearst what she planned to tell her baby daughter about her experiences when she grows up. "Maybe I won't tell her anything," Patty said. "Maybe I'll just let her find out about it for herself."

A person's chances of "making it" on television are better if he has some personal eccentricity or social-sexual deviance to offer up for discussion. He is then often presented as an amusing *divertissement,* with both host and audience allied in not-so-subtle ridicule of his odd behavior and/or appearance. Even so usually sensitive and sincere a host as Phil Donahue will occasionally indulge in this kind of sport. On one show, Donahue broke into a discussion among a trio of transvestites to inquire, "Where do you guys go to the bathroom?" The audience howled with delight. The female impersonators smiled and shrugged; the derision aimed at them seemed a reasonable price to pay for the opportunity, however brief, to "be somebody."

Eccentrics and oddballs have proved so successful on talk shows that a new kind of program was developed especially for them. An NBC executive describes "Real People" as "a celebration of American inventiveness and individualism." A close look at the content of the program suggests that the basic message communicated is somewhat less noble. A recent show featured a married transvestite couple saving up for dual sex-change operations. After brief interviews with the couple, the husband was shown wiggling down the street in a tight miniskirt, while the hefty wife was filmed repairing the roofbeams. As the film rolled, a soupy rendition of the song "Together" warbled in the background while the studio audience cackled and jeered. Other "Real People" "stars" have included a psychologist who specializes in enlarging women's breasts through hypnosis; a man who taught his bellybutton to whistle; a woman who stripteases for Christ; a man who keeps ten thousand flies in his kitchen and who is teaching a tarantula to dance; and a man who, anticipating the imminent destruction of the world, has built and designed his own spaceship in the shape of a banana. "Real People" producer George Schlatter claims that the intent is not to ridicule, but to celebrate these people as representative of the spirit of American individualism—rather like modern-day Thoreaus: "Americans . . . need to be brought back to themselves," Schlatter says, "to believe in the individual. In that sense we make a very patriotic statement—in a time when the mood is of a nation abandoned, we need to get back to individual achievements."[15]

Exactly what is meant by the word "achievement"? What of any social, scientific, artistic, or spiritual value has actually been "achieved"? The "achievement" of such people appears to be primarily in getting themselves on television. What is celebrated is celebration itself—rather like a hall of mirrors in which all is reflected images and no one and nothing is really there.

Lacking any other qualities that might gain them the spotlight, some people even offer up their lives for the chance to "be somebody." The show "That's Incredible" provides them with the opportunity. In the first year of broadcast alone, the show was responsible for several accidents: one man burned his fingers to stumps while attempting to run through a tunnel of fire; another ruptured his aorta in an unsuccessful motorcycle leap; a third nearly tore off his foot when he miscalculated a broad jump over two oncoming cars. The show broadcast the footage of the latter two catastrophes, including a slow-motion segment showing the man's shattered foot spinning all the way around his ankle. One network producer was prompted to remark, "This hasn't happened since they threw people to the lions."

Yet there's no shortage of people eager to volunteer for such honor. Deran Serafian, the associate producer of a now-defunct program ("Games People Play"), says he was constantly inundated by phone calls from people dying—literally —to get on TV. He describes one such call:

> One man wanted to jump out of an airplane a mile over the Florida Everglades without a parachute and land in the marshes.
>
> ". . . and *live*," he said.
>
> I told him, "That's suicide."
>
> He got mad. "Listen, if I die it's better for your show! What have you got to lose?"
>
> "My lunch," I replied.[16]

People who are unwilling to go quite so far to gain a brief flash of celebrity have an alternate route to fame and fortune:

They can become contestants on game shows. Game shows are the perfect embodiment of what it means to "be somebody" in America. First, they provide viewers with celebrity role models to admire and emulate. Because of the expense of importing "major" celebrities, these programs have created their own in-house variety—"game show celebrities," a species whose chief distinction appears to be in owning at least five changes of clothes, one for each day of the week. Nipsey Russell, Brett Somers, Gene Rayburn, and Nick Gautier, among others, serve as jolly if somewhat condescending companions to contestants in quest of riches and frost-free refrigerators.

Game shows do not merely encourage consumerism; they sanctify it. Before every "game," the product prize to be won is prominently displayed while organ music swells in the background and the announcer goes into born-again ecstasies while reading the litany of "special product features":

> Well, Bob, the lucky winner of the next game will receive . . . [suspenseful pause as the curtain slowly opens to reveal prize] . . . a luxurious SWINGOMATIC HAMMOCK!!!!! Yes, it's the fully automatic three-speed motorized hammock with sturdy self-expanding acrylic webbing for easy-care, easy-clean comfort. Rock your cares away during those long, hot summer days with SWINGOMATIC!!! And this beautiful luxury item can be yours if—YOUR GUESS IS RIGHT!!!!!

If anyone entertains any doubts as to the desirability of such a prize, they are swept away by the excitement of the contestants, who are often chosen for their willingness to squeal and whimper on cue.

One of the chief functions of the host is to play up a contestant's desperate desire to gain the prize. On a recent broadcast of "The Price Is Right," Bob Barker told a nervous contestant, "You're shaking. Put your hand out there. Look at that hand shake, ladies and gentlemen!" Monty Hall, host of "Let's Make a Deal," called up a young woman who immediately began to fall apart. "Richie, Richie," she moaned to her husband seated in the audience. "What if I don't choose right? What if we don't get it?" Hall milked the situation for several minutes, mimicking her cries and sidecracking to the audience, "If this is what she's like when she's happy, imagine what she's like when she's sad?" Often a game show host will feign embarrassment and distress at a contestant's antics: "Now, Bonita, control yourself. Whatever will these nice people think of you?" Actually, they try to draw out such exchanges as long as possible, knowing that they promote the *real* purposes of the show. For game shows are ingenious ways for the TV medium to circumvent the rule that only eight minutes of commercials are allowed on a half hour show. The game show *is* a half hour commercial. *Everything* on such a program—from the wardrobe of the host (donated by a clothing store credited at the end) to the manufactured glamour of the celebrity guests, to the product prizes donated free by eager sponsors—is part of a carefully crafted hype. And the monomaniacal emphasis on the importance of the acquisition feeds the great American dream of easy money and an abundance of material goods.

The "game" itself is secondary to this overriding message. Most of today's game shows are simply egalitarian guessing games in which contestants take stabs at questions that have no correct answers: "Name something in a fish tank"; "What's something that kids hate to do?"; "What's the best time of day for a nap?" If a question has a "correct" answer, it is often given to contestants as part of a "multiple choice," to guarantee that even the slowest of contestants will have one chance out of three or four of getting it right. Former game show host Art James describes a typical example:

> . . . the question given to a young married couple was, "Simple

Simon met a pieman going to the: school, fair, or church?"

After a moment the intense husband asked, "Could you repeat the question, please?"

It was given again and the couple thought very hard. Just as time was up, the man said "fair." When told he was right, the weary warrior turned proudly to his wife and gave a long "Whewwwwwwww."[17]

Another popular device is to provide most of the answers in the question itself: "One of the most famous pieces of American literature, written by Edward Everett Hale, was about a character called Philip Nolan, the Man Without a . . . what?" Even providing that much information cannot guarantee that a contestant will get the answer right. To that question, the contestant responded unhesitatingly, "The Man Without a Coat." Another memorable wrong answer is described by Art James:

> It was at a key point in the game and the pace was furious. The answer that we wanted was "The Statue of Liberty." The question: "Svelte is much admired in women. But there is a much-loved American woman, whose designer was Bartholdi and whose waist is 35 feet . . ." A buzzer sounded.
> "Yes?" I asked.
> "Kate Smith," came the answer.[18]

Contestants are chosen not for their cleverness or knowledge, but for their willingness to help sell the game show message. "We look for the person who will be open, who is not afraid to display their emotions, who is willing to let themselves go a little," says one game show producer. Usually, this means a willingness to appear silly. Since the game itself isn't of real interest or importance, viewers are kept entertained by oddball contestants who are likely to come up with amusing responses. Producers love contestants like the New Mexico ranchhand who, when asked to name a romantic-sounding instrument, responded, "Drums." Often, questions are deliberately phrased to exploit a contestant's limited vocabulary and intelligence. For instance, the host of the now-defunct "Newlywed Game" once asked a group of wives to "estimate the length of your husband's inseam." The first wife replied, "Oh, about 29 inches," at which point the camera, alert to the possibilities of the situation, closed in for a tight shot of wife number three's astonished look. Then wife number two estimated her husband's inseam to be 31 inches long. Wife number three's astonishment grew visibly—and was duly recorded by the cameras. When her turn came and the question was repeated, she finally replied, helplessly, "Well, gee, it just *can't* be any longer than seven inches!"

Watching her performance later, what must she have thought? Was she embarrassed? Chances are she was not overly distressed. Her appearance made her a kind of celebrity among her friends, and if she didn't actually manage to walk away with the Maytag washer and dryer, well, maybe the *next* time. For game shows hold out the eternal promise of happiness through having better products, and more of them, than one's neighbors.

Presumably, the offer of other kinds of rewards would promote other kinds of values. The people of a less materialistic culture might have little regard for a brand new car (particularly if they already had a perfectly functional means of transportation), but they might be thrilled with the offer of an opportunity to meet and talk with a great religious or spiritual leader, or the chance to take a course of study at a prestigious school of education, or a month's leave from routine work to spend in quiet reflection and meditation. Such "prizes," of course, sound absurd to most of us. Nevertheless, this is not a measure of their relative worth, but of how completely we have been "sold" the idea that the only true pleasures are material ones.

Consider how *you* got your present set of values—rarely by reflection, deduction, or argument, often not even from education in schools. For the most part, you have adopted the implicit assumptions of your society, assumptions that are constantly reinforced in the media that reflect and reinforce that society.

There is the story of a wealthy young daughter who accompanied her businessman father on a visit to Communist China—a society in which no one is supposed to make money from anyone's labor but his or her own. At a meeting with a young Chinese girl, the daughter was asked, "How many people work for your father in his business?"

"Nearly 400," the American girl replied.

"Aren't you *ashamed*?" the Chinese girl asked.

Everything depends on your point of view. A cockroach has its own opinion of a clean kitchen.

III

The Politicians

6

It Sells Soap, Doesn't it?

Two centuries ago when a great man appeared, people looked
for God's purpose in him; today we look for his press agent.
> Daniel Boorstin

I ask admen not to confuse candidates for the presidency with a
deodorant, or the White House with an armpit.
> John O'Toole, president of the
> Foote Cone & Belding
> advertising agency

In 1934, socialist writer Upton Sinclair ran for Governor of
California on the Democratic ticket. Initially dismissed as an
idealistic fringe candidate, Sinclair astounded everyone when
he won the primary election with a thumping majority, re-
ceiving more votes than all of his opponents combined. Republican businessmen, realizing they could no longer afford
to dismiss Sinclair and his "visionary" ideas, collected the
previously unheard of sum of $10 million to mount an adver-
tising campaign against him. All across the state they rented
two thousand billboards plastered with the alarming quota-
tion, "If I am elected governor, half the unemployed in the
country will hop the first freight to California—Upton Sin-

clair." Most voters believed that Sinclair himself had bought the billboards to communicate that message. The Republican Party produced a series of commercial newsreels hinting that Sinclair was an agent of Russian communism. In one, a mass of scruffy hobos gets off a freight train in California and begins celebrating because, as one puts it, "Sinclair says he'll take the property of the working people and give it to us." Another spot showed a roving reporter interviewing a motherly old lady knitting peacefully in her rocking chair. The reporter asks, "Who are you voting for, Mother?" She replies, "I'm voting for the Republican, Frank Merriam, because this little home may not be much, but it is all I have in this world. I love my home and want to protect it." The reporter then is seen interviewing a bedraggled old vagrant in a torn and soiled overcoat. "Who are *you* voting for, sir?" he asks. The vagrant replies in a heavy foreign accent, "I am voting for Seen-clair. His system vorked vell in Russia, so vy can't it vork here?"

Sinclair, whose candidacy had at first seemed so strong, was easily defeated in the election by a candidate whose own supporters described him as lackluster. It was by no means the first or the last time that a political candidate would be defeated by the combined power of advertising and corporate money.

Most early political advertising relied on crude brainwashing techniques. A 1933 commercial for Franklin Delano Roosevelt used cartoon animation to depict Mickey Mouse racing down an endless tunnel, whimpering in fear as visions of bank rushes and stock market panics fill his mind. Finally, Mickey arrives at the office of "Dr. Pill," and asks him, "Doctor, what will cure a depression?" The doctor points knowingly to a picture of FDR and says, "There's your doctor!" The next scene shows Mickey in the White House asking, "Mr. President, what will cure a depression?" Cheerful music swells and the cartoon FDR breaks into a little soft-shoe as he sings:

Confidence!
Can lick this whole depression.
Confidence!
And wear the right expression.

Smile!
Grin!
Laugh right out loud!
And watch the golden sunshine
Scatter every cloud.

Confidence!
Hey, hey!
Is our salvation.
Confidence!
The hope of our great nation.

Teach it!
Preach it!
Tout it!
Shout it!
Confidence!
Just have confidence!

A 1966 political commercial for California governor Pat Brown featured his opponent Ronald Reagan in clips from his old movies and from Boraxo soap advertisements and concluded with the line, "Remember, it was an actor who shot Lincoln!"[1]

Today's voters, more sophisticated in the uses of television, are subjected to subtler techniques. In the 1978 contest for mayor of New York, political media consultant David Garth pictured his client, Ed Koch, with a trench coat draped over his shoulders whether scenes were filmed in rain or shine. Thanks to movie stars such as Alan Ladd and Humphrey Bogart, the trench coat has become a symbol for a "tough guy," and this was the subliminal message Garth wanted to convey to voters. The commercials were success-ful. As a result of this and similar public relations techniques, the comparatively unknown Koch won over a field of better known candidates. One opponent, Mario Cuomo, exclaimed after the election, "What hath Garth wrought?"

Many political commercials work by forming these sub-liminal associations in the viewer's mind. One ad for Senator Malcolm Wallop showed him as a kind of legislative Marlboro Man, riding at the head of seventy-five horsemen through the hills of Wyoming to the accompaniment of rousing Western music. It ended with the slogan, "Ride with us, Wyoming!" Of course, that kind of advertising works only for a geograph-ical location with a suitably strong image: One can hardly imagine a senator from Iowa striding through grunting pig herds, or a representative from Abilene manfully picking his way through a field of cow droppings. Nor is it likely that a representative from a certain impoverished borough of New York City would care to campaign with the slogan, "Ride with us, South Bronx!"

Most people believe they are not influenced by political image-making. But a recent study revealed that more voters based their decisions on information received from TV adver-tising than on information received from any other source. One reason is that many people think political commercials are somehow related to "the news," particularly if they are broadcast in and around news programs. David Garth says, "A lot of times when we poll we ask people if they saw our commercials. They say, 'No, we saw you on the news. That was the news.'" He adds, "We use our commercials as a news vehicle."[2]

Part of the reason for this confusion is television coverage of party conventions. Conventions are treated as news events, though in fact they are nothing more than elaborately pro-duced advertisements. The media give party conventions more coverage than earthquakes, foreign revolutions, or famines. ABC, NBC, and CBS spent over $40 million covering the 1980 conventions, and more than 12,000 people from the media showed up to cover the Republican convention—more than six times the number of delegates! This disparity prompted Russell Baker to observe:

> A logical mind confronted with 12,000 news people covering 2,000 Republicans might reason as follows: six news people for every Republican means that a single Republican's twenty-four-hour day can be covered most efficiently if each of the six works a four-hour shift. At the end of it, however, only one person will have been covered. To wit, the Republican. The waste and inefficiency—two things that gall Republicans especially—are appalling. The sensible alternative is to have each Republican cover six news people. This would give us six reports for the price of one instead of, as under the present system, one for the price of six.[3]

Despite all this attention, nothing really happens at a political convention. All the real decision-making takes place in the months before the election. Most of the delegates have about as much freedom of choice as a freight car full of prime steers on its way to the stockyards. The only "news" at a convention is when the delegates ratify the presidential candidate's choice of a vice-presidential running mate. Yet the networks build special control rooms, anchor booths, engineering spaces to allow coverage of the event from every possible angle. Taking note of all the expensive equipment CBS had brought to the 1980 Republican convention, then-network President William Leonard remarked, "We have built this elephant gun, and we have aimed it squarely at a gnat."[4]

All this television coverage amounts to free advertising for the presidential candidate and his party. For four consecutive evenings, messages of promise, hope, and goodwill toward Republicans (or Democrats) are broadcast simultaneously on all three networks to a captive audience. Minor party candidates do not get equal time. To buy that much advertising time, the candidate of a minor party would have to pay over $10 million.* The result is that his chances in the election remain decidedly minor, edging toward impossible.

Party spokesmen admit freely that conventions are extended advertising vehicles. William Carruthers, media advisor to Presidents Nixon and Ford, says, "There is no reason that a convention should be laid out for prime time any differently than an entertainment special."[5] In keeping with this philosophy, Carruthers wrote a "script" for the 1972 convention that included pauses for applause, instructions for cheering, and even stage directions for nodding at the color guard as it went by.

The centerpiece of the convention is the party propaganda film. Ever since 1956 when networks "cut away" from the film to do some interviews, lights on the convention floor have been dimmed to prevent the broadcast of anything other than the film. Most news people today would show the film even without prodding. "The film is part of the convention," David Buksbaum of CBS News says. "I think the American people have a right to see it, even if it is a commercial. The whole week is a commercial."[6] The 1980 Democratic convention film offered the following paean to Jimmy Carter:

> (Pictures of Washington, Lincoln, Jefferson, FDR, Kennedy are flashed on the screen)
> Announcer's voice: Jimmy Carter, like his predecessors, came into office because the people saw something in him that they liked—something they trusted . . . What *are* the qualities that Americans search for in a President?
> Representative Henry Gonzalez: Jimmy Carter doesn't act like a politician is supposed to act up here in Washington, D.C.

---

*It is an advantage which the major parties jealously guard. When Independent candidate John Anderson was hired as a network commentator during the 1980 convention, the Democrats and Republicans complained that his appearance violated "equal time" provisions.

... But this is what the people wanted ... He has given us independence from the corrupted processes, from the vested interests ...

Representative Morris Udall: Jimmy Carter is one of those people I call a work horse rather than a show horse. He's good at the hard, tedious job that any executive has got to do. He's not all that good at bragging on himself and pointing out the achievements.

Lieutenant Governor Mario Cuomo: When he got low in the polls, that to me was his badge of honor because I knew it meant he was willing to do the right thing even if it wasn't, for the moment, the popular thing.

Representative Jim Wright: One of the things I've noticed about President Carter is that when he gets people together he appeals to the best instincts in each of them. There are leaders, of course ... who appeal to the worst in each of us—the fear, the hate, the dread. Not Jimmy Carter—he appeals to the hope, the faith, the future. He makes each of us feel like a better person for having sat and talked with him ...

"What's the difference between selling a President and selling soap?" asked the director of the Ford advertising campaign in 1976. "Frankly, the disciplines are basically the same." Leonard Hall, former chairman of the Republican national committee, advised public relations people to "sell your candidates the way business sells its products."[7] Most political advertising blends perfectly with the tone and style of product commercials, as in this mixture of Gerald Ford and a Coca-Cola advertisement:

I'd like to buy the world a home ...
There's a change that's come over America
And keep it company ...
It's better than it used to be ...
Grow up on trees and honey bees

I'm feeling good about America . . .
And snow-white turtle-doves
We are at peace
I'd like to teach the world to sing
We are at peace with the world
I'd like to give the world a Coke [Ford?]
We know we can depend on him . . .
And keep it company . . .
Is there anything more important?
It's the real thing . . .

As product advertising, political commercials feature people offering cheerful—and definitely solicited—testimonials to the candidate's virtues. Here are a few samples:

"An honest man . . . I trust him."
"I'm voting for Ford because I trust him . . . he's a decent man"
"I have faith in the man. I trust the man."
"I like him very much. He's a very honest man."
"He's about the most straightforward man I know . . ."
"He's just a downright, decent, honest person, seems to me."

One commercial for Jimmy Carter featured a sweet elderly couple saying, "I think he's going to fight for everything that's good in this country," and "I think Jimmy Carter's a man who could come in here and sit down in that chair and I could talk right along with him." (They probably don't want the whitener taken out of Final Touch Fabric Softener, either.)

Ronald Reagan brought in his running mate George Bush to testify for him: "He's a kind person, he's a compassionate person who cares deeply about others. He'll be a great President." (It is not bringing Bush's integrity into question to wonder what would have happened if he had said that he had come to know Ronald Reagan so well that he had decided to vote for Jimmy Carter.) Even Nancy Reagan was persuaded to get into the act: "I am offended by President Carter's comments about my husband's character . . . I am offended as a mother, a wife—and a woman."

Senatorial candidate Al D'Amato of New York takes the prize for producing the best testimonial to his virtues. That inestimable symbol of wholesomeness and American apple pie—Mommy—actually had a good word for her son. Antoinette D'Amato praised her Al's fine qualities, and pushed her pamphlet, "Antoinette D'Amato's Recipes for the Forgotten Middle Class" (the first known link between political aptitude and home cooking).

Perhaps the most startling approximation of product advertising was a commercial for the third-party candidate in the 1980 election. The TV commercial for John Anderson showed pictures of Anderson growing up in Rockford, Illinois, while the following subtitles rolled:

WORKED IN FAMILY GROCERY STORE
GRADUATED WITH HONORS
STAFF SERGEANT WITH FOUR BATTLE STARS
TWO LAW DEGREES
WIFE, CHILDREN, AND SON-IN-LAW

One half expected to see:

ALL THIS FOR ONLY $4.95. DAUGHTER-IN-LAW INCLUDED FREE
IF YOU ORDER TODAY!

Caveat emptor . . . As newsman Robert MacNeil says, "If a TV commercial makes you like the image of one brand of toothpaste enough to buy a tube, it is no great matter if you find you don't like the stuff after all. You can quickly revert to the brand you like. If a TV commercial makes you like the image of a politician, it may be six years before you can change him, and he is next to impossible to throw away."[8]

Since most political advertisements are only twenty to thirty seconds long, they must rely on catchy symbols and phrases: "Firm, Fair Fahey for County Court Judge"; "Durham delivers" (pizza? moo goo gai pan?). One candidate for a judgeship had a line which God might envy: "He had the proven ability to make all the right decisions." Jerry Brown's theme for his candidacy was no less exalted: he pledged to "protect the earth, serve the people, and explore the universe." A candidate with such ambitions should not have been campaigning for a mere political office.

The thirty-second commercial breathed new life into the political slogan: "The time is now," "This time, vote like your whole world depended on it," "Peace with honor," "Vote Republican—for a change." The latter is based on Eisenhower's 1952 slogan "Time for a change," a phrase which John Kennedy billed as "the weakest and least constructive slogan in the history of American political thought." But this catchall appeal is effective, because it appears to offer an answer to every form of discontent—with inflation, with diminishing American influence abroad, with nuclear armament, with the personality of the opposition candidate, or—you name it. As editor Harlan Cleveland told Eisenhower's adman Rosser Reeves, "You're sabotaging democracy. You're trying to take a complex presidential personality, trim it down to a few slogans, reduce it to fifteen seconds, and use your rat-ta-tat-tat technique."[9] Eisenhower's campaign was so successful in the use of marketing techniques that Marya Mannes celebrated the achievement in verse:

Hail to BBD and O
That Told the Nation How to Go
It managed by advertisement
To sell us a new President

Eisenhower hits the spot
One full General, that's a lot
Feeling sluggish, feeling sick

Take a dose of Ike and Dick
Philip Morris, Lucky Strike
Alka Seltzer, I like Ike[10]

There is one major difference in the way products and candidates are marketed to the public: product advertising has to meet certain minimum standards of truthfulness and accuracy; political advertising does not. In his excellent book, *The Duping of the American Voter*, Robert Spero analyzed many political commercials and found they contained statements which wildly violated network code regulations for product advertising. There was, for example, the 1976 Carter commercial called "Government Reorganization":

> Carter: When I was elected governor, I went into office not as a politician but as an engineer, a farmer, a businessman, a planter. We had 300 agencies and departments in the state government. We abolished 278 of them . . . That saved a lot of money . . . With a new budgeting technique called zero-base budgeting we eliminated all the old obsolescent programs. Put into effect long-range goals, planning, and cut administrative costs more than 50 percent. And shifted that money and that service . . . toward giving better government services to our people.
>
> Announcer: What Jimmy Carter did as governor, he'll do as President. If you agree that government should be reorganized, vote for Jimmy Carter.

This commercial failed to meet product advertising standards on at least three counts:

> *"When I was elected governor, I went into office not as a politician . . ."*
> Actually, Carter had been elected and served two terms in the Georgia Senate. He had also made a previously unsuccessful run for the governorship.

> *"We abolished 278 [of 300 agencies in the state govern-*
> *ment . . ."]*
> Many of the agencies he referred to here were not in opera-
> tion anyway. Several others were not funded by the State, as
> he claimed.
> *"[I] cut administrative costs more than 50 percent . . ."*
> During Carter's four years as Governor, the cost of running
> the state office grew by 49 percent. The number of state
> employees grew by 30 percent.

As Wendell Phillipps has said, "You can always get the
truth from an American statesman after he has turned seventy or given up all hope of the presidency." Revised for
truthfulness, the commercial would read like this:

> Carter: When I was elected governor, I went into office . . .
> Announcer: What Jimmy Carter did as Governor, he'll do as
> President.

One of Richard Nixon's former aides recalls, with a
twinge of conscience, that:

> In [one] commercial we spent a lot of time on Nixon ratifying
> the bill giving the vote to eighteen-year-olds. He's there mak-
> ing a speech about how he welcomes them, and if eighteen-
> year-olds can fight and die, they can vote, blah, blah, blah. We
> didn't think anything of it, but later I did. I mean, Nixon damn
> well *had* to ratify that bill. He spent a year and a half fighting it
> and *Congress* had given them the right. *He* didn't want the
> damn eighteen-year-olds to vote. At the time, the White House
> thought the eighteen-year-olds would kick him out. So when
> he *had* to put his signature on the bill, there we were having a
> commercial about taking credit for giving them the vote. Is
> that fair to do?[11]

Political commercials often present voters with a false or
unreal choice. In 1952, the choice was "Vote Republican or

Die." One commercial, for example, showed two GIs crouching on a battlefield during the Korean War. Frightened, they talk about the futility and pointlessness of the war, and their own disillusionment about what they are supposed to be fighting for. Suddenly, the enemy opens fire and one of them is hit, writhes, and dies. His buddy, in frustration and despair, exposes himself to the enemy fire and is also killed. Over the picture of the two dead bodies, a voice is heard announcing lugubriously, "Vote Republican."

When Harry Truman was asked his opinion of Batten Barton Durstine & Osborn, the ad agency which created this spot for General Eisenhower, he snapped, "What do I think of BBD & O? I think it stands for Bull, Baloney, Deceit and Obfuscation."

In 1964, politics flip-flopped, and the choice became "Vote Democratic or Die." One of the most controversial commercials ever made showed a pretty little girl, all innocence, picking petals off a daisy in a field. In a small, sweet voice, she counts the petals as she pulls them off, "One, two, three . . ." When she gets to ten, the picture is frozen, and a man's grim voice begins to count back down from ten (as in a nuclear blast countdown). At zero, the scene dissolves into a nuclear holocaust. Over the mushrooming cloud President Lyndon Johnson's voice is heard: "These are the stakes—to make a world in which all God's children can live or go into the dark. We must either love each other or we must die." Voters got the message: A vote for Johnson's opponent Goldwater is a vote for dead little girls. At last count, partisans of dead little girlhood did not constitute a large percentage of the electorate.

As the ad's creators point out, Goldwater was never mentioned in the commercial, but so strong was the impression that Goldwater had been directly attacked that more than eight years later *The New York Times* described the commercial as having said, "Whose finger do you want on the trigger?"

Other commercials for Johnson promoted the idea of

"peace on earth." Robert Spero describes these commercials as forms of "bait-and-switch" advertising. Voters are "baited" with offers of one product—peace—and then "switched" to a different product—Johnson.[12]

There was a clear difference between the two. On the very day the first "peace" commercial was introduced, Johnson and his national security advisors reached agreement that air attacks on North Vietnam would begin after the elections. Three days after his overwhelming victory as the "peace candidate," Johnson ordered covert military action against North Vietnam to begin.

Viewpoints contrary to established political thinking are often required to meet standards from which pro-Establishment advertising is exempt. At the peak of the Vietnam conflict, a group called the Business Executives Move for Peace tried to buy air time for one-minute commercials against the war. Their request was denied, with the explanation that the station had a "long-established policy of refusing to sell spot announcements dealing with controversial issues" and that, furthermore, "subjects of this type deserve more in-depth analysis than can be produced in ten-, twenty-, or sixty-second commercials."[13] There would be no quarrel with this high-minded policy if it were applied to both sides of the controversy. But in the world of the media, pro-Establishment opinions are never controversial.

Political commercials never attack the American system. One Reagan commercial showed an old black woman shopping in a grocery store, shaking her head, obviously unable to afford to buy the food she needs. "Why doesn't someone in Washington do something about prices? People are suffering." She isn't angry at an unfair social and economic order, however; she's just tired of the Democratic party. The announcer's voice comes on to suggest the solution: "Vote Republican. For a change."

The most effective political advertising avoids any specific statement of policy or purpose. An example is the "feeling bad" commercials, in which the candidate talks about a particular problem but does not suggest how to solve it. One 1976 commercial showed Carter saying, "I don't think we'll ever have a solution to our present economic woes as long as we've got eight and a half or nine million people out of jobs and looking for jobs. And another two or three million who have given up hope of getting work. And another million and a half on welfare who never have worked but are fully able to." He felt just awful about the whole thing. But no solutions were suggested; they would have seemed irrelevant in a spot clearly designed to project Carter's humanity and warmth, not his intelligence.

Media specialist Tony Schwartz describes the making of another "feeling bad" spot:

> When I was doing Gaylord Nelson's campaign, Abe Ribicoff's campaign, Mike Gravel's campaign, inflation was a concern of people. I asked each [candidate] what he would do about it. No one had a clear answer. I wasn't impressed. So if I wasn't impressed, I'm not going to use their answers. What I did was ask them how they *felt* about inflation. I did spots with Ribicoff and Gravel with their wives. I had them talk about the high cost of groceries. I had slides of them walking through a store. I had them say they would fight against it. They weren't giving answers of what they would do, but how they felt about it. And this did impress me.[14]

The perfection of this form may have been reached with the 1952 commercial for Eisenhower in which a "citizen" asks, "Mr. Eisenhower, what do you think of the cost of living?" Eisenhower replies, "My wife Mamie complains about it too. I tell her that our job is to change all that on November 4th." As Talleyrand observed, "Speech was given to man that he may hide his thoughts."

In a pointed strike at the rhetorical dodge, John Anderson took on a mock "running mate" in the 1980 election—

Yoda, the out-of-this-world creature from *The Empire Strikes Back* (once described as "a cross between a Hobbit samurai instructor, a midget Zen monk, and Paul Williams"). In an "interview" with screen writer Ellis Weiner, Yoda displayed an impressive command of rigamarole rhetoric:

> *Q:* What do you think should be done about inflation?
>
> *A:* Inflation you are worried about? Living in the future is what worrying is. Live where you are. Pay attention to now.
>
> *Q:* About détente with Russia?
>
> *A:* Confused are the Soviets. Perhaps it is the dark side they wish to serve. But the Force is not with them.
>
> *Q:* About oil shortages?
>
> *A:* Energy are these matters. The Force is Energy.
>
> *Q:* Could you be more specific?
>
> *A:* Always it is specific you want. A deadline you wish to meet—worry, worry, always rushing to write your story.
>
> *Q:* What is your position on world affairs?
>
> *A:* My position, is it? My position is, I serve the Force. There. Now no more questions. Eat.[15]

Ambiguity is useful in political advertising because it allows viewers to supply their own interpretation of what is meant. In the absence of any real information, they draw their own conclusions. In 1980, Ronald Reagan's promises to "cut back" on government spending were generally interpreted to mean he would give less money to welfare programs and other entitlements for the poor. When he began to reduce middle-class benefits such as college loans, social security payments, and farm subsidies, these people felt betrayed. Yet Reagan's statements on the subject had always been vague allusions to unspecified "waste" and "extravagance." A typical example:

> I believe that there is enough extravagance and fat in government . . . We've had the General Accounting Office estimate

that there is probably tens of billions of dollars that is lost in fraud alone, and they have added that waste adds more to that. We have a program for a gradual reduction of government spending based on these theories . . . I'm confident that it can be done and that it will reduce inflation . . .

"The best political commercials," says political media consultant Tony Schwartz, "are similar to Rorschach patterns. They do not tell the viewer anything. They surface his feelings and provide a context for him to express his feelings."[16] If the communication is sufficiently hazy, people will decide for themselves the real meaning of what is being said.

In his novel *Black Mischief,* Evelyn Waugh provides an amusing example of this. His story concerns the attempts of the Emperor of Azania to introduce his poverty-stricken people to the use of contraception. The Emperor mounts a massive advertising campaign using a poster that pictures:

> . . . on one side a native hut of hideous squalor, over-run with children of every age, suffering from every physical incapacity—crippled, deformed, blind, spotted, and insane; the father prematurely aged with paternity squatted by an empty cook pot; through the door could be seen his wife, withered and bowed with childbearing, desperately hoeing at their inadequate crop.
>
> On the other side a bright parlor furnished with chairs and table; the mother, young and beautiful, sat at her ease eating a huge slice of raw meat; her husband smoked a long Arab hubble-bubble . . . while a single healthy child sat between them reading a newspaper. Inset between the two pictures was a detailed drawing of some up-to-date contraceptive apparatus and the words: Which Home Do You Choose?

The advertising was enormously successful. The people bought contraceptives in such numbers that stores could not keep up with the demand. The Emperor was delighted—until one man explained to him the reason for the product's success:

> See: on the right hand, there is rich man: smoke pipe like big chief; but his wife she no good; sit eating meat: and rich man no good: he only one son.
> See: on left hand: poor man: not much to eat: but his wife very good, work hard in field: man he good too: eleven children: one very mad, very holy. And in the middle: Emperor's juju. Make you like that good man with eleven children.[17]

The rhetoric of political commercials is always safely middle-of-the road, in order to appeal to the broadest possible spectrum of voters. To take a clear position on any side of an issue is inevitably to alienate a certain percentage of the electorate. The safe course is to try not to offend anyone. The result is the kind of fence-straddling once satirized by Mark Twain, who said:

> I have no prejudices in politics, religion, or anything else. I'm in favor of anything and everything—of temperance and intemperance, morality and qualified immorality, the gold standard and free silver. There could be no broader platform than mine.

In an attempt to expose the vacancy of most political rhetoric, two professors at the University of Missouri programmed a computer to write a model political speech for the 1980 campaign. One of them explains, "We figured that if we did the proper market-type research and programmed the computer to write a speech reflecting the findings, the speech would end up sounding pretty much like the genuine article churned out by a pack of poll-watching speechwriters." Their purpose was to prove "that you can take any idiot, parade him around the country for twelve months, and get him elected."[18]

In 1980, several people running for political office—including one for governor and one for mayor of a major city—wrote to the professors asking if the computer could write a little something for them!

Candidates who have opinions deviating from "center" must be carefully coached to appear more moderate than they actually are. When Ronald Reagan was a spokesman for the General Electric Company, he made remarks such as, "There can be no justification for the progressive income tax." Once he became a candidate for political office, a host of advisors scurried to steer him toward more "acceptable" language. His pollster, Richard Wirthlin, sent Reagan a memo early in the campaign cautioning him to "stay away from specific and arguable statements."[19] Another Wirthlin memo read, "Without question, the electorate must view Ronald Reagan in less extreme conservative terms in the fall if we are to win. This can be done without altering any issue positions. By rounding out the perception of Ronald Reagan as a . . . human, warm, approachable individual, we can 'moderate' the arch-conservative characterizations of the Governor."[20]

Despite careful coaching, some of Reagan's old conservative rhetoric would occasionally slip out, and the press would make hay with it. A Reagan aid explained the problem with the candidate this way: "Rather than take advantage of a question to enhance himself, he tries to be responsive. Some of those things you call gaffes were attempts to get reporters to understand his thought processes. And that's not always the most helpful to himself." (The aide was apparently unaware of what this indicated about the quality of Reagan's thought processes.) Eventually, Reagan learned to stick to harmless epigrams and jests at which no one could take umbrage:

> One signer of the Declaration of Independence said, It's not important that we leave our children money; what is important is that we leave them liberty.

There's enough fat in that government that if you rendered it and made soap you could wash the world.

A balanced budget is like protecting your virtue—you just have to learn to say no.

The rush toward political center has made most political candidates indistinguishable from one another. Can you tell who was responsible for each of the following statements made in a political commercial?

1. This election is a choice between the politics of the past and a whole new approach . . . There's a new consensus growing in America that cuts across traditional political lines. That consensus wants a prosperous America, an America with low taxes, a balanced budget . . . It's time we left the old politics. It's time for a New Beginning.

2. Let the United States once again be a nation of Big Shoulders. We want to live in freedom and in peace. We want to see our children have at least the chance we had for advancement. We want the freedom to worship in our own way. I'm talking about what it means to be an American . . .

3. We've seen walls built around Washington, and we feel that we can't quite get through to guarantee the people . . . a government that's sensitive to our needs. And if there are things that you don't like in your own government, if we've made mistakes that you don't want to see made again, or if there are hopes . . . in your own lives, or in the lives of your children that you'd like to see realized, I hope that you will join me in a personal commitment to change our government for the better . . .

4. Let us resolve that this era will be what it can become: a time of great responsibilities, greatly borne, in which we renew the spirit and the promise of America . . .

The first statement is by Ed Clark, Libertarian candidate for President in 1980; the second is by Ronald Reagan; the third by Jimmy Carter; and the fourth by Richard Nixon. They are as interchangeable as a set of Lego blocks. They are effective because they are not threatening. The code words— "liberty," "freedom," "prosperity," "peace," "greatness"— soothe listeners with ideas that make them feel comfortable. As Murray Edelman says, the real message is that the candidate is "conforming and presents no risk of doing anything that will upset the established order or question its basic value premises."[21] Semanticist Don Hahn adds, "The politician who says nothing is not a threat; if he mouths language with which his audience is comfortable he can be assumed to be safe, to favor the right things and oppose the wrong ones. He is properly middle-of-the-road. His mediocreness recommends him."[22]

Nowhere is this more apparent than in presidential debates, which lack the vigorous give-and-take of the Lincoln and Douglas confrontations. Candidates in today's televised debates do not even question or respond to each other directly. Instead, they are gently prodded into a series of rehearsed responses by a panel of star journalists. During the 1980 debates, one panelist asked, "Specifically, what are the differences between the two of you on the uses of American military power?" Reagan replied:

> I'm here to tell you that I believe with all my heart that first priority must be world peace, and that use of force is always, and only, a last resort when everything else has failed. And then, only with regard to our national security.
>
> Now I believe in meeting this mission, this responsibility for preserving the peace, which I believe is a responsibility peculiar to our country, that we cannot shirk our responsibility because we're the only one who can do it. And therefore, the burden of maintaining the peace falls on us. And to maintain that peace requires strength . . .
>
> But I've seen four wars in my lifetime. I'm a father of sons.

> I have a grandson. I don't ever want to see another generation of young Americans bleed their lives into sandy beachheads in the Pacific or rice paddies and jungles in Asia or the muddy, bloody battlefields of Europe.

As a statement, this could only be "debated" by taking an opposing point of view. Viz: "I believe in the use of force when not absolutely necessary, and I think it would be nice to see another generation of young Americans bleed their lives into sandy beachheads and muddy, bloody battlefields." Carter did not avail himself of this unique opportunity. His response to the question was virtually indistinguishable from Reagan's:

> I'll always remember that the best weapons are the ones that are never fired in combat and the best soldier is the one who never has to lay his life down on the field of battle.

Journalists traveling with the Carter campaign had heard that line so often they took to joshing press secretary Jody Powell about it, calling out as he went to lunch, "Hey, Jody, did you know that the best hamburger is one that's never eaten and the best bun is one that's never toasted?"

Televised debates, like political commercials, are aimed at the lowest common denominator of the electorate. It's like marketing a perfume after conducting detailed sales surveys to determine which fragrance will offend the fewest buyers. Marketing the candidate in this way becomes easier with modern sophisticated polling techniques which discover exactly what people want to hear. Polling can deliver a complete picture of a given constituency—the average age, income, education, and beliefs of the voters. It reveals what the voters' opinions are on a host of different issues. It can tell a candidate the reaction to a given policy statement before he has uttered it. This allows a candidate to shape his campaigns to match voter preferences. Joe Napolitan, one of the media advisors who helped to develop "computer campaigning," describes how the technique helped the candidacy of former Pennsylvania Governor Milton Shapp:

> We did some polls, and we discovered that a strong percentage of voters were favorable to raising the age for drivers' licenses, but were against lowering voting age. So in our campaign material that year we underlined [Shapp's] position on drivers' licenses and ignored his position on lowering voting age.[23]

A candidate's devotion to success can make him a willing slave of public opinion polls. He begins to measure ideas not by their intrinsic quality, but by the number of people who can be expected to agree with them. He tries to determine what it is that voters want in order to shape his opinions— even his personality—around it. As Camille Desmoulins remarked during the French Revolution, "The mob is in the streets. Tell me where they are going so I can be their leader."

No one would suggest that politicians should be unresponsive to the wishes of their constituencies. But a politician without any ideas or convictions of his own is a sorry kind of leader. Adman Rosser Reeves, who designed media campaigns for several successful candidates, says:

> [Politicians] want to know what the public wants and then they change their beliefs much as you would change the color on a package of corn flakes if your research department said the public didn't like the color that's on it. These people simply want to get elected. They don't have any personal beliefs. The Kennedys didn't. I don't think Eisenhower did. I don't think any of them do. And if they did, their personal beliefs are crowded under to say what is going to get the maximum number of votes . . . Eisenhower, once he got into politics . . . wouldn't say "boo" without reading the polls.[24]

David Ogilvy, a famous adman, predicts that the day will come when candidates are elected by polls rather than polling booths. The aim is not to promote a policy but to get the most votes. A story told by Sidney Blumenthal illustrates the point:

> After Jimmy Carter won a few Democratic primaries Gerald Rafshoon [his media advisor] visited the Manhattan office of a high-powered political media consultant, seeking his help in the upcoming presidential campaign. The consultant, who has a reputation for being tough, smart, and pragmatic, asked, "What does the guy stand for?"
>
> Rafshoon replied, "Come on. Be serious. He stands for getting elected to the White House."
>
> "I know everyone wants the election," said the consultant, "but programmatically where would you put him?"
>
> "Be serious," said Rafshoon.[25]

It's not at all clear that public opinion even exists in the way polls indicate. The sea of public opinion is constantly shifting, developing new undercurrents, changing tides. Michael Wheeler, who has made an extensive study of opinion polling, believes, for example, that before the 1980 presidential conventions as many as 40 to 50 percent of voters were undecided about who to vote for. Pollsters who look for clean, sharp-edged results were not prepared to accept that. As Wheeler explains, It's not a good headline to say "50 percent Undecided in Poll;" "Harris Shrugs Shoulders," "Beats the Hell Outa Me, Says Gallup." So you say to the people who don't make up their minds: 'If you really *had* to choose, who would you say you're leaning toward?' As a consequence, you're altering people's first reactions. Not only is the poll a little dishonest in that regard, but people who are just barely leaning in one direction are lumped together with those who say, "Dammit, I'm for Reagan!'"[26]

Much depends on the way poll questions are phrased. In May 1980 one poll asked, "Who would you like to see elected President in 1980?" The results: "Not Sure" won with 25 percent, followed by Carter and Reagan tied at 24 percent and Anderson with 5 percent. An alternative candidate was specified by 22 percent. One week later a different poll asked, "If you had to choose right now, would you vote for Reagan, Carter, or Anderson?" Naming those three candidates in the question had a dramatic effect on the results: 39 percent favored Reagan, 34 percent Carter, and 24 percent Anderson. Only 3 percent were undecided. No one specified an alternative candidate as their choice for President. Herbert Schiller comments, "Polling . . . is a *choice-restricting* mechanism. Because ordinary polls reduce and sometimes eliminate entirely . . . the true spectrum of possible options, the possibilities and preferences they express are . . . 'guided' choices."[27]

The use of highly connotative or emotionally charged words can also affect the way a poll turns out. One poll asked respondents, "Would you favor a constitutional amendment prohibiting abortions?" Twenty-nine percent said yes. But when the same question was rephrased as "Would you favor a constitutional amendment protecting the life of an unborn child?" 50 percent of the very same respondents said yes.

Pollsters are not above slanting questions to increase the chances of getting a particular kind of response. The Television Information Office once commissioned a Roper poll on advertising during children's programs. The question put to viewers was: "Some people think there should be *no* commercials in any kind of children's programs because they feel children can be too easily influenced. Other people, while perhaps objecting to certain commercials, by and large see no harm in them and think children learn from some of them. How do you feel—that there should be *no* commercials on any children's programs or that it is all right to have them *if they don't take unfair advantage of children?*"

What a masterpiece of artful phrasing! The very point is in dispute—whether commercials take unfair advantage of children—is neatly sidestepped by including it as a "given" within the question itself! Not surprisingly, 74 percent of the people thus polled agreed with Roper that kids' commercials were "all right." The Television Information Office promptly released the poll results to the press as evidence of the nation's overwhelming endorsement of children's advertising.

Such biased polling is not at all uncommon. Pollsters, eager to have their information appear "newsworthy," often slant questions to increase the chances of getting a dramatic response. Albert H. Cantrell of the National Council on public polls says that even so well respected a pollster as Louis Harris is not free of a tendency to frame "questions likely to yield surprising results that make good copy."[28]

Polling fosters the idea that truth is measured in numbers. Yet all new ideas begin as minority opinions; at one time, most people believed the earth was flat. Old heresies often become new orthodoxies. By their very nature, polls are hostile not only to genius but to human idiosyncrasy and waywardness. Government by poll has a built-in bias toward the status quo: What is habitual or familiar is also "right." Gladstone, the famous British statesman, once remarked, "Looking over all the great achievements that have made the last half century illustrious, not one of them would have been effected if the opinions of the West End of London had prevailed."

If public opinion polls had existed during the American Revolution, the Declaration of Independence would never have been written, and America might still be paying taxes to the British monarch. In a pointed demonstration of what might have been, Dartmouth professor Noel Perrin penned this fanciful "Poll of 1774":

> On the fifth of September, 1774, the delegates to the Continental Congress commissioned a study of Publick Opinion in the thirteen colonies, that they might better know the will of the People. For no great Operation on the Body Politick should be approved, unless first there be a taking of the Pulse . . .
>
> To every man was put the question: Are you content with the present System of Government, that we be ruled from London? . . .

1,116 people did say they were satisfied with the present System, and that we should not change; 983 were not satisfied and said we should; and 422 did ask, "What System?" . . .

To our question, "Would you take up arms for Independence?" the replies were equally discouraging. Nine Hundred and sixty-two men either said flatly, Nay, or threatened to report our Interrogator to the Governor. Seven hundred and three, mostly in New England, said flatly, Yea. Another 839 said they might, "be that I get riled up," or if the pay is to be good . . . The remaining 259 were Females, and they were not asked the last question.

When the entire Survey is considered, the Interrogators are of the opinion that there doth not exist Publick Support for the proposed War . . . No cause can hope to succeed with so little Backing. We therefore recommend to the honourable Delegates that the Continental Congress be disbanded, and that plans for Independence be laid on the Shelf. If conditions warrant, another larger Survey might perhaps be profitably made in ten years.[29]

Polling—and the elaborate advertising campaigns erected around it—has ended meaningful discourse in American politics. People vote for a particular candidate for the same reason they buy a particular brand of cigarette—because the ad-manufactured image appeals to them. "I like him—I think he's the kind of guy who'll make a good President," they say. Image appeal matters much more than what a man actually stands for.

Campaigning through advertising means that only well-funded (thus, generally, pro-Establishment) candidates will be taken seriously. A single Senate race can cost a candidate $5 to $7 million, presidential contests many times more. As Will Rogers said, "Politics has got so expensive that it takes a whole lot of money just to get beat." Campaign managers speak candidly about "buying" the vote, as in this description by Carter aide Patrick Caddell of the 1976 presidential primary in South Dakota:

[Udall] assumed he was going to win South Dakota because Senators McGovern and Abourezk were for him. And the party was for him . . . But we outspent Udall in South Dakota. We didn't tell anybody . . . We just bought the state. It wasn't too much to buy . . .[30]

Third-party and Independent candidates stand even less of a chance. Without money to buy equal TV time, their candidacies literally become invisible to the great majority of voters. The situation is not unlike product advertising: bombarded with commercials for Democratic and Republican "brands," voters learn to disregard—even to distrust—lower priced "generic" candidates. "The right to speak is of little value if no one is listening," comments media critic Robert Cirino. "A person speaking to eighty million people has quite an advantage over someone with a conflicting view talking to a thousand people in an auditorium." He adds, "The idea that gets amplification and extension through the media—not necessarily the most reasonable idea—is the one which wins the endorsement of the people."[31]

The late Hubert Humphrey once said, "There is no surer way to corrupt American life . . . than to have the great decision of this nation as to who will be its leader and what its sense of direction determined by the size of a checkbook or a bank account. It's wrong; it is wrong, wrong, wrong to have to go around seeking large contributions from the few rich in order to conduct a campaign which you say is for the many. Can't do it. It's wrong."[32]

The Federal Election Campaign Act of 1974, passed after Watergate funding scandals, was supposed to remedy financial inequalities in presidential campaigns. Outside contributions were limited to $1,000, to lessen the influence of corporate financing. Total campaign spending was limited to $30 million, and candidates were provided with federal matching funds for every dollar they raised (monies collected from the one-dollar contribution taxpayers can check off on their income tax returns). Unfortunately, the Act had several loopholes: no limit was placed on the amount of personal wealth that a candidate could spend, and if candidates chose to turn down federal assistance, there was no limit to the amount he could spend. (Candidate John Connally, with the backing of big oil companies and other corporate contributors, chose this option.) Also, the Act did not apply to *party* advertising. In 1982, the Republican party planned to spend $12 million on paid TV commercials to sway the Congressional elections—ten times more than the Democratic party was able to raise for similar advertising.

The most serious drawback of the Election Campaign Act was that third-party candidates could not qualify for matching funds until after the election—and then only if they managed to get a certain percentage of the votes. This is rather like telling a driver with an empty fuel tank that he can get gas if he can drive as far as the filling station.

The media has turned political contests into personality contests. The victor is the man who can manage to make the most voters feel the most comfortable. As Patrick Caddell says:

> "I don't think we've necessarily improved the quality of politicians. I'm not convinced the new politicians are superior to the class they replace. That really troubles me a great deal. I know people in Congress who vote simply to survive. How many people there, regardless of party or ideology, worry about the United States of America? I've had congressmen tell me they know they're voting for things that are not in the national interest and that they're going to hurt the country. The problem is that they stay there to stay there. I've had young congressmen tell me they're embarrassed about what happens on the floor of the House. Survival at what cost? We have produced these people. I don't know why they're there and they don't know why they're there. Do these people really care about what happens to the country?"[33]

The remedy to this deplorable situation is simple, if not easy: prohibit all paid political advertising. That may sound drastic, but the fact is that America is one of the very few countries that permit campaigning for office through paid advertisements. No major European country allows purchase of television time for political purposes. Why, then, should we? Why not simply require networks to give free time to *all* qualified candidates for political office? Candidates could "qualify" for time in the same way they do for inclusion on a ballot—by petition. This would at least bring them to the attention of voters.

Naturally, broadcasters will not like the idea of providing free (i.e., unprofitable) time. But television broadcasting is an enormously profitable business (one observer has said that owning a TV station is like having a license to print money) and it is not unreasonable to suggest that some of this profit, reaped from use of the public airwaves, be harvested in the public interest. The networks have already proposed dropping gavel-to-gavel coverage of party conventions at a savings of about $40 million. This money would go a long way toward financing free television time for all qualified presidential candidates.

Robert Spero suggests some guidelines for free time appearances:

> The essence of free speech should be the essence of free time; unfettered, ungimmicked, robust, argumentative . . .
>
> Candidates must sink or swim strictly on their own merits, whether it be done through explanations of who they are, their qualifications, their goals, the people they would bring into government, and their interpretations of issues; debates with other candidates; or give-and-take questioning . . . not by the candidates' political managers but by nonpartisan groups. No pseudo-panelists would be allowed to ask rehearsed partisan questions of a candidate . . .
>
> All appearances by the candidates should be spontaneous

and, whenever possible, live. Candidates should be seen by the viewer as they are, not as the political media specialist would make them. Film and tape should be allowed only when the film or tape is an unedited duplicate of a previous live appearance. *No editing should be allowed in any event.*

No manufactured films that claim to represent a candidate's life and times and political accomplishments should be allowed, unless the station is prepared to offer a probing rebuttal.[34]

Some will argue that such regulation constitutes censorship, and threatens our First Amendment rights to freedom of speech. But there is a difference between the liberty to speak and a license to deceive—a difference well articulated by Walter Lippmann:

> If there is a dividing line between liberty and license, it is where freedom of speech is no longer respected as a procedure of the truth and becomes the unrestricted right to exploit the ignorance, and to incite the passions, of the people. Then freedom is such a hullabaloo of sophistry, propaganda, special pleading, lobbying, and salesmanship that it is difficult to remember why freedom of speech is worth the pain and the trouble of defending it . . . It is sophistry to pretend that in a free country a man has some sort of inalienable or constitutional right to deceive his fellow men. There is no more right to deceive than there is a right to swindle, to cheat, or to pick pockets.[35]

If the important issues of our day are not to be determined by small groups of moneyed men who finance the activities of an even smaller group of public relations men, then these issues must be debated in a forum that cannot be controlled, censored, or bought.

7
Hail to the Chief

The people are happy when attending a spectacle: this is the means by which we hold their mind and their heart.
Louis XIV

Neither Genghis Khan, nor Alexander the Great, nor Napoleon, nor Louis XIV of France, had as much power as the President of the United States.
Harry Truman

A group should venerate its chief; if they did not, it would be very wrong.
Mao Tse-Tung

Once the Selling of the President has been completed, selling *by* the President can begin. Today's Chief Executive is not merely a policy-maker, he is the premier salesman for Establishment policies and ideas. In this role he is aided by the media, which initially treats him with a deference and respect more appropriate for a monarch than an elected official.

Nowhere is this more apparent than on the day of inauguration. The media people reported the investiture of Ronald Reagan in cadences that were scriptural, as in this ABC commentary:

Ronald Reagan was a private citizen when he woke up this morning. But not for long. To the White House he drove. To the Capitol he rode. Ronald Reagan was a private citizen no longer.

This narrative was accompanied by numerous "jump shots" of Reagan—a camera angle which gives its subject appearance of tremendous power and stature. Reagan even included television directions on the advance text of his inaugural address so cameramen would be sure to maximize the majesty of the moment. Observing the occasion, Walter Cronkite was moved to remark, "This is the closest thing to monarchical tradition that we have in this country."

A new president is traditionally presented to the public in language that suggests his Olympian qualities, his superiority to mere mortals. Look at some of the "news reports" on Reagan in the weeks just following his inauguration:

> . . . Ronald Reagan looked like a dream. He was wearing a blue-and-green wool tartan jacket, a purple tie, white shirt, white handkerchief, black pants and black loafers with gold along the tops. Who else could dress that way? Reagan's face was ruddy, in bloom, growing younger by the second . . . His size seems an emblem of his modesty. Lyndon Johnson used to enter a room and rape it. Reagan seems to be in a . . . posture that makes strangers lean towards him . . . The voice goes perfectly with the body. No President since Kennedy has had a voice at once so distinctive and beguiling. It recedes at the right moments, turning mellow at points of intensity. When it wishes to be most persuasive, it hovers barely above a whisper so as to win you over by intimacy, if not by substance. This is style, not sham.
>
> *Time* magazine

The banker's hours that Ronald Reagan is keeping bespeak a brand of measured leadership long absent from the Executive

Mansion. The applause is drowning out scattered criticism . . . Jimmy Carter, Richard Nixon and other recent Presidents spent long hours immersing themselves in the details of problems—sometimes losing their sense of overall priorities in the process. Reagan's instinct, in contrast, is to keep his eye on the Big Picture at all times. And public-opinion polls show that the freshness and simplicity of this style is a solid hit with the public . . .

U.S. News & World Report

Of course, *Time* and *U.S. News & World Report* are fairly conservative publications, so their rhapsody over the newly elected Reagan is understandable. But television news reports of a newly elected president—any president—reveal a similar regard for his person and his office.

Media deference to the office and person of the president gives him unequaled power. Network news will cover almost any presidential action or appearance, whether or not it represents real "news." Knowing this, a president is free to arrange pre-planned "pseudo-events," as Daniel Boorstin has called them—occurrences which have no purpose or function other than to gain media attention. A classic example in 1956 was the broadcast of an Eisenhower "cabinet meeting" scheduled to appear on TV just before the election. In fact, there was no reason for the cabinet to convene just then. But a "meeting" was carefully staged, with Eisenhower, gravely presidential, calling on each cabinet member in order of rank to give prepared speeches stressing the administration's progress and plans for the future. The cabinet members had been advised that no ad libs would be permitted, and the entire broadcast fit neatly into one hour of broadcast time. As anyone who has worked in television will tell you, this kind of split-second timing does not happen without a great deal of pre-planning and rehearsal. Democrats, understandably, were outraged, since the event was so clearly intended as free advertising for the Republican administration—eight days before the national election. In contrast, the only way for Democratic candidate Adlai Stevenson to get any media coverage was to *buy* thirty minutes of television air time. And Stevenson never mastered the art of the pseudo-event: All too often, he was still talking when his thirty minutes were up and the screen went black. Voters were left with an impression of Stevenson as undisciplined and lacking in leadership.

Presidential pseudo-events are designed by media specialists trained in the art of creating popular images. After Carter's election, his private pollster, Patrick Caddell, determined that what people wanted was for Carter to be "different from other politicians, not part of the Establishment." To please these citizens, it was not necessary for Carter genuinely to reject Establishment values or policies; he merely had to *appear* to do so. This was accomplished through the skillful staging of appropriate pseudo-events. Caddell's memo on how to proceed reads like a script of the early days of the Carter administration:

> —I would suggest cutting back on "imperial" frills and perks. By symbolic actions you are sure to excite the public.
> —Fireside chats . . . build a sense of personal intimacy with the people.
> —Town meetings . . . I think it could have a dramatic impact on the public to see the president willing to go out and meet and talk and answer questions from the country.
> —Question periods . . . opportunities for people to question Carter on the media.[1]

Pseudo-events are the ultimate magic trick. The public eye is distracted while the president performs political sleights of hand. Machiavelli first recognized the importance of illusion in government, and advised his Prince: "Everyone sees what you appear to be, but few understand what there is within; and those few will not dare contradict the opinion of the majority, which is reinforced by the majesty of the State.

. . . Common men believe only what they see . . . *Therefore, a Prince will not actually need to have all the qualities previously mentioned, but he must surely seem to have them.*"2 [Italics added.]

In the art of creating illusion, the media is the president's all-too-willing conspirator. Coverage of a president's staged appearances amounts to an obsession. Any piece of information, no matter how trivial, becomes "news" if it is about the president—or his family. Listen to the way ABC News covered the moments before Ronald Reagan's inaugural address;

> Ann: Frank, they have cleared the driveway here as limousine number one rolls up, and what an historic moment . . . Here in this area the Carter aides wearing their radios and Secret Service buttons for the last time, a double phalanx of Secret Servicemen of course for the two Chief Executives or the Chief Executive and the Chief Executive-To-Be.
>
> President Carter is now shaking hands with the dignitaries here. As you can see, he is not wearing the same kind of formal outfit that President-Elect Reagan is. They are forming for a—no, not really a photo out here—but hurrying inside.
>
> No telling what the conversation was in the limousine, but no sign of real distress on any of the faces . . . but they are now inside the building on the way to holding rooms while Mrs. Carter out here, Mrs. Reagan in red, waiting to take their places inside.
>
> The last poignant moments for the Carters. Mrs. Carter handing off a coat to Senator Byrd to hold for her while she proceeds inside. It must be a very poignant moment for the Carters as they go into what they know was their last ride in official vehicles as the First Family. Frank?
>
> Frank: Yes, thanks, Ann. You notice that the President and the President-Elect separated. The President-Elect is being escorted by Senator Hatfield to room EF-00. Not that that means a great deal to you but that is more or less a holding

room where he will wait till he is given the signal to come out and go down the—quite a few stairs, actually—about thirty-five stairs. He'll walk through and then. . . .

If Ronald Reagan had stopped to pick his nose on the way down the steps, it would have become an event of historic moment.

Where the president is concerned, even no news is news. One Christmas Eve, Carter sent the press away, saying there was no news, and that fact was duly reported on the evening news, with the speculation about its possible significance. CBS once broadcast a story on a Rosalynn Carter speech which showed her telling her audience, "I called the President this morning to see if there were anything new about Iran, Afghanistan, about inflation. He said 'no.'" ABC White House correspondent Sam Donaldson says, "I have to argue *not* to be on the nightly news sometimes because I don't have a story." [3]

Let a president set foot out of Washington, D.C., and he will have a host of newsmen dogging his every step. A presidential trip is the ultimate pseudo-event—an elaborately staged spectacle designed to show off the president to maximum advantage. Before the trip, White House aides accompany network correspondents on a "pre-advance" (or advance-of-the-advance) trip. They fly to every city the president will visit and rehearse "walk-throughs" of every scheduled event. They instruct network correspondents on the president's best camera angles and arrange for little girls to bring him flowers. Jimmy Carter's 1978 trip to Venezuela is a case in point. The staged events, such as laying a wreath on the grave of Simon Bolívar, were all scheduled in time to make U.S. news deadlines, without concern for the preferences or convenience of Venezuelan leaders or media. Carter's address to the Venezuelan congress, for example, took place at 8:25 A.M.—far too early in the morning for the Venezuelans, but perfect timing to appear on U.S. morning news programs. The trip, billed as a "good neighbors" visit, actually earned the enmity of some Venezuelans who resented the "implied cultural arrogance" behind the Carter people's disregard for their interests. But Carter was pleased with the results of his journey, which accomplished his primary objective—not to improve diplomatic relations with Venezuela, but to promote his own popularity with the folks at home. Carter's ability to command media attention during the Venezuela trip caused his media advisor Gerald Rafshoon to remark, "It's almost as if TV went out and discovered the presidency as a series for TV. It's the best political show they can find—and they don't have to pay the talent."

Nixon commanded the same kind of media coverage during his 1972 trip to China. Every night Americans viewed extensive footage of Nixon's movements during that day, even if he had done nothing more significant than remark, as he did, on viewing the Great Wall of China for the first time, "That's a great wall!" Even Pat Nixon's remark, while she was being fêted at an elaborate Chinese banquet, "My, you're really cooking up a storm!" was faithfully recorded for posterity. After that trip, Art Buchwald penned the following satire:

> It was two days after President Nixon's return from China and the family went into the living room after dinner to watch television.
>
> My wife turned on the set and said, "That's funny. There seems to be something wrong with the TV. I can't get President Nixon on the tube . . ."
>
> "I can't understand it," I said. "President Nixon has been coming in loud and clear on prime time every evening. But tonight all I can get is a movie, Dean Martin, and a *Lucy* rerun."[4]

The president's control over and instant access to the media is powered in part by what some critics call the "death watch" factor. Media analyst Joel Swerdlow explains, "Ever since Dallas in November 1963, the one overriding fear of network correspondents is that it will happen again and they will not be there to record it." He gives the example of the time Jimmy Carter was scheduled for an afternoon of making television commercials. The filming session was closed to network cameras and press. But one network representative begged Gerald Rafshoon, Carter's television advisor, to let his crew come along just to observe. "We won't film anything." he said. "We just want to be there in case someone takes a shot at him. And if they did that, you wouldn't want to use that film for a commercial, anyway." Rafshoon saw the logic in that argument, and agreed.[5]

When Ronald Reagan became the target of an assassin's attack, his PR strategies were quick to turn the event into what one called "political capital." Reagan pollster Richard S. Beal comments, "What the crisis was about in terms of image was a totally unscripted event. It focused uniquely on the president. It did a lot to endear the president to the people."[6] The first reports of Reagan's condition from presidential aides were filled with anecdotal stories emphasizing his qualities of courage and humor. After the incident, one private presidential poll asked people, "As a result of the assassination attempt, have you changed your opinion of Ronald Reagan?" The results showed that Reagan's popularity had increased to a 3 to 1 favorable rating.

A president's most powerful tool of persuasion is the televised address. Up to 90 million people may watch a single presidential address. To reach such a vast audience without the benefit of television, it has been estimated that a president would have to appear before capacity crowds forty-eight times in each one of the twenty-six giant pro-football stadiums in the country—a total of 1,248 separate appearances.[7] As Fred Friendly has said, "No mighty king, no ambitious emperor, no pope, or prophet ever dreamt of such an awesome pulpit, so potent a magic wand."[8]

Presidential reliance on this "awesome pulpit" has been slowly and steadily increasing. Eisenhower made twenty-three prime-time television adresses in eight years. Kennedy made ten in less than three years. Johnson made twenty-four in five years. Presidential appearances in prime time have become a familiar part of a presidential repertoire; a president must learn to be a skilled performer. Alistair Cooke offers one refreshing example of how things were in the days before the media became so important:

> In 1924, President Calvin Coolidge and a radio announcer stood together on a railroad platform in Glendale, California. At once the radio announcer throbbed into the mike: "And *now*, ladies and gentlemen, for a real, new first in history, you will hear the voice of the President of the United States over the *radio.* . . . Mr. President, may I ask you to tell this audience on a nationwide hookup, just as you are about to board the train back to Washington after a prolonged trip around the country: What message do you have for the American people?"
>
> He tilted the microphone toward the pursed lips of President Coolidge, who opened them long enough to say, "Goodbye."
>
> They don't make presidents like that anymore.[9]

Coolidge could hardly have survived in today's media-oriented presidency. In 1965, Lyndon Johnson had a fully equipped television studio installed in the White House, staffed by a twenty-four-hour-a-day television crew trained to be ready to broadcast on a five-minute alert. Maintenance of the studio cost the TV networks $1 million a year. But Nixon was the president who first used the power of the "bully pulpit" to the fullest. In his first year and a half of office, he made more appearances than Eisenhower, Kennedy, and Johnson combined during their first year and a half. During Nixon's tenure, the Pentagon proposed an Orwellian plan to attach an electronic gadget to each of the nation's television sets that would allow the president to turn them all on at once. The idea was scrapped when an alert administration official argued that people might "misinterpret the intentions" of the project.

Presidential addresses are rather like extended sales pitches. The president tries to "sell" his programs by sheer force of his personality and conviction. "Trust me," the president says in effect. "I know what is best if you will only believe in me." As when Peter Pan appeals to us on behalf of Tinkerbell, we are moved to applaud, not understanding exactly what is meant but only that it is important we believe:

> . . . Something very exciting has been happening here in Washington and you are responsible. Your voices have been heard. Millions of you, Democrats, Republicans, and Independents, from every profession, trade, and line of work, and from every part of this land; you sent a message that you wanted a new beginning . . . All the lobbying, the organized demonstrations and the cries of protest by those whose way of life depends on maintaining government's wasteful ways were no match for your voices which were heard loud and clear in these marble halls of government . . .
>
> A recent poll shows that where a year-and-a-half ago only 24 percent of our people believed things would get better, today 46 percent believe they will. To justify their faith we must deliver the other part of our program . . . In these six months, we've done so much and have come so far. It's been the power of millions of people like you who have determined that we will make America great again. You have made the difference up to now. You will make the difference again.
>
> Let us not stop now. Thank you. God bless you. (Reagan address on Tax Cut Bill, July 27, 1981)

The language is not meant to inform, but to persuade without enlightenment. In the same speech, Reagan offered up the following anecdote, with its implicit suggestion that blind faith is a more appropriate response than knowledgeable doubt:

> A few days ago I was visited here in the office by a Democratic Congressman from one of our southern states. He'd been back in his district and one day one of his constituents asked him where he stood on our ecomomic recovery program . . . Well, the Congressman, who happens to be a strong leader in support of our program, replied at some length with a discussion of the technical points involved, but *he also mentioned a few reservations he had on certain points.* [Italics added.] The constituent, a farmer, listened politely until he'd finished and then said, "Don't give me an essay. What I want to know is are you for 'em or agin 'em?"
>
> Well, I appreciate the gentleman's support and suggest his question is a message your own representatives should hear.

One observer comments, "In the eyes of some leaders, the voter is unable to understand what is really at stake . . . it would be vain to explain the real problems and dangers to him. Since every society hates a Cassandra, it could also be dangerous. So it is better to make promises, even demagogic ones, leaving the issues aside. This way, leaders exercise a euphoric function, administering tranquilizers to the body politic."[10]

In a speech made not long after taking office, President Reagan decried "those Chicken Littles who proclaim that the sky is falling" and he insisted that "there is a rising tide of confidence in America." Exactly one month later, he was forced to admit that a recession was under way—in other words, that the Chicken Littles were not entirely wrong. Moral: It doesn't pay to be too cocky-locky.

An "effective" presidential address substitutes form for content, relying on McLuhan's theory that "the medium is the message." Reagan, a master of the technique, fills his addresses with homely anecdotes that appear to have been culled directly from the pages of *Reader's Digest:*

> Some years ago when we were a young nation and our people began visiting the lands of their forefathers, these American tourists were rather brash, unsophisticated by European standards but blessed with a spirit of independence and pride.
>
> One such tourist, an elderly, small town gentleman and his wife, were there in Europe listening to a tour guide go on about the wonders of the volcano Mount Etna. He spoke of the great heat that it generated, the power, the boiling lava, etc. Finally the old boy'd had enough of it, turned to his wife and he said, "We got a volunteer fire department at home—put that thing out in fifteen minutes."
>
> But he was typical of those Americans who helped build a neighbor's barn when it burned down. They built the West without an area redevelopment plan and cities across the land without federal planning.

Note how skillfully the language used plays on our most treasured myths: American innocence vs. European sophistication; independence; spunk; pride; neighborliness; pioneering courage. How this artful anecdote actually relates to any specific programs or policies is left reassuringly vague. Does it mean cuts in urban development funds? In funds for public transportation? As Nixon speech writer William Gavin explains, the idea behind such rhetoric is to "leave blanks in [viewers'] minds, elementary concepts based on emotion without any need to worry about analysis or reasoning." The "content" of such a message is supplied by the viewer, who, massaged into a mood of acceptance with familiar bromides, naturally assumes these words will "translate" into an action he himself approves of. After the presidential address in which Reagan was forced to abandon his proposals for cutbacks in Social Security due to a united opposition from Democrats and some members of his own Republican party, an "on the street" interview with an old woman showed her remarking, "I just *knew* he would defend my Social Security. That's just what I expected from this president." As one longtime political analyst says, "If you approach people the right way, you could get them to applaud their own hanging."

Reagan's reliance on jokes and stories to communicate led William Safire to devote an entire *New York Times* column to the president's "anecdotage." "At their worst," said Safire, "Mr. Reagan's colorful anecdotes betray either a simplistic approach to complex matters, which is dismaying, or a willingness to use stump speech routines on politically savvy associates, which is insulting."[11]

Nevertheless, such anecdotes are powerful rhetorical tools—so powerful that Reagan himself complained when they were used to great effect by television news. Contending that television networks were focusing too heavily on "individual cases of hardship," Reagan asked, "Is it news that some fellow out in South Succotash someplace has just been laid off, that he should be interviewed nationwide, or someone's complaint that the budget cuts are going to hurt their present program?" Later, presidential communications aide David Gergen was asked why it was not similarly unfair for Reagan to use anecdotes to make his points. Gergen replied that whereas the news media had an obligation to "describe reality," the president did not![12]

All of this doesn't even take into account the fact that most presidential utterances aren't even, strictly speaking, the president's own. Presidential addresses are elaborate sales packages, products designed and executed using the most advanced marketing techniques. First, a president engages the services of a private pollster, whose research reveals such information as "targets of opportunity" (issues and events which the public will approve of if acted on immediately), "resistance ratios" (the degree of approval the public can be expected to bestow on a presidential action), and "sequencing" (how to schedule a series of actions to achieve maximum favorable "fallout"). Armed with this information a president can now assemble ideas and opinions that he knows the public wants to hear. A team of speechwriters goes to work crafting a speech that will make the president appear not only wise, but also witty and wonderful. Theodore Sorensen, aide to President Kennedy, describes how the fabled Kennedy "charm" was systematically injected into his speeches:

> I had a large "humor file" that kept on getting larger. Since the texts of his speeches given to the press usually had anecdotal material removed, we could use it in other speeches . . . Besides our humor archives, we kept a collection of conclusions, usually quotations from famous persons or allusions to historical events that, accompanied by a brief peroration, could serve as the ending to any speech on any given subject.[13]

Kennedy did, of course, have native wit, and composed much of his speeches himself. Other presidents have had to rely more heavily on the talents of others. Roger-Gerard Schwartzenberg describes the laborious preparations for one address by President Ford:

> Well before D-Day, Robert Hartmann, White House advisor and chief speechwriter, went to work with five writers from his team. Two weeks before . . . Ford and Hartmann began to meet to . . . adapt the speech to the President's oratorical style. Phrases were recast, syntax simplified, complicated rhetorical turns deleted . . .
>
> One week before the day of the speech, Ford began working on his oral delivery. First, he read the speech to an audience of three persons: Robert Hartmann, his assistant Robert Orben, and media consultant Don Penny, a former

comic actor. Then he recorded it on videotape and went over it several times to polish his presentation. All this time, his advisors worked hard to get him to cut down on his favorite rhetorical tricks of lowering his voice to a melodramatic whisper or using grandiose flourishes.

The president took the tape with him to Kansas City to practice with it up to the last minute. Result: a performance so good that his team decided to buy a half hour of TV time in September to broadcast it as part of his campaign. Hartmann's comment: "If I had two weeks to work on every one of his speeches, they would all be that good."[14]

This kind of marketing of the presidential "package" reduces political action to no more than a reflex. The chief concern becomes not what people need to know, but what they are willing to hear; not what must be done, but how it will appear. What can we say we know about a man when we do not learn what he really thinks? When words are used not to clarify but to mystify? George Reedy, for one, thinks that meaningful dialogue requires that a president not write his speeches at all:

I think [they] should get up and give them off-the-cuff because when a man is asking for my vote I want to know what he really thinks and what he really feels. I am perfectly willing to forgive him any minor slips that he may make. But the fact is when you see a political leader on television today, the whole thing is merely a performance. The speech has been prepared and at least ten people have had a direct hand in it; lighting and makeup experts have been consulted; and each word has probably been submitted to Batten Barton Durstine Osborn and three other firms . . . I believe this is one of the major factors in the decline of the democratic dialogue.[15]

This is the politics of the spectacle, with the president as star performer, taking directions from a host of producers, directors, and stage managers. It is a concept which is nourished and reinforced by television. After one speech by Jimmy Carter, NBC's Chris Wallace introduced two network commentators with the remark, "These are two of the drama critics of American politics, part of that group that will tell us in the next few days whether Jimmy Carter has a hit or a flop." ABC's Charles Gibson added, "We can tell you a little bit about how it played in Pittsburgh." Even before Ronald Reagan, former actor, assumed the mantle of office, news writers had billed him as a star. *Newsweek* magazine carried this story on Reagan's pre-inaugural trip to Washington:

> REAGAN WINS RAVE NOTICES ALL AROUND
> For the first time since America cast him as its 40th President, Ronald Wilson Reagan played Washington last week . . . His vehicle was a tightly booked five-day tour in which he shook hands and made up with Jimmy Carter, massaged the barons of both parties in both houses of Congress, sipped white wine with the Justices of the Supreme Court, and swept the city's civic and cultural glitterati off their feet . . .

Time magazine's story headlined, "Reagan Gives a Boffo Performance in His First Appearance in the Capital," and said, "Barnstorming Washington for the first time, the President-Elect gave an Oscar-winning performance as he charmed the city . . . Not in all his years as an actor had Reagan so wowed a tough audience . . . Reagan has this role rehearsed to perfection . . ."* The language used—"rave notices," "Oscar-winning performance," "rehearsed to perfection," is straight out of *Variety* and other show-biz publications.

Focusing on presidential star quality helps divert the public from genuine political concerns. The president is

---

* Not everyone agreed with the casting for the part. Jack Warner, movie producer and former Reagan employer in his acting days, is said to have remarked, on first hearing of his candidacy, "No, no. *Jimmy Stewart* for President; Ronald Reagan for his best friend."

judged not on actual executive ability, but on how well he enacts the role he was elected to play. The ultimate accomplishment is to look presidential. During the 1976 debates, Gerald Ford was so determined to maintain a "presidential" posture that when the sound system broke down and the debate was temporarily halted, he stood rocklike throughout the entire twenty-eight-minute delay—though a stool was available right behind him. Presumably, some media advisor had informed him that the electorate does not respect a president who bends in the middle.

Some people have speculated that many of our earlier Chief Executives would hardly have excelled at televised government. Lincoln, for example, had a very high-pitched voice that would have been extremely unpleasant on television. FDR would have been revealed as a hopeless cripple. Writer E.M. Halliday once envisaged what might have transpired had television been around during Washington's incumbency:

> Make-up man: General, I think just a *touch* of the brush on the bridge of your nose would put the finish on it. It cuts down the reflection a bit. You have, if I may say so, sir, a . . . *magnificent* nose.
>
> Washington: Well, well, do it and be done with it! I reiterate that all this falderal over appearances, in my estimation, is a pack of stuff and nonsense. A man is, sir, what he is. How many people did you say will be watching tonight, Henry?
>
> Knox: Estimated at four million, sir.
>
> Washington: Hmmm. Four million. But who are they? Riff raff, no doubt, for the most part.
>
> Hamilton: We all know that your people, sir, is a great beast. But as things go in this so-called democracy, sir, this beast can nourish a man or devour him. The beast must be pleased.
>
> Washington: You have a gift for metaphor, Hamilton. How's my wig?

Makeup Man: The wig is *perfect*, General. Please remember not to try to adjust it after we go on the air. Don't even *touch* it.

Washington: Have I got time to take these damnable teeth out for a moment? They hurt my gums.

Knox: Two minutes to go, General. Take them out for one minute, but make sure to reset them firmly. Otherwise there is an unhappy sibilance attendant upon your enunciation of the s, sir, that the microphone tends to amplify. The sound men don't like that.

Washington: (false teeth in hand) Damn the thound men, thir! They care for nothing but effecth!

Technician: One minute! One minute![16]

A modern president's access to the airwaves constitutes a virtual monopoly on the manufacture of public opinion. Alone of all our elected officials, the president can commandeer all the prime-time broadcasting he wants and use it to propagandize his views, his party, his programs. His speeches are broadcast simultaneously on all three networks, which means that, short of turning off the set, there is no way that viewers can tune him out. In contrast, opposition views are rarely broadcast in prime time, and when they are, they are scheduled on one network—usually one which has abandoned all hope of competing with a rival network's stronger programming at that hour anyway. The Democratic response to Reagan's State of the Union Address, for example, was buried in the "graveyard" slot opposite CBS's "Dallas." The Committee for Fair Broadcasting of Controversial Issues has stated that this disparity in the nature and extent of TV coverage between the president and his opponents is "as if the president has a megaphone and a soapbox while everyone else is required to whisper."[17] Senator William Fulbright adds, "Television has done as much to expand the powers of the president as would a constitutional amendment formally abolishing the co-equality of the three branches of government."

But what is the president trying to sell? The message is so well concealed in familiar rhetoric that to most it appears not as a sales message at all but as the expression of plain truth and reason. If that is so, how is it that on most issues these days the majority of nations are opposed to us? Are they so addicted to untruth and unreason, so blinkered by the dogma sold to them by *their* leaders that they cannot recognize a plain and simple fact?

We have been so sold on the basic message delivered to us that all contrary opinion is regarded as extremist or revolutionary. In effect, what *we* believe is truth, and what *they* believe is propaganda. Roger-Gerard Schwartzenberg explains why the president's sales message is so effective: it "offers the simple pleasures of conformity, the reassuring platitudes increasing the public's feeling of security. As a virtuoso of the conventional, zealously promoting notions popular with the masses, [the president] tends to unify the nation by reinforcing its cherished beliefs. His stage trick is to tranquilize with routine."[18]

What every president is "selling" us, what he is in the White House to represent, is the American Way, which means capitalism and parliamentary democracy. Presidents may differ on details: whether it is better for us to have détente with Russia and/or China, whether it is better to spend more on defense and less on social programs, whether there should be more or less consumer protection, more or less concern about the environment, lower taxes for corporations or for individuals—but they are totally in agreement on the necessity of selling the American system.

The president's message is amplified by his natural allies in the world of business, who work behind the scenes to promote the basic product being sold. One Reagan aide estimates that the administration has about 1500 companies lobbying on its behalf—what he calls a "grass-roots" business network. He says that the resources of the network are "almost scary, they're so big." When, for example, Reagan was battling for passage of his tax-cut package through Congress, his "business coalition" used its sophisticated intelligence-gathering capabilities to keep track of the leanings of individual Congressmen. With this information (in some instances transmitted via brokers' display terminals), the coalition was able to mobilize members to make over 35,000 phone calls to pressure wavering Congressmen. Reagan's eleventh-hour presidential address was just the frosting on a cake which had already been carefully baked following a detailed—and largely secret—recipe.

Theoretically, of course, people wishing to express opposition viewpoints can *buy* air time to respond to a presidential address. To get equal time for a typical presidential address any other individual or group would have to pay over $200,000—which doesn't include the cost of producing the program.* And there would be no hope of attracting even a small fraction of the president's audience. Anyway, in practice, the networks won't sell air time to anyone wishing to express what they call "controversial views." Often, this means views that are contrary to policies which the president has decided are best for the country. For example, during the time when President Johnson repeatedly used TV to "sell" his Vietnam policy to the American public, Senator Harold Hughes tried to buy air time to present anti-war arguments. He was always refused. As he comments, "I could buy time to sell soap or women's underwear, but not to speak as a United States Senator on issues of war and peace."

Once, it is true, CBS did try to provide free time to air viewpoints contrary to the president's. They were careful,

* The cost of trying to match presidential newspaper coverage is even more prohibitive. A presidential press conference is guaranteed to produce headlines in the next day's newspapers. Even a casual remark may do that. The cost of the space provided a president, free of charge, would be in the tens of millions of dollars to his opponents.

however, to avoid the suggestion of real controversy: the programs were titled "The Loyal Opposition," as if to reassure viewers that while some of the things they might hear were not in agreement with the president, the viewpoints offered were not radical or subversive. The first program featured then-Democratic National Committee Chairman Lawrence O'Brien responding to a televised address by Nixon on the Vietnam War. O'Brien did not confine his remarks to the question of war, however, also discussing a number of different points of Democratic disagreement with the president. Because of this, the Republican National Committee demanded time to respond to the Democratic National Committee's response. Whereupon CBS, panicked by the prospect of providing free air time to endless counter-arguments, terminated the "Loyal Opposition" programming.

The lack of any effective opposition response is compounded by the fact that newspeople often do not provide any penetrating discussion or analysis of a president's statements in the minutes following presidential addresses. Frequently commentary focuses on style, not substance; on image, not idea. Take, for example, the following commentaries on then President Carter's famous address on "the flagging American spirit":

> Lesley Stahl (CBS): I did hear a new voice. I was told that he would be speaking with a louder voice from now on, and I did hear one. I heard a firmer voice than I've heard . . .
>
> Sam Donaldson (ABC): This was an extraordinary performance by this man. I mean, he gave it a heck of a shot . . . he used gestures; he tried to sound forceful; at times he even shouted at us a little bit.
>
> Roger Mudd (CBS): He certainly gave the impression that he was acting and leading.

This is "safe" commentary: It gives the impression of providing "analysis" of the president's remarks, without risking the kind of serious questioning or discussion which might arouse White House ire. Networks are sensitive to presidential complaints about their coverage of an address. On one occasion, Cassie Mackin of NBC provided a point by point analysis of a Nixon address during which he had attacked opponent George McGovern. She explained how each of Nixon's claims about McGovern's positions on the issues was misleading and in what way. Minutes after she went off the air, Herb Klein, the White House Communications Director, called NBC to complain. She never did that again.

By carefully avoiding controversy in analyzing a presidential address, network news becomes by default a propaganda arm for the government. Media critic Michael Arlen comments, "I wonder if television news people really understand the degree of complicity with official government policy that they achieve by presenting government statements at face value and then simply *not asking* the questions that intelligent men are bound to be concerned about."

Fred Friendly, for one, is convinced that the lack of essential analysis of one of President Johnson's televised addresses may have contributed to the tragedy of the Vietnam War. He explains:

> . . . I give CBS News and myself a D for effort and performance on the night of August 4, 1964, when President Johnson, in his Tonkin Gulf speech, asked for a blank check on Vietnam. In spite of the pleas of our Washington bureau, I made the decision to leave the air two minutes after the president had concluded his remarks. I shall always believe that, if journalism had done its job properly that night and in the days following, America might have been spared some of the agony that followed the Tonkin Gulf Resolution. I am not saying that we should have, in any way, opposed the president's recommendations. But to quote Klauber's doctrine of news analy-

sis, if we had "out of common knowledge or special knowledge . . . pointed out the facts on both sides, shown contradictions with the known record," we might have explained that after bombers would come bases, and after bases, troops to protect those bases, and after that hundreds of thousands of more troops . . .[19]

A study by Louis Harris showed that support for Johnson's Vietnam policy rose by 30 percent after he was permitted to promote it, unquestioned and unchallenged on television.

Theoretically, one counterbalance to the presidential address is the presidential press conference, in which the press has the chance to question the president directly. In practice, it doesn't work that way. For one thing, the president gets to make an "opening statement" at the beginning of every press conference. Since most reporters come to the conference with their questions written in advance (sometimes given to them by their publisher or editor), that statement is rarely challenged. Jimmy Carter called a press conference one month before the national election in order to file this advertisement for himself:

> Good afternoon. Although attention has naturally focused on domestic politics, events around the world and here at home still demand my attention and action in ways that affect the well-being of American citizens . . .
>
> Yesterday, *the second anniversary of the signing of the Camp David accords*, I met with [Israeli and Egyptian diplomats] as efforts continue in our quest for a lasting peace in the Middle East, which is so important to the future of Americans and to the entire world . . .
>
> Here at home there are some encouraging economic signs: the unemployment rate has been steady, or slightly down, for the last four straight months . . . In the last month, *we've added some 470,000 new jobs.* Housing starts are up now for the third month in a row. New orders for durable goods

were up sharply in July. And for the past nineteen days, retail sales have also shown increases . . .

But I will continue to press ahead to strengthen our economy, to increase productivity, and to revitalize our American industrial system . . .

Finally, I'm working with the Congress for the passage of critical bills. I think we will have a good legislative year . . . In domestic and international affairs, the progress of America goes on. [Italics added.]

I will now be pleased to answer any questions you may have for me.

Reagan's campaign manager, William Casey, appealed to the networks for equal time, arguing that the statement was "an obvious partisan announcement, not responsive to questions from the press, separate from the press conference." He added, "It could not have been a more political commercial if [Carter] had paid for the time." He lost the appeal. A CBS spokesman added that the network would have charged Carter $81,000 for a comparable political commercial.

Another difficulty with press conferences is that reporters who have a White House beat are dependent on the president's goodwill in gathering their stories, and they generally don't want to risk alienating him with hostile or probing questions. Many of the questions asked at a press conference are "softball pitches" designed to help the president make a solid hit with the public. For example, this question directed at Ronald Reagan:

Mr. President, as I think you're aware, a number of black leaders in this country have expressed some reservations about your policies—and I wonder if you might have something to say today to reassure the blacks in this country concerning your attitude and your policies?

Note how the question is phrased: No real information or

detailed accounting is called for; instead the reporter asks for less clearly defined (and inevitably, more propagandistic) "reassurance." This question allowed Reagan to launch into his favorite rhetorical mode, the personal anecdote:

> . . . I have been gratified by the support that evidenced to me through mail, through calls, through personal meetings with members of the black community that have told me they believe in the program. I had one letter just a few days ago from a sixteen-year-old boy who identified himself as black and he said, "I am wholeheartedly behind what you are trying to do and I think it means much for my own future." I had another from a young black man who had just become the father of a baby girl, and he was telling me that he—and he had come all the way over from being a diehard Democrat to support this program because, he said, "I think it means a better world for my daughter."

The question was so perfectly designed to meet Reagan's public relations needs that he might just as well have written it himself.

And, in fact, presidents, or their aides, do write questions and plant them with compliant members of the press. Television reporters, who are under pressure from their networks to appear on camera, are particularly willing to cooperate. Newsman Robert MacNeil reports that one of President Johnson's aides once told him that while newspaper reporters would sometimes refuse to ask questions planted by the White House staff, television reporters never refused.[20]

George Reedy, former aide of Lyndon Johnson, acknowledges that questions are planted with the press, but adds that the practice is really unnecessary because

> . . . as long as [a press conference] is on television the president dominates it so thoroughly that it would really be foolish for him or his assistants to plant things.

He is standing physically on a higher level; he is flanked by the American and presidential flags; the setting inspires awe; and every single newspaperman when he arises to ask a question knows that he is being viewed by 110 to 120 million people. He will be rather genteel about his questions. He doesn't want to look like a lout rubbing the president's nose in some triviality.

The president can very easily skip from person to person and there cannot be any follow-up questions. The modern press conference format is a very bad one. It's one in which the president has such complete control inherent in the situation itself that there is no need for planting questions. They are not necessary.[21]

Pierre Salinger, John Kennedy's press secretary, once confessed that he used a system of mobile partitions to reduce the size of the conference room on days when fewer newsmen showed up. That way, Kennedy's press conferences always appeared to be "standing room only."

With such control over the proceedings, a president is, in effect, able to say just about anything he likes, free from an impromptu challenge. At one recent press conference, for example, Ronald Reagan described some Lebanese weapons as "offensive" and added, "We know which way they're pointed." Not one newsperson followed up on this, though many presumably knew that the weapons referred to were actually earth to air missiles, and so could hardly be termed "offensive" unless one was suggesting that they might perhaps one day be used to blow flocks of migrating Middle Eastern birds to oblivion.

On another occasion, Reagan stated, "The Soviet Union has made it very plain that among themselves they believe a nuclear war is winnable." Again, no one asked him to defend that statement, nor to explain on what he had based it. Writing in the *New York Times* after the event, Anthony Lewis remarked: "The Soviet Union is dangerous in many ways, but that madness is not one of them—not on any evidence that I can find." He quoted a leading student of Soviet strategy as saying:

> Official Soviet doctrine is that nuclear war cannot be controlled and that it is inherently unwinnable. On a lower level of military science they think the best deterrence is a nuclear war-fighting capability; that is very identical with the United States view . . . I could not find anything about victory in a nuclear war in modern Soviet writings.[22]

Yet for millions of Americans, Reagan's statement stands as the only appraisal of Soviet thinking, because it went unchallenged. To ask President Reagan, for example, how he knows what the Soviet Union believes "among themselves" or even what that means would be disrespectful. As Howard K. Smith says, "The Chief of State is like the flag. You have to be deferential."[23]

Yet if the important questions do not get asked, or alternative viewpoints aired, how is anyone to judge whether what is being said is true? Our constitutional checks and balances on power did not take into account the invention of television, pollsters, and public relations advisors. The founding fathers had no way to foresee advances in technology that would enable one man so to dominate the available news channels to the public. A recent U.S. Court of Appeals ruling on presidential access to the media warns:

> If the words and views of the president become a monolithic force, if they constitute not just the most powerful voice in the land but the only one speaking for a nationwide point of view, then the delicate mechanism through which an enlightened public opinion is distilled . . . is thrown dangerously off balance. Public opinion becomes not informed but instructed, not enlightened but dominated.[24]

*　　*　　*

Former Carter press aide and media critic Hodding Carter put it more simply: "When the president and the press lie down together, it's the public that rises up with fleas."[25]

If we are not to become a government of the president, by the president, and for president, then something must be done about the White House stranglehold on the media. Opposition viewpoints must be given equal hearing, even if all they provide is a token opposition. If the president's message is broadcast simultaneously on all three networks, the opposition response should be too. Britain has used such a system for years. After the prime minister presents a "ministerial broadcast," the opposition party is automatically given the same time slot to respond the following evening, and on the third evening there is a panel discussion among members of Parliament representing both views. Sweden has even tighter controls on executive access to television. There, the prime minister goes on TV only at the request of the Swedish Broadcasting Corporation, which then offers equal time to any opposition parties.

Presidential press conferences should be extended to an hour, to allow for some follow-up questions from reporters. In addition, the president should hold informal untelevised talks with the press at least once a month which would make for more genuine dialogue and less pose-striking.

Above all, people should be educated, beginning as schoolchildren, to recognize propaganda. There is a distinction between argument and sophistry, between persuasion and demagoguery, between information and dogma. A rational democracy requires that people be able to recognize that distinction. As Jacques Ellul says in his famous book *Propaganda*:

> The only truly serious attitude . . . is to show people the extreme effectiveness of the weapon used against them, to rouse

them to defend themselves by making them aware of their frailty and their vulnerability, instead of soothing them with the worst illusion, that of a security which neither man's nature not the techniques of propaganda permit him to possess . . . the side of freedom and truth for man has not yet lost, but . . . it may well lose—and . . . in this game propaganda is undoubtedly the most formidable power, acting in only one direction (toward the destruction of truth and freedom), no matter what the good intentions or the good will may be of those who manipulate it.[26]

IV

Conclusion

8

Shadows on the Wall

I see no virtue in having a public that cannot distinguish fact from fantasy. When you start thinking fantasy is reality you have a serious problem. People can be stampeded into all kinds of fanaticism, folly and warfare.

Isaac Asimov

Why sometimes I've believed as many as six impossible things before breakfast.

Queen to Alice in Lewis Carroll's *Through the Looking Glass*

In Book Four of *The Republic,* Plato tells a story about four prisoners who since birth have been chained inside a cave, totally isolated from the world outside. They face a wall on which shadows flicker, cast by the light of the fire. The flickering shadows are the only reality they know. Finally, one of the prisoners is released and permitted to leave the cave. Once outside, he realizes that the shadows he has watched for so long are only pale, distorted reflections of a much brighter, better world. He returns to tell the others about the world outside the cave. They listen in disbelief, then in anger, for what he says contradicts all they have known. Unable to accept the truth, they cast him out as a heretic.

Today, our picture of the world is formed in great part from television's flickering shadows. Sometimes that picture is a fairly accurate reflection of the real world; sometimes it is not. But either way, we accept it as real and we act upon it as if it were reality itself. "And that's the way it is," Walter Cronkite assured us every evening for over nineteen years, and most of us did not doubt it.

A generation of Americans has grown up so dependent on television that its images appear as real to them as life itself. On a recent trip to a widely advertised amusement park, my husband, daughter, and I rode a "white-water" raft through manufactured "rapids." As we spun and screamed and got thoroughly soaked, I noticed that the two young boys who shared our raft appeared rather glum. When the ride ended, I heard one remark to the other, "It's more fun on television."

As an experiment, Jerzy Kosinski gathered a group of children, aged seven to ten years, into a room to show them some televised film. Before the show began, he announced, "Those who want to stay inside and watch the films are free to remain in the classroom, but there's something fascinating happening in the corridor, and those who want to see it are free to leave the room." Kosinski describes what happened next:

> No more than 10 percent of the children left. I repeated, "You know, what's outside is really fantastic. You have never seen it before. Why don't you just step out and take a look?"
>
> And they always said, "No, no, no, we prefer to stay here and watch the film." I'd say, "But you don't know what's outside." "Well, what is it?" they'd ask. "You have to go find out." And they'd say, "Why don't we just sit here and see the film first?" . . . They were already too corrupted to take a chance on the outside.[1]

In another experiment, Kosinski brought a group of children into a room with two giant video screens mounted on the side walls. He stood in the front of the room and began to tell them a story. Suddenly, as part of a prearranged plan, a man entered and pretended to attack Kosinski, yelling at him and hitting him. The entire episode was shown on the two video screens as it happened. The children did not respond, but merely watched the episode unfold on the video screens. They rarely glanced at the two men struggling in the front of the room. Later, in an interview with Kosinski, they explained that the video screens captured the event much more satisfactorily, providing close-ups of the participants, their expressions, and such details as the attacker's hand on Kosinski's face.[2]

Some children can become so preoccupied with television that they are oblivious to the real world around them. UPI filed a report on a burglar who broke into a home and killed the father of three children, aged nine, eleven, and twelve. The crime went unnoticed until ten hours later, when police entered the apartment after being called by neighbors and found the three children watching television just a few feet away from the bloody corpse of their father.

Shortly after this report was released, the University of Nebraska conducted a national survey in which children were asked which they would keep if they had to choose—their fathers or their television sets. *Over half* chose the television sets!

Evidence of this confusion between reality and illusion grows daily. Trial lawyers, for example, complain that juries have become conditioned to the formulas of televised courtroom dramas.

Former Bronx District Attorney Mario Merola says, "All they want is drama, suspense—a confession. Never in all my years as a prosecutor have I seen someone cry from the witness stand, 'I did it! I did it—I confess!' But that's what happens on prime-time TV—and that's what the jurors think the court system is all about." He adds, "Such misconceptions make the work of a district attorney's office much harder than it needs to be."[3] Robert Daley describes one actual courtroom scene in which the defendant was subjected to harsh and unrelenting cross-examination: "I watched the jury," he says. "It seemed to me that I had seen this scene before, and indeed I had dozens of times—on television. On television the murderer always cracks eventually and says something like 'I can't take it any more.' He suddenly breaks down blubbering and admits his guilt. But this defendant did not break down, he did not admit his guilt. He did not blubber. It seemed to me I could see the jury conclude before my eyes: ergo, he cannot be guilty—and indeed the trial ended in a hung jury . . . Later I lay in bed in the dark and brooded about the trial . . . If [television courtroom dramas] had never existed, would the jury have found the defendant guilty even though he did not crack?"[4]

Television actors are frequently treated by their fans as though they actually were the characters they are paid to portray. Confusion of the actor with his role occurs at the very highest levels. Consider the following examples:

—Robert Young, the actor who played Marcus Welby on the long-running television series, is asked to deliver the commencement address at Harvard Medical School.
—Normal Fell, the actor who played landlord Mr. Roper on "Three's Company," is hired to appear in a series of commercials promoting tenants' class action suits against the Department of Housing and Urban Development.
—Nichelle Nichols, former ballerina, supperclub singer, and actress in the old "Star Trek" series, is made a member of the Board of Directors of the National Space Institute, and a consultant for NASA.
—John Gavin, an actor whose command of Spanish resulted in a lucrative series of television spots advertising rum in South America, is appointed United States Ambassador to Mexico.

Television drama seems to be trying to blur further the fading distinctions between reality and fiction. In the minds of millions of Americans, the television production of "Shōgun" became an accurate account of Japanese history, tradition, and thought. Yet Professor Henry Smith, a specialist in Japanese history, who was in Japan at the time the show aired there, reported that the Japanese found the program to be "bad if not insulting."[5] Before the first broadcast in Japan, Yoko Shimada, the actress who played the lead role of Mariko, and former U.S. Ambassador to Japan Edwin O. Reischauer appeared on the screen to appeal for audience indulgence toward this naive and error-ridden "Western view" of Japan. But most Americans readily accepted that view, because, as *The New York Times* suggested, it "provided stereotypes that Americans could recognize, feel comfortable with, and accept as authentic."[6]

At least the television drama of "Shōgun," derived from James Clavell's best-selling novel, never claimed to be anything but a work of fiction. But other forms of entertainment, such as "fact-based" or "docu-" dramas, are far less clear about where fact ends and fiction begins. Originally, fact-based dramas were imaginative reconstructions of great historical events, of the kind satirized by Russell Baker:

The army of the Israelites is gazing at a distant city. "Hath yonder distant city a name, O Joshua?"

"That, sergeant, is a place called—JERICHO!"

*   *   *

Behind his desk in the Oval Office Franklin Roosevelt glances up from dispatches. "Well, bless my soul," he says to a man entering, "if it isn't HARRY HOPKINS, THE MOST CONTROVERSIAL FIGURE IN THE NEW DEAL."

"I hear there is bad news, chief."

"True, my CONTROVERSIAL YET CLOSE FRIEND. The Japanese have bombed a place."

"What place, chief?"

"A place called—PEARL HARBOR!"

*   *   *

"General Washington," asks Colonel Travers, "what is that town ahead?"

"Scaggsville, Maryland, if you must know, and hereafter I'll thank you not to ask me that question again until we come to a certain place in southeastern Virginia."

"Do you mean a place called—"

"That's my line," says Washington. "A place called—YORKTOWN!"

"Do you ever dream of the future, General?"

"My dream, Colonel, is of a great country, a place called—THE UNITED STATES OF AMERICA—a place where, FOURSCORE AND SEVEN YEARS FROM NOW we will be called—OUR FOREFATHERS."[7]

The popularity of this form of entertainment proved to be so great that rights to "real life" properties were bought up at an astonishing rate. Promising news events were "dramatized" even as they unfolded. The story of Jean Harris, the school headmistress convicted of murdering diet doctor Herman Tarnower, was written, produced, and broadcast less than four months after her trial ended. On the very afternoon *Newsweek* published a story on the death of a Los Angeles college student during a fraternity hazing, four dramatized versions of the story were filed with the Writers Guild. Last year alone, three news features from CBS's "60 Minutes" were turned into television docudramas. Writer Lance Morrow comments, "At times television seems a kind of history-devouring machine scooping up great sections of reality and then reconstituting them, made for TV . . . Dozens of public events, issues, and figures have been filtered through the sophisticated docudramatizing process. In millions of viewers' minds the televised account has now become surrogate reality."[8]

Many docudramas invite this reaction by deliberately trying to create a "real-life" atmosphere. "The Rideout Case," a dramatization of the widely publicized court case in which a wife sued her husband for rape, used documentary techniques such as providing the exact hour and date for specific scenes—"October 6, 1978, 2:30 P.M." Other "fact-based" dramas assure viewers, "The names have been changed. But the story is true."

Bill Moyers comments, "Docudramas cross the line between art and reality without telling you that they have done so. They are done for the sake of commerce instead of illumination and are a very disturbing mélange of fact and fantasy. Without discriminating respect for what actually happened, they can set back the cause of public understanding by giving an *illusion* of what happened. They are done hastily with little regard for the nuances and subtleties that make history intelligible."[9]

They also permit opinion to masquerade as fact. The producers and writers of docudramas can, in effect, ensure that their interpretation of the meaning of events will be seen as the "correct" one. History Professor Eric Foner says, "I think the first thing that ought to be done by people who are involved in the docudramas is to realize that your selection of the facts is an interpretation. The very subject you choose to present is itself a political decision."[10]

Given the social and economic status of television's illusion-makers, it is not surprising that their interpretation of history is often pro-Establishment. Take, for example, "The Missiles of October," a docudramatization of John F. Kennedy's handling of the Cuban missile crisis. The program depicted Kennedy as a Lincolnesque hero capable of making difficult decisions and sticking by them. For millions of people, that vision has become the reality, though libraries are filled with books that give very different—and less favorable—interpretations of Kennedy's actions and motives.

Or there is the example of "The Marva Collins Story," a docudrama based on the experiences of a black schoolteacher who, disgusted with the inadequacies of the ghetto public schools, quit and set up her own highly successful private school. The program clearly identified the reason for the public schools' dismal failure adequately to educate ghetto children: teachers so overwhelmed with bureaucratic regulations and unnecessary paperwork that they have no time left "for our *real* jobs—teaching!" All the other social and economic factors that might cause the inadequacy of ghetto schooling were entirely overlooked. This left a clear political message: We should leave the school system exactly as it is, but try to cut down on unnecessary and harmful regulation by the federal government.

Still another example of pro-Establishment propaganda was seen in the docudrama series "Backstairs at the White House," which dealt with the intimate personal lives of twentieth-century American presidents: Teddy Roosevelt, Taft, Wilson, Harding, Coolidge, Hoover, and Franklin Roosevelt. Ostensibly based on "the facts" about these men, much of the dialogue necessarily had to be invented, because it consisted of private conversations between family members. Yet many people regarded these conversations as matters of factual record. After the broadcast, I questioned a group of my freshmen college students about their understanding of what they had seen:

Q: How much of it do you think actually happened?
A: *All* of it. I mean, it said it was based on the facts, didn't it?
Q: How do you think the writers knew exactly what President Wilson said to his wife at that point?
A: I don't know. I guess maybe they interviewed people and stuff like that. And aren't all White House conversations recorded on tape?
A: Maybe those weren't the *exact* words they said, but they must have said something very close to it or else they couldn't get away with saying it was a "true story."

As far as these students were concerned, the dialogue was real, not invented. The invented dialogue portrayed the presidents as benign statesmen with no identifiable party affiliations or political convictions beyond an altruistic concern for the welfare of the nation. Critic Frank Rich comments, "I'm willing to accept the premise that every fact in "Backstairs at the White House" was accurate, but what was that show telling us? What did they do with those facts? It was telling us that all the presidents in this century were a bunch of cuddly guys . . . and they had no particular strong political positions. It wasn't clear how they got us in the wars and took us out of the wars and so on. That show was a complete disservice to history . . ."[11]

Responding to remarks made by docudrama producer Alan Landsburg, journalist Richard Reeves said, "[This was] one of the most extraordinary statements I've ever heard . . . What he said was that he had toiled in the vineyards of documentaries and he got terribly frustrated by photographing the outside of the White House and not being allowed in the Oval Office to find out what happened. Then he said, 'Thank God docudrama came along . . . and allowed me to guess what was happening in the Oval Office.' He then continued to say what a marvelous opportunity this was and ended by saying, 'And now I can tell the truth. I can tell what's really going on in the Oval Office.' That to me is a political story—that many Americans are going to be told one man's guess."[12]

Docudramas and similar forms of entertainment that mix fact and fiction allow storytellers to propagandize for established political and social viewpoints. No one alerts viewers that this is what they are doing. As psychologist Victor Cline explains, "The very real danger of docudrama films is that people take it for granted that they're true and—unlike similar fictionalized history in movies and theater—they are seen on a medium which also presents straight news. No matter how much they call these movies 'drama,' they're really advocacy journalism. They can't help reflecting the point of view of the writer or the studio or the network."[13]

The impact of such propagandizing is enormous because

so many of us accept what we see as truth, not illusion. Writer Paddy Chayevsky railed against this kind of folly in his award-winning movie *Network*:

> Television is not the truth . . . We lie like hell . . . We deal in illusions, man. None of it is true. But *you* people sit there day after day, night after night . . . We're all you know. You're beginning to believe the illusions we're spinning here. You're beginning to think that the tube is reality and that your own lives are unreal. You *do* whatever the tube tells you. You dress like the tube, you eat like the tube, you raise your children like the tube. This is mass madness, you maniacs. In God's name, *you* people are the real thing; *we're* the illusion![14]

Looking back through history, it is easy to see how people erred because the "pictures in their heads" did not correspond with reality. Because they believed God was offended by "pagan" art, Egyptian Christians burned the greatest repository of knowledge in the ancient world, the library at Alexandria. Because they believed that witches walked the earth, the Salem settlers drowned old women and children. Because they believed a disastrous economy and mounting social problems were caused by a lack of racial "purity," Nazis exterminated six million Jews.

Today we view the illusions on which these irrational actions were based as ludicrous. We flatter ourselves that our own mental maps are far more accurate guides to the actual territory. Yet the discrepancy between the pictures in our heads and the world outside is just as wide as that of our predecessors. We revere our founding fathers as "patriots," when in fact they were revolutionaries who overthrew an existing government and replaced it with a new one; we pride ourselves on our Constitution and Bill of Rights, though in fact we often disapprove the practice of its fundamental tenets; we accuse "big government" of being the source of our economic and social woes, though in fact we suffer and complain when government funds and services are withdrawn; we believe we are the champions of liberty throughout the world, though in fact we actively support oppressive governments.

We are the victims of the most extravagant of all illusions: that every kind of human distress can be solved with an appropriate pill, and that a simple and easy solution exists for even the most complex problem.

A poster popular during the time of the hostage crisis in Iran pictured actor Clint Eastwood as "Dirty Harry" holding a .44 magnum gun to the head of the Ayatollah Khomeini and saying, "Say goodnight, Khomeini." This type of "poster thinking" reduces the complexity of world affairs to the level of understanding of a five-year-old child. And five-year-old children, charming and funny as they are, are not equipped to deal with the intricacies of foreign policy. Daniel Boorstin comments, "Now, in the height of our power, we are threatened by a new and peculiarly American menace. It is not the menace of class war . . . of poverty, of disease, of illiteracy . . . It is the menace of unreality. We risk being the first people in history to make their illusions so vivid, so persuasive, so 'realistic' that we can live in them."[15]

There is a great danger whenever simplistic illusions displace reality. The manufacturers of those illusions acquire enormous power over the rest of us. Semanticist Alfred Korzybski says, "Human beings are a symbolic class of life. Those who rule our symbols rule us." The danger is magnified when, as with television broadcasting, the illusion-makers constitute a very small and unrepresentative social group. Jerry Mander says, "Television technology is inherently anti-democratic. Because of its cost, the limited kind of information it can disseminate, the way it transforms the people who use it, and the fact that a few speak while millions absorb, television is suitable for use only by the most powerful corporate interests in the country. They inevitably use it to redesign human minds . . ."[16]

It is still possible to free ourselves from this insidious manipulation of our minds. Commercial broadcasters do not, after all, *own* the airwaves; they license them. The mechanisms for revoking those licenses if broadcasters fail to serve "the public interest" are clearly defined in the Federal Communications Act. These mechanisms have not been used, not because they won't work, but because powerful groups are opposed to having them work.

There is much that can be done. An important first step is to accept the fact that change *is* possible, that the current state of affairs does not represent a fixed and immovable order. All of this century's important political achievements, from women's suffrage to civil rights legislation, appeared at the outset to be mere tilting at windmills. To start with a small, easily achieved goal: Antitrust proceedings can be instituted to compel networks to sell the five stations each now owns and operates outright. As journalist and television critic Jeff Greenfield asks, "Should suppliers of programming also have instant control over a quarter of the American viewing population?"[17]

Further antitrust action can be taken to require networks to accept news stories and programs from freelance agencies. Networks argue that they use news features they produce themselves because they must be sure of their accuracy and truthfulness. In reality this is another way to consolidate their control over the free flow of information. Important documentaries have been made by independent producers, and many more have been proposed, only to be kept from the public view by the network blackout of outside news sources.

The number of hours that any one licensee uses on a given channel can be legally restricted. Greenfield says, "There is no reason why Channel 2 in New York must be programmed from dawn to dawn, seven days a week, by the same corporation, particularly when a broadcast band represents a government-licensed monopoly of a terribly scarce and enormously valuable 'property.'"[18] Broadcast time could be shared by groups of licensees occupying alternating time periods. Such a move would be in keeping with the Supreme Court ruling that truly democratic communication requires a variety of information from "diverse and antagonistic sources."

Obviously, so thorough a shaking of The Powers That Be will not come about without a struggle. But it is a struggle well worth waging. What is at stake is not merely the issue of who will control the media but who, ultimately, will control America. Consider the words of former FCC Chairman Nicholas Johnson, who believed that the mass media should not hold us hostage to our old dreams but lead us toward new ones:

> The issue before us ought to be stated quite starkly. It is, quite simply, who is to retain the potential to rule America. We know, if we are honest with ourselves, which segments of the economic and social structure have the loudest voices . . . But the potential for popular check remains. It remains, however, only so long as the people can obtain education and information, only so long as they can communicate with each other, only so long as they can retain potential control over the mass media of this country. So long as we preserve the people's *potential* to rule—their potential opportunity to participate in the operation of their mass media—there is some hope, however small, that some future generation—perhaps the next— will use this potential to rebuild America.

Notes

(If a full citation for a monograph is not given with the note in this section, see the bibliography at the end of the book.)

Introduction

1. Doris Graber, *Mass Media and American Politics*, p. 135.
2. Joseph Keeley, *The Left-Leaning Antenna*, p. 47.
3. Adam Smith, *An Inquiry Into the Nature and Causes of the Wealth of Nations* (New York: Modern Library, 1937), p. 537.
4. Jerry Mander, *Four Arguments for the Elimination of TV*, p. 152.
5. Erik Barnouw, *The Sponsor*, p. 140.
6. Ibid., p. 141.
7. A. Q. Mowbray, "Free Press in Fancy Packages," *The Nation*, Dec. 11, 1967, pp. 621–623.
8. "Public Relations Today," *Business Week*, July 2, 1960, p. 42.
9. Herbert Schiller, *The Mind Managers*, p. 135.
10. "A Case for Professionalism," *The Bulletin*, American Society of Newspaper Editors, November–December 1970.
11. James Monaco, *Celebrity*, p. 5.
12. Schiller, *Mind Managers*, p. 19.
13. Ibid., pp. 23–24.

Chapter 1: Profits Without Honor

1. Daniel Boorstin, *The Image*, pp. 208–209.

2. Jonathan Price, *The Best Thing on TV*, p. 9.

3. Jeffrey Shrank, *Snap, Crackle and Popular Taste*, p. 93.

4. Ibid., p. 100.

5. Helen Woodward, *Through Many Windows*, p. 298.

6. Russell Baker, "Sunday Observer," *New York Times Magazine*, May 18, 1980, p. 24.

7. "Selling It," *Consumer Reports*, January 1981, p. 48.

8. Ibid., p. 48.

9. *New York Times*, September 8, 1981, p. 23.

10. Ibid.

11. Edward Buxton, *Promise Them Anything*, pp. 234–235.

12. Mark N. Grant, "I Got My Swimming Pool by Choosing Prell Over Brand X," in *American Mass Media*, eds. Robert Atwan, Barry Orton, and William Vesterman (New York: Random House, 1978), p. 62–64.

13. Ibid., p. 67.

14. Ibid.

15. Ibid., p. 62

16. Frederick Pohl, *The Space Merchants* (New York: Ballantine Books, 1952), pp. 47–48.

17. Shrank, *Snap, Crackle, and Popular Taste*, p. 55.

18. "Raymond Rubicam Enters Ad Hall of Fame," *Advertising Age*, July 1, 1974.

19. Woodward, *Through Many Windows*, p. 204.

20. Christine McGaffrey Frederick, *Selling Mrs. Consumer* (New York: Business Bourse, 1929), pp. 275–285.

21. Price, *Best Thing*, p. 59.

22. Frank Mankiewicz and Joel Swerdlow, *Remote Control*, pp. 238–239.

23. Newsweek, August 10, 1981, p. 63A.

24. *Village Voice*, April 12, 1976.

25. Arthur Asa Berger, *The TV-Guided American*, p. 5.

26. George W. S. Trow, "The Bobby Bison Buy," in *Media Culture*, ed. James Monaco, p. 113.

27. Barnouw, *The Sponsor*, p. 71.

28. Price, *Best Thing*, p. 146.

29. *Advertising Age*, July 19, 1965, p. 42.

30. Price, *Best Thing*, p. 158.

31. John Kenneth Galbraith, *The New Industrial State,* 2nd edition,

revised (Boston: Houghton Mifflin, 1971), pp. 379–380.

32. Stuart Chase, *Danger: Men Talking* (New York: Parent's Magazine Press, 1969), pp. 191–192.

Chapter 2: All the News That Fits

1. Aldous Huxley, *Brave New World Revisited* (London: Chatto and Windus, 1959), p. 55.

2. "TV News As Metaphor," *ETC*, Winter 1980, p. 321.

3. Ron Powers, *Newscasters*, p. 4.

4. *Chicago Sun Times*, March 5, 1972, Sec. 2, p. 7.

5. "Sex and the Anchor Person," *Newsweek*, December 15, 1980, p. 65.

6. Russell Baker, "Sunday Observer," *New York Times Magazine*, March 8, 1981, p. 20.

7. Tony Schwartz, "Are TV Anchormen Merely Performers?", *New York Times*, August 1, 1980, p. C3.

8. James David Barber, *Race for the Presidency*, p. 194.

9. Powers, *Newscasters*, p. 40.

10. "Uninformed Voters," *The Wilson Quarterly*, 3 (Summer 1979), p. 29.

11. Powers, *Newscasters*, p. 79.

12. William Adams and Fay Schreibman, eds. *Television Network News*, p. 2.

13. "The Miami Riots: Did TV Get the Real Story?" *TV Guide*, August 30, 1980, p. 20.

14. Robert Henry Stanley and Ruth Graeme Ramsey. "TV News: Format as a Form of Censorship," *ETC*, Winter 1978, p. 35.

15. *Media Probes*, broadcast on public television, May 5, 1982.

16. Eric Michael/Levin, "Chopper Fever," *TV Guide*, April 26, 1980, p. 16.

17. John Weisman, "Stories You Won't See on the Nightly News," *TV Guide*, March 1, 1980, p. 8.

18. Ibid.

19. Robert Cirino, *Don't Blame the People*, p. 138.

20. David Saltman, "Next Up: 107 Dogs, 2 Cats, and Other Come-Ons To Keep You Watching," *TV Guide*, August 8, 1981, p. 15.

21. Powers, *Newscasters*, p. 83.

22. Mander, *Four Arguments for the Elimination of TV*, p. 274.

23. Gaye Tuchman, *Making News*, p. 139.

24. "Has 'MacNeil/Lehrer' Found a Better Way to Do the News?" *TV Guide*, March 14, 1981, p. 7.

25. "The Miami Riots," *TV Guide*, August 30, 1980, p. 21.

26. Mankiewicz and Swerdlow, *Remote Control*, p. 113.

27. Richard M. Levine, "Why Unconscious Racism Persists," *TV Guide*, July 25, 1981, pp. 27–28.

28. John Weisman, "Blind Spot in the Middle East," *TV Guide*, October 24, 1981, p. 12.

29. Thomas Griffith, *How True*, p. 115.

30. "An Angry Young Congressman Criticizes Special Interest Groups," *New York Times*, January 11, 1980, p. 32.

31. David Altheide, *Creating Reality*, p. 176.

32. Ibid., p. 69.

33. Graber, *Mass Media and American Politics*, p. 261.

34. *Newsweek*, December 3, 1979, p. 88.

35. *Newsweek*, November 17, 1980, p. 69.

36. Robert MacNeil, *The People Machine*, p. 47.

37. Barber, *Race for the Presidency*, p. 181.

38. "The Risks of Interpretation," in *The Mass Media Book*, Rod Holmgren and William Norton, eds., p. 159.

39. Robert Cirino, *Power to Persuade*, p. 201.

40. *New York Times*, November 18, 1981, p. 24.

41. MacNeil, *The People Machine*, p. 61.

42. Ibid., p. 289.

43. Fred Friendly, "Thoughts on Vice-President Agnew," in *The Mass Media Book*, p. 96.

44. "The Happy Ending (Maybe) of 'The Selling of the Pentagon,'" in *The Mass Media Book*, p. 154.

45. Ibid.

46. MacNeil, *People Machine*, p. 272.

Chapter 3: Let Me Entertain You

1. *Re:act*, 9, No. 3 and 4 (Spring/Summer 1980), p. 16.

2. Joseph F. Littell, ed., *Coping with the Mass Media*, p. 16.

3. Cirino, *Power to Persuade*, pp. 89–90.

4. Barnouw, *The Sponsor*, p. 55.

5. Shrank, *Snap, Crack, and Popular Taste*, p. 37.

6. Barnouw, *The Sponsor*, pp. 106–107.

7. Ibid., p. 196.

8. Ibid., p. 57.

9. Ibid., p. 4.

10. Michael Moore, "B & B's Buyer's Guide to TV Network Advertising," *Broadcasting*, April 28, 1975.

11. Barnouw, *The Sponsor*, p. 114.

12. Richard Levinson and William Link, *Stay Tuned*, p. 38.

13. Cirino, *Power to Persuade*, pp. 205–206.

14. Ibid., p. 113.

15. Levinson and Link, *Stay Tuned*, p. 108.

16. Ibid., p. 119.

17. Bradley S. Greenberg, *Life on Television*, p. 11.

18. David Dempsey, "Social Comments and TV Censorship," in *The Mass Media Book*, Holmgren and Norton, eds., p. 375.

19. Rose Goldsen, *The Show and Tell Machine*, p. 7.

20. Schiller, *Mind Managers*, p. 162.

21. John Neary, "The Dogfights are Fake—The Fatalities Aren't," *TV Guide*, October 3, 1981, p. 19.

22. Goldsen, *Show and Tell Machine*, p. 7.

23. Barnouw, *The Sponsor*, p. 54.

24. "The Men Who Run TV Know Us Better Than You Think," in *The Mass Media Book*, Holmgren and Norton, eds., pp. 328–329.

25. Ibid.

26. Doug Brode, "Interview with Jack Lemmon," *Syracuse New Times*, February 14, 1981, p. 5.

27. Levinson and Link, *Stay Tuned*, p. 31.

28. Barnouw, *The Sponsor*, p. 120.

29. Tom Nolan, "Keep Those Troubles Coming," *TV Guide*, August 8, 1981, p. 10.

30. Mankiewicz and Swerdlow, *Remote Control*, p. 266.

31. Goldsen, *Show and Tell Machine*, p. 233.

32. Mankiewicz and Swerdlow, *Remote Control*, p. 267.

33. *New York Times*, September 30, 1981, p. A28.

34. "Administration's Crime-Fighting Proposals Would Violate Rights Without Reducing Crime," *Civil Liberties*, 340, December 1981, p. 1.

35. Mankiewicz and Swerdlow, *Remote Control*, p. 263.

36. Ibid., p. 256.

37. Nicholas Johnson, *How To Talk Back To Your TV Set*, pp. 88–89.

38. Cirino, *Don't Blame the People*, p. 237.

39. Cirino, *Power to Persuade*, p. 43.

40. Schiller, *Mind Managers*, p. 1.

Chapter 4: Sin, Suffer, and Repent

1. Keeley, *Left-Leaning Antenna*, p. 67.

2. Lance Morrow, "History-Devouring Machine," in *Media and Methods* (New York: Simon and Schuster, 1975), p. 63.

3. Ellen Torgerson, "Don't You Just Want to Scratch Their Eyes Out?" *TV Guide*, July 7, 1979, p. 12.

4. Goldsen, *Show and Tell Machine,* p. 17.

5. James Thurber, "Onward and Upward with the Arts," *The New Yorker*, May 29, 1948, p. 33.

6. Ibid., p. 31.

7. "The Angst of the Upper Class," *Journal of Communication*, August 1979, p. 41.

8. Mary Cassata, "In Sickness and Health," *Journal of Communication,* August 1979, p. 50.

9. "The Angst of the Upper Class," *Journal of Communication*, August 1979, p. 41.

10. Thurber, "Onward and Upward with the Arts," *The New Yorker*, May 29, 1948, p. 33.

Chapter 5: Being Somebody

1. Boorstin, *The Image*, p. 61.

2. George Eels, *Hedda and Louella* (New York: G.P. Putnam's Sons, 1972), p. 295.

3. Ibid., p. 144.

4. Terry Galanoy, *Tonight!* (New York: Doubleday, 1972), pp. 113–114.

5. Craig Tennis, *Johnny Tonight!*, p. 99.

6. Frank McLaughlin, "Cavett Caveats: The Winsome Wisdom of Dick Cavett," *Media and Methods*, October 1978, p. 14.

7. "The Future of National Debates," in *The Great Debates*, ed. Kraus (Bloomington, Indiana University Press, 1970), p. 168.

8. Saul Braun, "Until Joey Bishop, Merv Griffin, and Johnny Carson Do Us Part," in *Celebrity*, ed. James Monaco, p. 43.

9. Griffith, *How True*, p. 82.

10. Galanoy, *Tonight!*, p. 214.

11. "Entertainment," Feedback 5, The Network Project, *Performance*, no. 3 (July/August 1972), p. 91.

12. Monaco, *Celebrity*, p. 10.

13. Tennis, *Johnny Tonight!*, p. 138.

14. Mankiewicz and Swerdlow, *Remote Control*, p. 168.

15. Jack Hicks, "This is a Big Slice of American Life," *TV Guide*, August 2, 1980, p. 24.

16. "Warning: Prime Time Fame Can Be Fatal," *TV Guide*, November 8, 1980, p. 7.

17. "Meet Don Coyote, Werner Brothers, and The Man Without a Coat," *TV Guide*, January 17, 1981, p. 28.

18. Ibid., p. 30.

Chapter 6: It Sells Soap, Doesn't It?

1. MacNeil, *People Machine*, p. 146.

2. Sidney Blumenthal, *The Permanent Campaign*, p. 79.

3. Russell Baker, "Sunday Observer," *The New York Times Magazine*, August 3, 1980, p. 14.

4. "Convention Update," *TV Guide*, Syracuse edition, August 9, 1980, p. 14.

5. *TV Guide*, August 9, 1980, p. 29.

6. Ibid.

7. Roger-Gerard Schwartzenberg, *Superstar Show of Government*, p. 181.

8. MacNeil, *People Machine*, pp. 193–194.

9. Robert Spero, *The Duping of the American Voter*, p. 32.

10. Sig Mickelson, *The Electric Mirror*, p. 60.

11. Spero, *Duping of the American Voter*, pp. 118–119.

12. Ibid., p. 85.

13. Cirino, *Don't Blame the People*, p. 213.

14. Blumenthal, *Permanent Campaign*, p. 128.

15. Ellis Weiner, "On the Campaign Stump With Yoda," *The New York Times Magazine*, August 3, 1980, p. 30.

16. Blumenthal, *Permanent Campaign*, p. 123.

17. Evelyn Waugh, *Black Mischief* (Boston: Little, Brown and Co., 1977) pp. 192–193.

18. *Newsweek*, August 20, 1979, p. 83.

19. Elizabeth Drew, *Portrait of an Election*, p. 356.

20. Ibid., p. 365.

21. Don F. Hahn, "Why Politics Bore Us," *ETC*, Winter 1980, p. 335.

22. Ibid.

23. Joe Napolitan, *The Election Game and How to Win It* (New York: Doubleday, 1972), p. 121.

24. Spero, *Duping the American Voter*, p. 35.

25. Blumenthal, *Permanent Campaign*, pp. 45–46.

26. Rod Townley, "TV Campaign Polls: How Much Can We Believe?" *TV Guide*, September 6, 1980, p. 26.

27. Schiller, *Mind Managers*, pp. 121–122.

28. Rod Townley, "TV Campaign Polls," *TV Guide*, September 6, 1980, p. 23.

29. "The Poll of 1774," in *The Mass Media Book*, eds. Holmgren and Norton, pp. 221–224.

30. Blumenthal, *Permanent Campaign*, p. 37.

31. Cirino, *Don't Blame the People*, p. 2.

32. UPI, *Stars and Stripes*, Fulda, Germany, February 3, 1969, p. 8.

33. Blumenthal, *Permanent Campaign*, p. 57.

34. Spero, *Duping the American Voter*, pp. 199–200.

35. Walter Lippmann, *The Public Philosophy* (Boston: Little, Brown, 1955), p. 10.

Chapter 7: Hail to the Chief

1. Blumenthal, *Permanent Campaign*, p. 42.

2. Niccolò Machiavelli, *The Prince*, French edition (Paris: Seghers, 1972), pp. 62–63.

3. *Inside Story*, broadcast on public television November 18, 1981.

4. *Chicago Sun Times*, March 5, 1972, sec. 2, p. 7.

5. Mankiewicz and Swerdlow, *Remote Control*, p. 84.

6. Richard S. Beal, *New York Times Magazine*, September 13, 1981, p. 112.

7. Newton Minow, John Bartlow Martin, and Lee M. Mitchell, *Presidential Television*, p. 19.

8. Ibid., p. vii.

9. Alistair Cooke, *World*, August 15, 1972, p. 13.

10. Schwartzenberg, *Superstar Show of Government*, p. 172.

11. William Safire, "Reagan's Anecdotage," *New York Times*, March 8, 1982, p. A19.

12. *New York Times*, March 18, 1982, p. 22.

13. Theodore Sorensen, *Kennedy* (New York: Harper and Row, 1965), pp. 53–54.

14. Schwartzenberg, *Superstar Show of Government*, pp. 195–196.

15. George Reedy, *The Presidency in Flux*, p. 59.

16. E. M. Halliday, "Backward Look at the New Politics: G. Washington's Preparation for a TV Appearance," *American Heritage*, 19, No. 112 (October 1968), p. 112.

17. Minow, Martin, and Mitchell, *Presidential Television*, p. 14.

18. Schwartzenberg, *Superstar Show of Government*, p. 37.

19. Fred Friendly, "Thoughts on Vice President Agnew," in *The Mass Media Book*, Holmgren and Norton, eds., p. 96.

20. MacNeil, *People Machine*, p. 299.

21. Reedy, *Presidency in Flux*, p. 63.

22. Anthony Lewis, *New York Times*, October 4, 1981, p. A21.

23. *Time*, January 18, 1971, p. 36.

24. *New York Times*, August 23, 1981, p. D25.

25. *Inside Story*, broadcast on public television November 18, 1981.

26. P. 263.

Chapter 8: Shadows on the Wall

1. David Sohn, "A Nation of Videots," in *Coping with the Mass Media*, Joseph F. Littell, ed., pp. 20–21.

2. Ibid., p. 22.

3. "Who'd Beat on a Suspect While the Camera's Running?" *TV Guide*, July 25, 1981, p. 17.

4. Mankiewicz and Swerdlow, *Remote Control*, p. 272.

5. *New York Times Magazine*, September 13, 1981, p. 90.

6. Ibid., p. 90.

7. Russell Baker, "Sunday Observer," *New York Times Magazine*, June 15, 1980, p. 12.

8. "The History-Devouring Machine: Television and the Docudrama, *Media and Methods*, Oct., 1978, p. 19.

9. Ibid., p. 20.

10. Link and Levinson, *Stay Tuned*, p. 42.

11. Ibid., p. 142.

12. Ibid., p. 143.

13. Bill Davidson, "Docudrama: Fact or Fiction?", in *Celebrity*, James Monaco, ed., p. 62.

14. Sam Hedrin, *Network*, p. 151.

15. Boorstin, *The Image*, p. 240.

16. Mander, *Four Arguments for the Elimination of TV*, p. 349.

17. "TV is *Not* the World," *Columbia Review of Journalism*, May 1979, p. 34.

18. Ibid., p. 34.

BIBLIOGRAPHY

Adams, William, and Schreibman, Fay, eds. *Television Network News: Issues in Content Research.* Washington, D.C.: Television and Politics Study Program, School of Public and International Affairs, George Washington University, 1979.

Alitheide, David. *Creating Reality: How TV News Distorts Events.* Beverly Hills: Sage Publications, 1976.

Altheide, David, and Johnson, John M. *Beureaucratic Propaganda.* Boston: Allyn, 1980.

Barber, James David. *The Pulse of Politics: Electing Presidents in the Media Age.* New York: W.W. Norton, 1980.

———, ed. *Race for the Presidency: The Media and the Nominating Process.* Englewood Cliffs: Prentice-Hall, 1978.

Barnouw, Erik. *A History of Broadcasting in the United States.* New York: Oxford University Press. (Volume 1: *A Tower in Babel,* 1966. Volume 2: *The Golden Web,* 1968. Volume 3: *The Image Empire,* 1970.)

———. *The Sponsor: Notes on a Modern Potentate.* New York: Oxford University Press, 1978. Berger, Arthur Asa. *The TV-Guided American.* New York: Walker, 1976.

Blumenthal, Sidney. *The Permanent Campaign.* Boston: Becon Press, 1980.

Boorstin, Daniel. *The Image, or What Happened to the American Dream.* New York: Atheneum, 1962.

Bunce, Richard. *Television in the Corporate Interest.* New York: Praeger, 1976.

251

Buxton, Edward. *Promise Them Anything.* New York: Stein and Day, 1972.

Cirino, Robert. *Don't Blame the People.* Los Angeles: Diversity Press, 1971.

———. *Power to Persuade: Mass Media and the News.* New York: Bantam Books, 1974.

Comstock, George; Chaffee, Steven; Katzman, Nathan; McComb, Maxwell; and Roberts, Donald. *Television and Human Behavior.* New York: Columbia University Press, 1978.

Drew, Elizabeth. *Portrait of an Election.* New York: Simon and Schuster, 1981.

Ellul, Jacques. *Propaganda: The Formation of Men's Attitudes.* New York: Vintage, 1965.

Epstein, Edward Jay. *News from Nowhere.* New York: Random House, 1973.

Ewen, Stuart. *Captains of Consciousness.* New York: McGraw-Hill, 1976.

Femina, Jerry Della. *From Those Wonderful Folks Who Gave You Pearl Harbor.* New York: Simon and Schuster, 1970.

Friendly, Fred. *Due to Circumstances Beyond Our Control.* New York: Random House, 1967.

Gans, Herbert. *Deciding What's News: A Study of CBS Evening News, NBC Nightly News, Newsweek and Time.* New York: Pantheon Books, 1979.

Goldsen, Rose. *The Show and Tell Machine: How Television Works and Works You Over.* New York: Dial Press, 1975.

Graber, Doris. *Mass Media and American Politics.* Washington: Congressional Quarterly Press, 1980.

Greenberg, Bradley S. *Life on Television: Content Analyses of United States TV Drama.* Norwood, N.J.: Ablex Publishing Corporation, 1980.

Griffith, Thomas. *How True: A Skeptic's Guide to Believing the News.* Boston: Little, Brown, 1974.

Hedrin, Sam. *Network.* (Screenplay by Paddy Chayevsky.) New York: Pocket Books, 1976.

Herschensohn, Bruce. *Gods of Antenna.* New Rochelle: Arlington House, 1976.

Hodgson, Godfrey. *All Things to All Men: The False Promise of the Modern American Presidency.* New York: Simon and Schuster, 1980.

Holmgren, Rod, and Norton, William, eds., *The Mass Media Book.* Englewood Cliffs: Prentice-Hall, 1972.

Johnson, Nicholas. *How to Talk Back to Your TV Set.* Boston: Little, Brown, 1970.

Keeley, Joseph. *The Left-Leaning Antenna: Political Bias in Television.* New Rochelle: Arlington House, 1971.

Levinson, Richard, and Link, William. *Stay Tuned: An Inside Look at the Making of Prime-Time Television*. New York: St. Martin's Press, 1981.

Lippmann, Walter. *Public Opinion*. New York: Harcourt, Brace, 1922.

Littell, Joseph F., ed. *Coping with the Mass Media*. Evanston: McDougal, Littell, 1975.

MacNeil, Robert. *The People Machine: The Influence of Television on American Politics*. New York: Harper and Row, 1968.

Mander, Jerry. *Four Arguments for the Elimination of TV*. New York: William Morrow, 1978.

Mankiewicz, Frank, and Swerdlow, Joel. *Remote Control: TV and the Manipulation of American Life*. New York: Times Books, 1978.

Metz, Robert. *CBS: Reflections in a Bloodshot Eye*. Chicago: Playboy Press, 1975.

————. *The Today Show*. Chicago: Playboy Press, 1977.

Mickelson, Sig. *The Electric Mirror: Politics in an Age of Television*. New York: Dodd, Mead, 1972.

Minow, Newton; Martin, John Bartlow; and Mitchell, Lee M. *Presidential Television*. New York: Basic Books, 1973.

Monaco, James, ed. *Celebrity*. New York: Delta Press, 1978.

————. *Media Culture*. New York: Delta Press, 1978.

Mueller, Claus. *The Politics of Communication*. New York: Oxford University Press, 1973.

Ogilvy, David. *Confessions of an Advertising Man*. New York: Ballantine Books, 1976.

Patterson, Thomas. *The Mass Media Example*. New York: Praeger, 1980.

Phelan, John M. *Mediaworld: Programming the Public*. New York: Seabury Press, 1977.

Powers, Ron. *Face Value*. New York: Delacorte Press, 1979.

————. *The Newscasters*. New York: St. Martin's Press, 1977.

Price, Jonathan. *The Best Thing on TV: Commercials*. New York: Penguin Books, 1978.

Reedy, George. *The Presidency in Flux*. New York: Columbia University Press, 1973.

Rubin, Bernard. *Political Television*. Belmont, California: Wadsworth, 1967.

————, ed. *Questioning Media Ethics*. New York: Praeger, 1978.

Schiller, Herbert. *Mass Communications and American Empire*. New York: Augustus, Kelley, 1969.

————. *The Mind Managers*. Boston: Beacon Press, 1973.

Schwartz, Tony. *The Responsive Chord*. New York: Doubleday/Anchor, 1973.

Schwartzenberg, Roger-Gerard. *The Superstar Show of Government.* Woodbury, New York: Barron's, 1980.

Shrank, Jeffrey. *Snap, Crackle, and Popular Taste: The Illusion of Free Choice in America.* New York: Delta Press, 1977.

Small, William. *To Kill a Messenger: Television News and the Real World.* New York: Hasting House, 1970.

Soares, Manuela. *The Soap Opera Book.* New York: Harmony Books, 1978.

Spero, Robert. *The Duping of the American Voter: Dishonesty and Deception in Presidential Television Advertising.* New York: Lippincott and Crowell, 1980.

Stein, Benjamin. *The View From Sunset Boulevard: America As Brought to You by the People Who Make TV.* New York: Basic Books, 1979.

Tennis, Craig. *Johnny Tonight!* New York: Pocket Books, 1980.

Tuchman, Gaye. *Making News: A Study in the Construction of Reality.* New York: Free Press, 1978.

Tunstall, Jeremy, and Walker, David. *Media Made in California: Hollywood, Politics and the News.* New York: Oxford University Press, 1981.

Wakefield, Dan. *All Her Children.* New York: Avon Books, 1976.

Woodward, Helen. *Through Many Windows.* New York: Harper, 1926.